SEEKING SUPREMACY

The emergence of the judiciary as an assertive and confrontational centre of power has been the most consequential new feature of Pakistan's political system. This book maps out the evolution of the relationship between the judiciary and military in Pakistan, explaining why Pakistan's high courts shifted from loyal deference to the military to open competition, and confrontation, with military and civilian institutions. Yasser Kureshi demonstrates that a shift in the audiences shaping judicial preferences explains the emergence of the judiciary as an assertive power centre. As the judiciary gradually embraced less deferential institutional preferences, a shift in judicial preferences took place and the judiciary sought to play a more expansive and authoritative political role. Using this audience-based approach, Kureshi roots the judiciary in its political, social and institutional context, and develops a generalizable framework that can explain variation and change in judicial-military relations around the world.

Yasser Kureshi is the John and Daria Barry Postdoctoral Fellow in constitutional theory and law at the University of Oxford. His research concerns the military and the judiciary and their impact on constitutional configurations and democratic outcomes in authoritarian and post-authoritarian states. His other research interests include democratic backsliding in South Asia, coup legitimation strategies, federalism and the making of legal cultures. His work has appeared in the *Journal of Comparative Politics*, the *Journal of Conflict Resolution* and *Democratization*.

T0382463

CAMBRIDGE STUDIES IN LAW AND SOCIETY

Founded in 1997, Cambridge Studies in Law and Society is a hub for leading scholarship in socio-legal studies. Located at the intersection of law, the humanities, and the social sciences, it publishes empirically innovative and theoretically sophisticated work on law's manifestations in everyday life: from discourses to practices, and from institutions to cultures. The series editors have longstanding expertise in the interdisciplinary study of law, and welcome contributions that place legal phenomena in national, comparative, or international perspective. Series authors come from a range of disciplines, including anthropology, history, law, literature, political science, and sociology.

Series Editors

Mark Fathi Massoud, *University of California, Santa Cruz*

Jens Meierhenrich, *London School of Economics and Political Science*

Rachel E. Stern, *University of California, Berkeley*

A list of books in the series can be found at the back of this book.

SEEKING SUPREMACY
The Pursuit of Judicial Power in Pakistan

Yasser Kureshi
University of Oxford

Shaftesbury Road, Cambridge CB2 8EA, United Kingdom

One Liberty Plaza, 20th Floor, New York, NY 10006, USA

477 Williamstown Road, Port Melbourne, VIC 3207, Australia

314–321, 3rd Floor, Plot 3, Splendor Forum, Jasola District Centre, New Delhi – 110025, India

103 Penang Road, #05–06/07, Visioncrest Commercial, Singapore 238467

Cambridge University Press is part of Cambridge University Press & Assessment, a department of the University of Cambridge.

We share the University's mission to contribute to society through the pursuit of education, learning and research at the highest international levels of excellence.

www.cambridge.org
Information on this title: www.cambridge.org/9781009016445

DOI: 10.1017/9781009025515

First published 2022
First paperback edition 2024

A catalogue record for this publication is available from the British Library

Library of Congress Cataloging-in-Publication data
Names: Kureshi, Yasser, author.
Title: Seeking supremacy : the pursuit of judicial power in Pakistan / Yasser Kureshi, University of Oxford.
Description: Cambridge, United Kingdom ; New York, NY : Cambridge University Press, 2022. | Series: Cambridge studies in law and society | Based on author's thesis (doctoral - Brandeis University, 2018) issued under title: Judging the generals : judicial-military interactions in authoritarian and post-authoritarian states. | Includes bibliographical references and index.
Identifiers: LCCN 2021058038 (print) | LCCN 2021058039 (ebook) | ISBN 9781316516935 (hardback) | ISBN 9781009016445 (paperback) | ISBN 9781009025515 (epub)
Subjects: LCSH: Political questions and judicial power–Pakistan–History. | Judges–Political activity–Pakistan–History. | Civil-military relations–Pakistan–History.
Classification: LCC KPL3499 .K87 2022 (print) | LCC KPL3499 (ebook) | DDC 347.5491/014–dc23/eng/20220207
LC record available at https://lccn.loc.gov/2021058038
LC ebook record available at https://lccn.loc.gov/2021058039

ISBN   978-1-316-51693-5   Hardback
ISBN   978-1-009-01644-5   Paperback

To Ami and Abou

CONTENTS

FIGURES

TABLES

ACKNOWLEDGEMENTS

This book and the professional and personal path leading to its completion began when I was a young Pakistani undergraduate student in the USA, watching from a distance, as a national movement demanding judicial independence and democracy unfolded. The unforgettable image of black-coated lawyers out in the streets, and judges being greeted with boisterous cheers and showered with flowers, inspired my long-term obsession with the complicated figure of the judge in Pakistan and beyond. Over a decade later, Pakistan's courts continue to elate and enrage, but never bore, and I am indebted to all those who enabled me to turn my youthful fascination into such a profound intellectual journey.

To begin with, I would like to express my sincere gratitude to the various institutions that provided funding and support for the research and writing of this book. This book was born out of my dissertation, and the original research in Pakistan was made possible by funding and support from Brandeis University and the Andrew Mellon Foundation. I would not have been able to complete my fieldwork in Pakistan without the generous support provided by the law firm Fazle Ghani Advocates. The firm graciously provided me with a desk in their state-of-the-art law library in Karachi and allowed me to carry out my case law research. Through the lawyers there, I immersed myself in the raucous and exciting world of Pakistani litigation. I would also like to thank the Dawn Group of Newspapers for providing me with access to their archive of newspaper clippings that proved a treasure trove of useful information. As a postdoctoral scholar, I was also privileged to have access to the resources of the libraries of the University of Oxford, through Trinity College and the Oxford School of Global and Area Studies. Thanks to the funding from the John and Daria Barry Foundation and the support from Trinity College, I have been able to complete my follow-up research and writing of this book.

During my time at Brandeis, Eva Bellin and Jeffrey Lenowitz were wonderful advisers, and Eva's committed mentorship and cheery optimism helped me see this project through. Outside Brandeis, Lisa Hilbink's intellectual imprint can be found across this project, and her advice, feedback and encouragement have all been indispensable in turning my dissertation into the book. My graduate school friends, Victoria McGroary, Matthew Isaacs, Kelly Stedem, Adam Smith and Paul Spalletta, were also an invaluable source of support. Finally, I have learned a lot from the lawyers, judges, journalists and activists I met in the field in Karachi, Lahore and Islamabad, who helped me understand the often bewildering culture and politics of Pakistan's bar and judiciary and went out of their way to help me gain access to interviewees through their networks. These include Salahuddin Ahmed, Raheel Kamran Sheikh, Hasnaat Malik, Munir Malik, Waqqas Mir, Faisal Siddiqi, Hasnain Chaudhry, Justice (retd) Jawwad Khawaja, Justice Mansoor Ali Shah, Abdullah Malik, Ali Almani, Saroop Ijaz, Summaiya Zaidi, Sara Malkani, Abdul Moiz Jaferii, Jeeva Haroon, Ahad Zuberi, Yousuf Nasim, Maryam Khan, Rana Asadullah, Qaiser Abbas, and Kamran Noorani.

At Cambridge University Press, Jens Meierhenrich was immensely encouraging, and Finola o' Sullivan, Marianne Nield, Chloe Quinn, Divya Arjunan and the rest of the editorial team have provided me with vital editorial support. Their guidance and the comments I received from four anonymous reviewers have also greatly improved the quality of the final product.

Finally, I am blessed to have a family that has nurtured both my interests and my ambitions and patiently supported me on the long and uncertain path of research and writing. I owe an enormous debt of gratitude to my parents. My father, Salman Kureshi, has been discussing and debating politics with me since I was a child, instilling in me, and encouraging, a passion for the study of politics. My mother, Ambreen Kureshi's endless energy and tireless efforts as a teacher and as a mother made the path I have taken possible, and have been a source of inspiration for me in my own academic career. My sister, Kiran Kureshi, is one of the warmest and most reassuring and resourceful people I have known, and her unflinching support has been invaluable.

I am especially indebted to my loving wife, Zoha Waseem. We met when we were both doing fieldwork for our dissertations, and now we are turning our dissertations into books together. Without her guiding me in my fieldwork, brainstorming ideas, providing feedback on drafts of chapters and reassuring me through this overwhelming process,

I would have never been able to see this project through, and I cannot wait to see her book in print as well.

I am fortunate to have so many other family members and friends who have been so generous to me over these past few years. In Lahore, Nadir Khan, Aisha Malik and Aizaz Khan welcomed me, opened their home to me and made my fieldwork in Lahore and Islamabad possible. Amar Khan supported me through my extended, and seemingly endless, education, and Waseem Ahmed and Talat Waseem facilitated several of my most fruitful interviews and provided care and support in Karachi and London. Other friends and relatives in Karachi, London and Boston, including Nadir Siddiqui, Zane deSouza, Huma Mehmood, Madeeha Channah, Anika Lakhani, Mehreen Mehmood, Maqbool Mehmood, Haniya Khan, Sadia Akram, Zamir Akram, Nadir Iqbal, Moeen Mehmood, Dania Khan, Faizan Diwan, Syed Ali Danial Jafri, Sana Khan and Zamir Khan, and many others, have all supported me along this journey.

The biggest challenge with such a project is completing it and seeing it leave your hands and go out into the world. I am thankful to all those who have helped this project progress to this point today, and I hope the book will do justice to all their generosity.

INTRODUCTION

> *The will of the people is above the constitution ... We as judges of the Supreme Court are sitting here as representatives of the will of the people.*
>
> Justice Jawwad Khawaja, twenty-third chief
> justice of Pakistan

Like many other post-colonial states, Pakistan's political system has experienced domination by its military, and other political power centres have needed to define their roles vis-à-vis the armed forces. An especially significant institution, and one whose role vis-à-vis the military has evolved and changed over time, has been the higher judiciary. On 3 November 2007, General Musharraf, Pakistan's fourth military ruler (since 1999), proclaimed a state of emergency in the country and suspended Pakistan's constitution. Musharraf's proclamation was motivated by a growing confrontation with Pakistan's judiciary and its activist twentieth chief justice, Iftikhar Chaudhry. The regime ordered the judges of the high courts and the Supreme Court to take an oath to uphold his new Provisional Constitutional Order, and dismiss any legal challenge to the powers and authority of Musharraf's military regime. Any judges who refused to take this oath were to be immediately removed from judicial service. Yet, in an impressive show of defiance, a majority of the judges refused to take the oath, and suffered removal from office. The now-iconic image of Justice Chaudhry being manhandled by security officials galvanized public support for the judiciary in its growing confrontation with the military.

1

As the confrontation between the two institutions escalated, Pakistan's lawyers mobilized across the country, celebrating the judiciary's new-found commitment to socio-economic activism, encouraging its grow-ing assertiveness against the military regime and resisting efforts by the military to subdue the judiciary. As a former leader of the Lahore High Court Bar Association from this period explained:

> It started with November 3rd 2007. Police broke into the High Court premises. They took us to the Anti-Terrorist court the next morning. All of us lawyers were sent to Kot Lakpat jail. After the arrests, there was no moving back even an inch, even a millimetre ... Restoration (of the Chief Justice) was the first agenda. Independence (of the judiciary) after that. We all wanted rule of law ... This Chief Justice (Iftikhar Chaudhry), he was a symbol of justice because he stood up to everyone ... even the military. By now lawyers had started thinking of themselves as a political party. From Communist lawyers to Islamist lawyers they were all united as one.[1]

The events of November 2007 highlighted just how potent a threat an assertive judiciary posed to the authority and stability of Pakistan's military regime, as well as how willing Pakistan's superior court judges were to confront the regime. What made the events of 2007 so puzzling was that Pakistan's judiciary had historically repeatedly upheld multiple military coups, provided legal cover to the authority and actions of preceding military regimes, and collaborated in main-taining military supremacy in the Pakistani state. Why did Pakistan's judiciary shift from collaborating with to confronting Pakistan's military?

This shift by the judiciary demands an explanation for several reasons. First, the courts contested the military's authority at a time when the military regime was relatively stable and without a clear political opening to explain increasing judicial assertiveness. Second, the pattern of contestation between the judiciary and military was characterized by jurisprudence that paid little attention to procedural constraints or jurisdictional limitations. A judiciary that had in the past veered in the direction of a formalist approach to decision-making now prioritized the nebulous concept of the 'public interest' over any con-cern about the constitutional limits of judicial power. Third, the judiciary's clash with the military demonstrated the importance of

[1] Interview No. L-11, 20 January 2017.

civil society in shaping interinstitutional dynamics, as the events of 2007 were actively encouraged and even coordinated by Pakistan's community of lawyers.[2]

The question of the judiciary's shift becomes even more significant given the outcome of the confrontation between the judiciary and the military. Musharraf's actions against the judiciary and the resistance from the judiciary and legal community helped galvanize a mass movement against his regime, which had been firmly entrenched for eight years. Within a few months of Musharraf's emergency proclamation he was forced to step down as president and the military had to accept the resumption of democratic rule. Further, the years since the fall of Musharraf's regime have proven that the surprisingly assertive populist judiciary was hardly an aberration created by the unique political circumstances of a late-stage authoritarian regime or prompted by the leadership of a single maverick chief justice. Instead, the judiciary continued to challenge civilian and, occasionally, military centres of power, even removing two elected prime ministers from office, and thereby furthering the judicialization of politics, as it pursued a preeminent role in Pakistan's political system. Thus, understanding the shift in the judiciary's relationship with the military in Pakistan helps us understand how the quest of judicial power can both further *and* undermine democratization in authoritarian and post-authoritarian states. Therefore, the central theoretical question this book addresses is: *under what conditions do courts muster the willingness to challenge politically powerful militaries?*

In examining the dramatic and consequential transformation in the role of Pakistan's judiciary in Pakistan, this book helps shed light on several questions that are central to comparative politics and public law. These include the sources of high-risk judicial assertiveness, the causes of the judicialization of politics, the sources of judicial preferences and how the construction of the judiciary's role and institutional relationships can impact democracy and the rule of law.

---

[2] 'You are our heroes!' remarked senior lawyer Naz Mohammadzai as she met the Peshawar High Court judge, Justice Dost Mohammad Khan, one of the judges who refused to take oath under the Provisional Constitutional Order (PCO), at his official residence in Peshawar. See 'Judges as Heroes', *The News*, 9 November 2007.

JUDICIAL ASSERTIVENESS IN AUTHORITARIAN AND POST-AUTHORITARIAN STATES

Scholars of judicial politics have demonstrated a growing interest in understanding the emergence of assertive judiciaries outside the context of established democracies, including in authoritarian and post-authoritarian states, where the political context shaping judicial decision-making is less fluid, and the institutional safeguards protecting judicial independence and authority are less secure (Ginsburg 2003; Chavez 2004; Helmke 2005; Hilbink 2007; Moustafa 2007; Trochev 2008; Kapiszewski 2012; Trochev and Ellet 2014). The two primary approaches to explaining judicial decision-making focus on *interests* and *ideas* (Woods and Hilbink 2009; Hilbink and Ingram 2019). Interest-based approaches focus on judicial strategies to maintain or expand the authority judges need to realize their policy preferences. Strategic judges will rationally adjust their behaviour in accordance with calculations about how other political actors will respond to their decisions, thereby minimizing any risk to their authority to achieve their policy goals (Epstein and Knight 1998; Helmke 2005; Vanberg 2015). The interests-based approach cannot, however, explain the high-risk judicial activism observed, where the judiciary risks likely defiance and retaliation, but acts assertively anyway. Why would a judge knowingly put his or her interests at risk by acting assertively? Explaining high-risk assertiveness requires engaging with the other interests of judges, interests that go beyond the instrumental preservation and acquisition of power to include reputation-building and job satisfaction.

Ideas-based explanations focus primarily on the sincere attitudes and legal and policy preferences judges hold, and how they motivate or dissuade judicial assertiveness. The attitudinal approach (e.g. Segal 2008) uses individually held policy preferences of judges to explain their assertive decisions. However, this attitudinal approach treats judicial attitudes as exogenous and does not explain how these attitudes are formed and change (Hilbink 2012).

Institutionalists argue that both ideas and interests are shaped by the institutional setting in which they develop (Hilbink 2009). Institutionalist scholars acknowledge that the legal and policy preferences of judges are not exogenous to judicial institutions but are constructed or constituted within the structure of the judiciary (Clayton and Gillman 1999; Hilbink 2007; Kapiszewski 2012). Different institutional settings allocate power and resources across different actors, empowering and constraining them differently. In doing so, institutional settings guide the behaviour and expectations of actors within these institutions by determining both which actors have more authority over the other actors, and which actors' norms and ideas regarding justice and rationality have primacy (March and Olsen 2011). Those actors whose authority is established and preferences are legitimized within the judiciary would then shape what behaviour is appropriate for judges. Institutionalist scholars have shown that the rules of appropriate behaviour are entrenched in the judiciary through history-dependent processes of adaptation, such as learning or selection. Through these processes, the institutional settings encode legal and policy preferences which then guide the actions of the judiciary. However, we need to build on these institutionalist insights, to better understand how external actors in state and society can shape both the formation of, and change in, institutional preferences within the judiciary

In this book I draw on both the ideas-based and interest-based literature to: (1) outline the mechanisms through which actors outside the judiciary, such as the military, can shape the norms and preferences governing appropriate behaviour within the judiciary, and thus guide both sincere and strategic judicial behaviour; and (2) develop a generalizable framework to understand the history-dependent processes through which legal and policy preferences that are encoded within the judiciary can change over time.

OVERVIEW OF THE ARGUMENT

The main argument put forth in this book is that the shift in judicial assertiveness towards the military in Pakistan is best explained by a change in the *audiences* with which judges interact, both individually and institutionally. I argue that the judiciary converges on a set of institutional preferences in response to the preferences of the institutions and networks, or 'audiences', with which judges interact. I build on the concept of an *audience* as developed by Baum (2007). An audience, for the purposes of this discussion, could be political institutions, civil and political organizations or social and professional groupings that are attentive to the decisions that judges make, and among which judges have reasons to build their reputations. The judiciary's affinity with the military diminishes as the audiences from which judges seek approval grow more independent from the military.

Before delving into the theory and application to the Pakistani case, a few definitions are necessary. This project is a study explaining variation in judicial assertiveness. Kapiszewski (2007: 18) defines judicial assertiveness as 'the degree and frequency with which courts challenge powerful actors in their rulings, that is, decide cases in ways that seek to nullify, restrict or change the behaviour of those actors'. This is not to be conflated with judicial activism, which is the tendency towards issuing rulings that legally innovate by straying away from established precedents or narrow readings of statutory and constitutional law (Kapiszewski 2007).[3]

This book primarily focuses on variation in judicial assertiveness towards the military.[4] In applying the concept of judicial assertiveness to the context of civil–military relations, it describes an increase in judicial assertiveness towards the military, as an increase in the judicial contestation of military prerogatives. Borrowing from the work of Stepan (1988) on civil–military relations and democracy, it defines 'military prerogatives' as the powers or privileges the military presumes it has, and it defines judicial 'contestation' as disagreements between the military and the judiciary over the extent of the military's prerogatives. These disagreements manifest themselves in judicial decisions challenging the military's prerogatives.

The key argument is that an increase in judicial contestation of military prerogatives is a product of a shift in audiences shaping judicial legal and policy preferences, away from the military. As the military's *institutional interlinkages* with the judiciary decrease, the military's role as an audience shaping judicial preferences decreases.

Institutional interlinkages are defined as links to the internal rules and processes of the judiciary that allow the military, and allied elites, to shape the internal structure and culture of the institution. Two types of institutional interlinkages are discussed: *utilitarian* and *normative*. If institutions, organizations or networks have a role in the appointments, promotions, transfers and disciplining of judges, I describe this as a

---

[3] While the two phenomena differ, often an increase in judicial assertiveness happens when a judiciary embraces judicial activism as a norm. In Pakistan's case, as I show in subsequent chapters, the judiciary grew more assertive as it grew more willing to deviate from established precedents that favoured deference and subservience to the Pakistani military.

[4] The book also discusses jurisprudence pertaining to civilian governments and institutions, where relevant.

utilitarian interlinkage with the judiciary. Social and professional net-works from which judges are recruited and with which they identify have normative interlinkages with the judiciary, as these networks can affect judges' esteem if judges do not manifest a commitment to a shared set of norms and preferences. Thus, the institutions, organizations and networks that have interlinkages with the judiciary are the audiences with which judges aim to build their reputations, for both material and non-material purposes, and thus are the critical audiences for the judiciary. Through these interlinkages, these audiences shape judicial behaviour.

In authoritarian and post-authoritarian states, the military seeks to shape the willingness of judges to contest the military by designing judicial institutions in such a way that the military or its societal allies are the key audiences for both judicial careers and esteem. If the military or allied elites are in a position to affect judicial careers, then the military possesses utilitarian interlinkages with the judiciary. If the judiciary is recruited from social and professional networks that are tied to and benefit from the military, then the military possesses normative interlinkages with the military. Through these interlinkages, the mili-tary can shape the legal and policy preferences underlying judicial behaviour.

The book develops a typology of different relationships between the judiciary and the military that shape the judiciary's jurisprudential approach to the military. This typology outlines both how different institutional arrangements shape the variation in judicial assertiveness towards the military in different countries and how judicial preferences regarding the military may change over time. When the institutional interlinkages between the military and the judiciary change, judicial preferences in favour of the military shift, and the judiciary moves between the categories in the typology.

The first category is the *controlled court*, where the military and judiciary enjoy utilitarian interlinkages, that is, the military and affili-ated elites shape the judicial legal and policy preferences through the appointment and promotion process. The second is the *collaborative court*, where the military and judiciary enjoy normative interlinkages, that is, the military shapes the judicial preferences since judges are recruited from networks aligned with the military. The third is the *loyal court*, where the military and judiciary enjoy both utilitarian and normative interlinkages. The fourth is the *confrontational court*, in which neither the military nor its affiliates are in primary control of

7

the appointment process, nor are the judges recruited from professional networks closely tied to the military. The military and the judiciary enjoy no institutional interlinkages and thus the military cannot shape the preferences of the judiciary.[5]

The Pakistani case helps outline both how institutional interlinkages shape the judiciary's approach towards the military, and how shifts in audiences change the judiciary's approach towards the military. Over the course of Pakistan's history, the judiciary's relationship with the military shifted across these categories, as the judiciary most closely approximated a loyal court in the years after independence, transitioned towards a controlled court in the 1980s and finally shifted towards a confrontational court by the turn of the century. In the first twenty years after Pakistan's independence, the military and affiliated elites were the critical audiences shaping the judiciary's legal and policy preferences, which ensured that a norm of upholding the military's interests and political supremacy was entrenched within the judicial system. However, since then, the Pakistani judiciary has transitioned away from the military, as the military and affiliated elites saw their role as audiences for the judiciary diminish, while the politically active *lawyer's community* became an increasingly critical audience shaping the judiciary's preferences. The result of this transition has been a concomitant shift in judicial preferences, as the judiciary embraced a less deferential and collaborative approach and sought to play a more expansive and authoritative political role in Pakistan's political system that increasingly placed it at odds with the military. Thus, the change in judicial audiences generated a change in judicial preferences, which led to increased contestation and confrontation between the judiciary and both military and civilian centers of power. This is not to say that other factors did not play important roles in explaining the variation in judicial assertiveness towards the military, as the judiciary was also responsive to variations in the unity and political strength of the

---

[5] These categories represent constructed ideal-types that approximate reality. In most states, the judiciary will usually have multiple audiences of varying importance, and it is unlikely that the military and affiliated elites will either be the sole audience for the judiciary, or, alternatively, have no interlinkages with the military or affiliated elites. However, the category that each state most closely approximates will depend on how dominant an audience the military is for the judiciary in that country, that is, how strong the normative and utilitarian interlinkages are between the military and the judiciary, in comparison to the linkages between other external actors and the judiciary in that state.

military, interruptions in the constitutional framework, changes in judicial leadership and the growth of electronic media. However, to account fully for the variation in judicial assertiveness towards the Pakistani military it is necessary to understand the audiences shaping institutional preferences.

What processes drove the Pakistani judiciary's movement from loyal court to confrontational court? Three processes led to a change in judicial audiences. First, institutionally, a separation of the judiciary from executive control through a series of constitutional reforms and judicial decisions endowed the former with significantly more autonomy, granted senior judges more control over judicial careers and reduced the military's influence in judicial careers. Second, demographically, the increasing indigenization of the judiciary led to a commensurate shift in the judiciary's priorities and preferences. There was a shift in the composition of networks from which judges were primarily recruited, from an elite cadre of lawyers and bureaucrats closely aligned with the military elite to a locally educated middle-class network of lawyers, more distant from the military and more attentive to mass politics and preferences. This shift reduced the military's role in the networks with which judges sought to build a reputation. Third, politically, at the same time that the private legal sector became a primary pipeline for judicial appointments, Pakistan's bar associations of private lawyers became increasingly politically active entities that embraced opposition to unfettered military rule and unregulated electoral supremacy. As the bar had by now become the major recruiting site for Pakistan's judiciary, this meant that judge-hopefuls increasingly had to fall in line with these norms and to some degree assert their independence from the military and embrace the more activist and interventionist postures prevalent in the bar. Thus, as a result of these three processes the military's institutional interlinkages with the judiciary were diminished, and the bar of activist lawyers became an increasingly importance audience shaping the legal and policy preferences of the judiciary.

This work deepens our understanding of the process through which legal and policy preferences are formed, institutionalized and disrupted within the judicial system, and provides a systematic explanation for the way in which the judiciary's relationship with external actors shapes this process. The audience-based approach, presented in this book, sheds light on the critical role of reputation-building in shaping judicial behaviour. Understanding the significant role of reputation-building helps connect institutions, organizations and networks outside the judiciary to the process of preference formation and transformation within the judiciary. Thus, the audience-based approach properly embeds the judiciary in its political, social and institutional environment, and explains how this environment shapes the legal and policy preferences underlying judicial behaviour. In doing so, it contributes to our understanding of judicial institutions and behaviour in four ways.

First, this study reveals how politically powerful militaries shape the willingness and ability of the judiciary to assert civilian control over the military. There is a robust literature on the strategies military regimes use to co-opt and control political institutions in order to consolidate their rule (Gandhi and Prezworski 2007; Gandhi and Lust-Okar 2009; Geddes, et al., 2014). Another strand of literature examines how, during democratic periods, post-authoritarian militaries carefully manage their political capital to preserve their prerogatives within the political system (Hunter 1997; Pion-Berlin 2001). Neither of these literatures pays adequate attention to how militaries strategize to co-opt, control or resist judiciaries, in order to consolidate their rule or preserve their prerogatives. Even the limited scholarship dealing with judicial–military relations has focused either on variation in the political space available to judiciaries under military regimes (Helmke 2005; Pereira 2005; Ginsburg and Moustafa 2008; Hamad 2019), or on the role the post-authoritarian judiciary plays in mediating between the military and elected governments (Rios-Figueroa 2016). This scholarship does not consider how politically powerful militaries seek to increase the willingness of judges to collaborate with, or defer to, military power, that is, how politically powerful militaries shape judicial ideologies. Understanding developments and changes in judicial preferences towards the military requires understanding the judiciary's interactions with state institutions, the legal profession and society more broadly, and locating the place of the military within this web of formal and informal relations that shape the internal culture of the judiciary. The audience-based approach does exactly this, and thus provides a generalizable framework that can explain variation and change in judicial–military relations across authoritarian and post-authoritarian states.

Second, this study highlights the role of the legal community in shaping judicial behaviour. I do not just consider moments where the legal community rallies in support of the judiciary, legitimizing and protecting the judiciary when it challenges politically powerful actors (Epp 1998; Moustafa 2007; Ghias 2010; Karpik and Halliday 2011), but also when the legal community effects changes in the legal and policy preferences underlying judicial behaviour (Ocantos 2016). I closely study the organization, sociology and culture of the lawyers' community in Pakistan to understand how ideas regarding political activism emerged and spread within the bar, and I show the conditions under which the lawyer's community's role as a key audience for the judiciary increased over time. I describe the informal but consequential power of the bar to make and break the reputations of judges, and the ways in which judges and aspiring judges adapted their behaviour in response to the bar. Thus, the book sheds light on how dominant values and preferences in the legal community percolate upwards, to become hegemonic within the internal culture of the judiciary. In doing so, this book also contributes to a better understanding of informal relationships within judges' social and professional networks (Popova 2012; Urribarri 2012; Dressel et al. 2017). It adds new insights to a growing interest in the less observable but often more consequential informal ties that bind judges to other state and societal elites, and that shape the internal culture of the judiciary and impact its jurisprudence.

Third, this book shows that judges are motivated by both material and non-material goals, and that non-material goals shape judicial behaviour far more than many scholars of judicial politics acknowledge. There is a growing body of research showing that judges are motivated by the non-material goal of building esteem (Baum 2007; Ginsburg and Garoupa 2009, 2015; Epstein and Knight 2012). Judges care about what the people they work with and socialize with think of them, and this concern has a tangible impact on their judgments. Further, with the development of electronic media and the proliferation of social media, the actions of judges come under ever greater scrutiny, and the challenge of gaining the esteem of one's social and professional networks has become a more demanding and salient priority for judges. The audience-based framework incorporates a judge's desire for esteem into explaining judicial willingness to uphold and endorse certain norms and preferences in their jurisprudence, in spite of the political risks. The study of Pakistani judges reveals the extent to which judges are cognizant of the esteem of their networks, and illustrates how this motivation affects their behaviour.

Finally, one of the driving forces behind the renewed interest in ideas in the institutional development of judiciaries is the increasing willingness of activist courts to not just move beyond formalistic understandings of the legal texts and rules in judicial decisions, but also to embrace new non-traditional roles within political systems, and address a growing range of public policy questions and political controversies (Hirschl 2008; Woods and Hilbink 2009; Couso et al. 2011; Couso and Hilbink 2011; Bhuwania 2016; Ocantos 2016; Landfried 2019). Courts are reinterpreting both their place among state institutions, and their position in the relationship between state and society, which impact debates about the meaning of the rule of law, sources of jurisprudence and public expectations of the judiciary. This book contributes to this dialogue about new judicial role conceptions and the judicialization of politics by explaining how Pakistan's judiciary shifted from a commitment to upholding the procedural requirements of a colonial-era legal framework designed to uphold executive power and discretion, towards a commitment to championing its conception of the 'public interest'. In service of this new populist role conception, the judiciary de-emphasized procedural and jurisdictional constraints on its authority, and intervened in the politics and policymaking of both civilian and military executives. This doctrinal transformation cannot be understood simply by tracking changes across the court's jurisprudence. This doctrinal transformation and the consequent judicialization of politics and governance and confrontations with military and political institutions is rooted in changes in the internal culture of the judiciary, and the sociological, political and institutional processes underlying these changes.

METHODOLOGY OF THE STUDY

This book seeks to refine our understanding of the causal process that leads historically deferential courts to confront politically powerful militaries. Explaining a shift in judicial behaviour requires investigating shifts in the institutional preferences underlying judicial behaviour. To do so, we must understand the formal and informal relationships between the judiciary, state institutions and civil society, which shape the internal culture of the judiciary. The goal is to show that a shift in the external audiences of the judiciary motivates judges, for both strategic and sincere reasons, to adopt new preferences that reorient their preferences regarding the role of the military within the political system and the role of the judiciary in confronting military and political power within that system, and that these preferences manifest themselves in the court's jurisprudence.

The empirical chapters offer a longitudinal analysis of judicial behaviour towards the military in Pakistan since its independence till 2017. Pakistan makes an illuminating case for studying judicial–military interactions for a number of reasons. First, the Pakistani military has been at or near the helm of Pakistan's political system for most of its history, with a range of prerogatives, including political prerogatives, economic prerogatives and security prerogatives, allowing us to study how the judiciary deals with a wide range of military-related legal questions. Second, Pakistan's judiciary shifted from collaborating with, to challenging the military, providing an opportunity to study and reveal the conditions under which the judiciary's institutional preferences, and relationship with the military, shift over time. Third, the Pakistani judiciary contested the military's authority, when the military directly ruled the state, facing few political challengers, which meant that judicial contestation of such a powerful military carried great risks. Fourth, upon confronting military power, the judiciary did not look back, subsequently overruling and undermining even elected civilian governments, thus highlighting both the promise and the perils of the judiciary's pursuit of power within a political system. Political factors alone cannot explain the judiciary's shift towards greater contestation of military supremacy or interventions into political governance. So, studying Pakistan allows me to focus on the implications of changing institutional relations and preferences for judicial behaviour.

The methodology guiding this book is to focus on the critical role of judicial audiences in shaping institutional preferences and demonstrate the impact of these legal and policy preferences on variations in judicial assertiveness. The book delves into the internal dynamics of the judiciary to shed light on how judges think about and pursue reputation-building, and connects the logic of reputation-building with the adoption and institutionalization of legal and policy preferences within the judiciary. The exploration of these micro-dynamics within judicial institutions, and their connections to broader processes of change in regime structure and shifts in jurisprudence, required canvassing a range of empirical sources.

This book is based on eighteen months of field research in Pakistan, in which I collected, coded and analysed over a thousand Supreme Court and High Court judgments; conducted over 130 interviews with lawyers, judges, politicians and journalists; and constructed an archive of thousands of newspaper articles, bar association resolutions, judges' speeches and judicial biographies. I used the evidence from these streams of data to carefully trace the processes by which changes in the institutional environment impacted a transformation in judicial preferences, which then caused variations in judicial assertiveness towards the military.

The collection of High Court and Supreme Court decisions that I analysed included a coded dataset of all reported judgments that dealt with challenges to military prerogatives between 1973 and 2015.[6] I began with 1973 as the start date for collecting judicial decisions for this dataset because, although there have been several constitutional amendments and suspensions, Pakistan has been under the same constitutional framework since then.[7] These judgments were then subjected to two types of analysis. First, I coded each judgment based on the extent to which it contested the military's prerogatives. This allowed me to assess variation in judicial assertiveness towards the military over time, and how this variation manifested itself across different types of military prerogative. Second, I studied the content and legal reasoning of these decisions, to understand the reasoning and priorities of the judges in these decisions.

The archive of newspaper articles, judicial speeches, judicial biographies and bar association resolutions, collected from the 1950s till today, allowed me to delve deeper into the impact of the judiciary's changing relationships with state institutions and civil society on the institutional culture and dynamics within the judiciary.[8] Newspaper articles provided a useful historical overview of the Pakistani judiciary and legal community, and they supplied context for the judiciary's most publicized decisions. Bar association resolutions and judicial speeches in both English and Urdu helped me understand changing

---

[6] I only consider reported judgments by the superior judiciary. A large number of High Court decisions go unreported and are therefore simply unavailable for consideration. Thus, this is not an exhaustive study of all High Court judgments pertaining to the military during this period. Restricting the dataset to only reported judgments does not create a selection bias because the choice to report a judgment is not based on the outcome of the decision, or the salience of the issue, but on an assessment that the decision will have an impact on the jurisprudence on that particular question, that is, that the judgment will have value as a legal precedent for subsequent decisions.

[7] I collected these decisions from the following law reporters: *Pakistan Law Decisions* (PLD), *Pakistan Law Journal* (PLJ), *Supreme Court Monthly Report* (SCMR), *Civil Law Cases* (CLC), *Pakistan Criminal Law Journal* (PCrLJ), *Yearly Law Review* (YLR), *Pakistan Law Commission*, *Key Law Reports* and *Sindh and Balochistan Law Review*. I located relevant decisions using their citations that were compiled in the *Annual Law Digest* (ALD).

[8] I collected newspaper articles from the following eleven newspapers: *Dawn*, *The News*, *Morning News*, *Pakistan Times*, *The Muslim*, *The Leader*, *Daily News*, *The Nation*, *Express Tribune*, *Star* and *Pakistan Today*.

14

relationships, priorities and preferences in the bar and bench. Judicial speeches and judicial biographies provided insights on the way judges thought about their reputations and were also useful sources of information on the educational and professional backgrounds of judges.

The third source of data was semi-structured interviews with lawyers and retired judges conducted in both English and Urdu. I used a method of snowball sampling to recruit more than 130 lawyers, judges, politicians and journalists for interviews. The judges and lawyers I interviewed came from different generations on the bench, from the 1960s till today. I interviewed lawyers who had worked in different sectors of the profession and had participated in relevant court decisions, and lawyers who had played important roles in the politics of the bar associations. I also interviewed several current and former political officeholders, who had been in positions where they were involved with the working of the judiciary. Finally, I interviewed journalists who had spent years reporting on the high courts and Supreme Court for print and electronic media. Thus, my interview sample gave me a diverse range of perspectives and experiences pertaining to judicial–military relations. The interview data enriched the narrative constructed through case law and archival data, by providing insights into the politics, norms and preferences informing bar–bench relations and judicial decisions regarding the military that are unavailable through studying public records. To protect anonymity, interviews with judges, lawyers, political office holders and reporters were assigned the letters J, L, P and R, respectively, along with a random number between 1 and 100 that was generated and assigned to each interview. All interviews are referenced only by that code and the interview date.[9]

I collected and combined information from these sources to: (1) track changes in the judicial appointment processes, changes in the political environment in which the judiciary was operating and changes in the ideas, organization and culture of the legal community within which the judiciary was embedded; (2) understand changes in the internal dynamics of the judiciary, including the politics surrounding judicial appointments, the demographic and educational backgrounds of judges and the reputation-building strategies judges used with their audiences; and (3) track patterns in judicial contestation of the military over time, and

---

[9] Thus, for example, an interview with a judge would be referenced by a code such as J-91, 4 January 2017, and an interview with a lawyer would be referenced by a code such as L-40, 20 December 2016.

examine how the court's perception of its role, its procedural and jurisdictional constraints and its relationship with the military and society changed over time. Bringing these three streams of information together allowed me to trace the process by which the changing audiences of the judiciary affected the legal and policy preferences underlying variation in the judiciary's behaviour towards the military over time.

A longitudinal tracing of institutional development and change over decades has its limitations. First, using publicly available data to analyse an institution's internal culture means one cannot account for unrecorded private bargains or deals within opaque state institutions that may shape important judicial outcomes but are largely unverifiable. Second, a longitudinal analysis does not afford the opportunity to exhaustively explain the process and context of judicial decision-making in individual cases, and account for all the actions of judges that run counter to the expectations of the audience-based thesis, which also merit explanation. My goal here is not to propose that the audience-based thesis provides a comprehensive explanation of all aspects of judicial behaviour towards the military. Instead, I demonstrate how a shift in jurisprudence towards the military in Pakistan cannot be explained without understanding the role of changing audiences in shaping the institutional preferences underlying judicial behaviour.

STRUCTURE OF THE BOOK

This book proceeds as follows. Chapter 1 surveys the literature on judicial behaviour and then argues for: (1) examining the effect of the institutional environment in which the judiciary operates in authoritarian and post-authoritarian states on judicial preferences; (2) incorporating a wider range of judicial motivations into studying judicial behaviour; and (3) teasing out the mechanism by which judicial relations with state institutions and society can reconfigure the legal and policy preferences of the courts. I then detail the audience-based approach to understanding judicial behaviour and outline how it addresses the three concerns discussed above and applies to the context of states where the military is a powerful and autonomous political actor. Finally, I probe the utility of this audience-based approach in the case of Pakistan.

The following chapters trace the shift in judicial audiences shaping judicial preferences in Pakistan between 1947 and 2017, outline the consequent changes in legal and political preferences held by the judiciary and demonstrate the impact of the shifting preferences on variation in judicial assertiveness towards the military in Pakistan.

16

Chapter 2 examines the first twenty years of Pakistan's history, and applies the audience-based explanation to explaining why the judiciary was *loyal* to the military during this period, supporting the military's rise to power and its pre-eminence. In the final part of this chapter, I discuss Pakistan's first period of constitutional democratic rule between 1973 and 1977 and outline the beginning of the judiciary's institutional separation from the military.

Chapters 3 and 4 describe and explain changes in the Pakistani judiciary's behaviour towards the military between 1977 and 1999. Chapter 3 shows, through examination of all areas of military-related jurisprudence during this time, that the judiciary was gradually shifting towards staking out a somewhat more independent position from the military, preserving and cautiously expanding its own role and jurisdiction. Chapter 4 traces the change in judicial audiences, and shows that as the military's institutional interlinkages with the judiciary diminished, and the judiciary's interlinkages with the politically active bar of professional lawyers grew, the legal and policy preferences of the judiciary changed.

Chapter 5 describes and explains the judiciary's increasing assertiveness and clashes with the military during the period from 1999 to 2017. Through this period, I show that the judiciary adopted a more *confrontational* approach towards both military and civilian centres of power, and argue that the changing audiences of the judiciary manifested themselves in the activist and populist legal and policy preferences in the judiciary, which explains the increased judicial assertiveness during this period. I also show how the institutional preferences that motivated the judiciary to confront the military also drove it to challenge and undermine post-authoritarian elected governments.

Chapter 6 briefly assesses how the judiciary's new role conception has fared in the context of autocratization in Pakistan since 2017. I show that the judiciary has both contributed to and been compromised by the process of autocratization, as assertive judicial interventions weakened elected governments, providing the space for a revival of military power, and enabling the military to disrupt the internal dynamics of the judiciary.

Chapter 7 summarizes the analysis of judicial–military relations offered in this book, applies the audience-based framework to the context of other authoritarian and democratic contexts and develops the theoretical implications of the arguments. It demonstrates that the audience-based explanation provides leverage in explaining judicial–military relations and judicial assertiveness in other authoritarian and democratic contexts, including Egypt, Turkey and India.

CHAPTER ONE

THE JUDICIARY, RULE OF LAW AND THE MILITARY

INTRODUCTION

Pakistan's military has been the country's dominant power centre for most of its post-colonial history, shaping the politics and policies of the state. But the military's dominance is neither unconstrained nor uncontested. The military is unable to maintain its authority and influence without relying on a coalition of allied bureaucrats, judges, political parties, urban and rural capitalists and civil society organizations. In Pakistan, many use the shorthand term 'the establishment' to describe this entrenched coalition of formal institutions, associations and interest groups, aligned around a mutual interest in supporting the military's political agenda. On the other hand, other political parties and segments of civil society have long worked to limit the military's authority and counter its political agenda. The struggle over maintaining or displacing the military as the primary power centre within the political system has been the axis around which Pakistan's politics has revolved for decades.

In the last fifteen years, this civil–military dynamic has been disrupted by the emergence of another power centre: the judiciary. Pakistan's judiciary is no longer the 'junior partner' of the military or a site upon which the military and its political allies and opponents compete for political leverage. The judiciary is now a power centre in its own right, seeking to expand and legitimize its authority, influence policymaking and compete with civilian and military authorities to shape the state. The emergence of the judiciary as an assertive and active centre of power has been the most consequential feature of

18

Pakistan's new political system, and the military has had to adapt its ambitions and strategies accordingly.

This book maps out the evolution of the relationship between the judiciary and military in Pakistan to explain why Pakistan's high courts shifted from loyal deference to the military, to open competition, and confrontation, with military and civilian institutions. To understand the emergence of the judiciary as an assertive power centre within Pakistan's political system, I delve into the processes by which the preferences that underlie judicial behaviour towards the military shifted over time. Judges are both officers in formal judicial institutions and members of a legal community embedded in informal social and professional networks. Both these identities place judges in a web of formal and informal relationships with other institutions and networks. The ties that connect the judiciary to institutions and networks within both the state and society shape judges' understanding of their role, ambitions and reper-toire within the political system. Delving into these relationships, and the processes by which these relationships evolve, allows us to under-stand how shifts in these relations shape the institutional preferences of the judiciary. Locating the military within the judiciary's web of formal and informal relationships allows us to understand how judicial norms and preferences towards the military emerge and evolve. This chapter develops the theoretical apparatus necessary to accomplish this task. I introduce the concept of judicial 'audiences', originally coined by Lawrence Baum (2007), to better describe the dynamics of the relation-ship between judges and external actors in state and society and their influence on judicial behaviour. I then demonstrate how variation in the relationship between the judiciary and the military is best explained by variation in the extent to which the military acts as a critical audience linked to the internal workings of the judiciary and shaping judicial preferences. Finally, I probe the applicability of this theory for explaining the evolution of the judiciary's relationship with the military in Pakistan and the emergence of competition and confrontation between these two unelected institutions.

Although the analysis is primarily focused on Pakistan, it was motiv-ated by and speaks to broader theoretical concerns. The task of estab-lishing the 'rule of law' is both urgent and complex in many authoritarian and post-authoritarian states because of the testing polit-ical circumstances typically found in these states (Teitel 2001). Where democracy has not been established, authoritarian rulers rule in a state of legal exception without many constraints, or they construct legal and judicial frameworks to project and entrench their power and control (Ginsburg and Moustafa 2008; Helmke 2009). In states where democracy has recently been established, the rule of law is undermined by the continued strength and influence of former ruling elites and the weaknesses of new representative institutions – a disparity that is frequently enshrined in the post-authoritarian legal or constitutional framework (Hirschl 2004). Most authoritarian regimes have been ruled by military leaders, and in many new democracies the military retains special powers, and the coercive authority of the military allows it to undermine the rule of law when and where it does not suit its interests (Geddes 1999; Pion-Berlin and Martinez 2017). Therefore, given that strong coercive institutions and weak representative institutions characterize most authoritarian and post-authoritarian states today, understanding the conditions under which the judiciary is willing to challenge a ruling or formerly ruling military is essential to understanding how the rule of law can be established (Rios-Figueroa 2016).

THE MILITARY'S JUDICIAL AGENDA

What relationship does a politically powerful military seek with the judiciary? Unlike political parties, the military is a state institution, and remains a state institution during periods of democracy and dictatorship. This means the military seeks to sustain a wide range of institutional prerogatives, regardless of regime type, although the scope of prerogatives varies depending upon regime type.[1]

When military regimes come to power, they set about reorganizing state institutions so as to consolidate and project their power.[2] Military regimes can use judiciaries to exercise state power against the opposition, advance administrative discipline within state institutions, maintain cohesion among factions within the ruling coalition, bolster regime legitimacy and facilitate market transitions (Ginsburg and Moustafa 2008; Trochev 2008; Moustafa 2014; Hamad 2019). However, the regime will only choose to empower the judiciary to carry out such functions once it can limit any risk that the judiciary will act assertively against the regime. The regime has two options: it can create either a

---

[1] By military prerogatives, I mean the powers the military presumes it has.
[2] There is an expansive literature on how military regimes create rubber-stamp parliaments through rigged elections and the engineering of loyal political parties (Gandhi and Prezworski 2007; Gandhi and Lust-Okar 2009; Boix and Svolik 2013).

weak judiciary *unable* to act assertively against the regime or a loyal judiciary *unwilling* to act assertively against the regime.

The literature on judiciaries under authoritarian regimes has focused on the tactics regimes used to weaken judiciaries. This includes fragmenting the judicial system by creating parallel judicial systems, immunizing regime actions from judicial scrutiny and reducing judicial authority by altering legal standing requirements, the structure of the judiciary and the scope of judicial review (Ginsburg and Moustafa 2008; Crouch 2020). All these actions ensure the judiciary fulfils the functions the regime needs it to but weaken the judiciary's ability to challenge the regime itself.

However, the military seeks to retain authority and influence during periods of both military rule and civilian democracy. During democratic periods, the military has moved out of a position of formal power and cannot legislatively weaken the judiciary's authority. If the military is interested in preserving its prerogatives it must ensure the judiciary does not challenge its interests, even during periods of civilian rule when the judiciary's powers are restored. Thus, the ideal relationship is one where the judiciary would uphold military interests, both when the judiciary's powers are weakened and when the judiciary's powers are restored. Thus, it is important to understand how military regimes shape a judiciary's ability to ensure their loyalty, rendering them unwilling to act assertively against the military.

UNDERSTANDING JUDICIAL BEHAVIOUR

How can the military shape judicial behaviour? Judicial behaviour is shaped by preferences and interests. There are two types of preference: (1) policy preferences and (2) legal preferences. Policy preferences refer to judges' preferences on questions of state actions and policymaking, and legal preferences orient a judge's approach to sources of law and legal procedure and condition their understanding of their role and the reach of the judiciary (Epstein and Knight 1998; Ocantos 2016). Judicial interests refer to judges' interest in (1) preserving and expanding their authority to realize their policy preferences, (2) advancing their careers and (3) building esteem (Epstein and Knight 2012). Scholarship on judicial behaviour is divided between strategic scholars, who focus on how external actors shape the judiciary's willingness to act on its preferences, and attitudinalists and institutionalists, who focus on the content of legal and policy preferences underlying judicial actions and the processes through which these preferences are constructed within the judiciary.

Strategic scholars pay special attention to how judges, motivated by their interest in realizing policy preferences, will (1) act on their sincere policy preferences when they can but (2) will adjust their behaviour in accordance with calculations about how other political actors will respond to their decisions, to minimize any risk to their authority to realize their policy preferences as closely as possible (Epstein and Knight 1998; Helmke 2005; Carruba and Gabel 2014; Vanberg 2015). Accordingly, courts are unlikely to assert themselves against the military when political power within the political system is centralized within the military and allied political institutions, strengthening the military's ability to undermine the authority of the judiciary. Conversely, courts are more likely to assert themselves against the military when political power is fragmented across the political system, weakening the military's ability to undermine the authority of the judiciary (Tsebelis 2002; Ferejohn et al. 2007; Rios-Figueroa 2007). The assumption that judicial behaviour is shaped by external political conditions leaves rational-choice institutionalists ill-equipped to explain why courts engage in high-risk confrontations with other branches of government, even when they are unlikely to win these contests, or how courts select legal justifications for interventions and judgments.

Attitudinalists and institutionalists look closely at the role of ideas about law and policy in the judicial decision-making process. Attitudinalists use judges' individually held policy preferences to explain assertive decisions (Segal and Spaeth 2002). Thus, a leftist judge will act assertively to challenge a right-wing government, and an activist judge will intervene in a wider range of policy issues than a restrained judge (Segal 2008). This approach suggests that courts are more assertive when the majority of judges ideologically oppose the policies underlying the laws or state actions under scrutiny.

Institutionalists do not treat judicial preferences as exogenously determined but seek to explain the historical and sociological processes through which judicial preferences are constituted (Clayton and Gillman 1999; Whittington 2007; Ocantos 2016). They shift the explanatory focus to the institutional design, norms and internal culture of the judiciary, to explain the construction of judicial preferences shaping judicial behaviour. The judicial institutions act as sites for preference formation, and institutional designs incentivize judges to take particular ideological positions and adopt particular conceptions of the role of the judiciary within the political structure of the state (Clayton and Gillman 1999; Ginsburg and Garoupa 2009). Institutional settings guide the behaviour and expectations of judges by determining which actors' norms and understandings of justice and rationality gain primacy and become entrenched as the norms and preferences of the institution over time (March and Olsen 2011). Scholars have explored the sources and consequences of the entrenchment of particular judicial norms (Stone 1992; Clayton 1999) and legal doctrines (Bussiere 1997) within a judicial system or explained how judicial appointment systems shape the character (Epstein et al. 2001; Kapiszewski 2012; Nathan 2013) and internal culture within the judiciary (Kapiszewski 2010; Jillani 2012). They have also probed the judicial education and training and promotion systems within which judges are trained, and the professional community of judges, prosecutors and lawyers within which judges work and socialize, to understand how these systems and communities facilitate the development of a particular conception of the role of the courts among judges (Hilbink 2007; Woods 2009; Ocantos 2016).

However, attitudinalist and institutionalist scholars' focus on the judicial institutions, the policy and legal preferences held by judges and the formation and institutionalization of these preferences leaves out the role of external actors. Instead, the extant literature primarily views state institutions and societal actors as actors upon which the judiciary seeks to exert its authority (Vondoepp 2006; Moustafa 2007; Kapiszewski 2012) or against which the judiciary seeks to protect its authority (Vanberg 2000; Ginsburg 2003; Helmke 2005). But external actors outside the judiciary do not simply constrain judicial strategies, they also constitute judicial preferences, and while institutionalists acknowledge that groups within the legal community can play a role in entrenching legal preferences (Kapiszewski 2010; Ocantos 2016), the process through which external actors construct judicial preferences remains inadequately theorized. This preference-shaping role has critical implications for understanding judicial behaviour, as, for example, if the military succeeds in shifting judicial preferences, it can ensure favourable jurisprudence over time, even after the authority of the military to influence the judiciary wanes.

Therefore, in order to fully understand and explain judicial interactions with other state institutions, and variation in judicial decision-making towards other state institutions, it is not enough to focus either on the power of external actors to compel the judiciary to act with strategic restraint or on the preferences of judges to act assertively or with restraint. We need to understand the role of external actors in *shaping* judicial preferences to act assertively or with restraint. Therefore, I propose a theory for explaining the role external actors play in shaping judicial preferences, predicated on two claims. First, judges' interests and preferences are interlinked, and the pursuit of judicial interests shapes the process through which certain preferences gain primacy, while entrenched judicial preferences shape the approach judges take in pursuing their interests. Second, each judge carries a combination of policy and legal preferences, which typically varies from judge to judge, but there is a certain combination of policy and legal preferences around which the judiciary builds an institutional consensus and that judges within the institution will largely adhere to, for both sincere and strategic reasons. Using this theory, I explain how external actors can shape institutionally held judicial preferences.

JUDGES AND THEIR AUDIENCES

The audience-based explanation for judicial decision-making builds on the awareness that individual judges are not simply interested in policy maximization, they are also interested in reputation-building. Ginsburg and Garoupa (2015 : 15) define reputation as the 'stock of assessments about an actor's past performance'. Judicial reputation conveys information about the quality of the judiciary and fosters esteem for the individual judge. Baum (1997) introduced the concept of audiences: the political institutions, civil and political organizations or social and professional groupings that are attentive to the decisions that judges make and with which judges seek to build a reputation when making decisions. Why do judges care about their reputation? Reputation-building has both material and non-material purposes. Materially, judges seek to advance their careers by gaining promotions and increasing pecuniary and non-pecuniary benefits. Therefore, they would seek to build their reputations with audiences who are in a position to control the process of appointment, promotion and budgetary allocation for the judiciary. Non-materially, judges also seek to build their reputations as 'able' judges to gain the esteem of those social and professional networks they are closely tied to, as their own esteem and satisfaction in the job is tied to gaining such respect (Cass 1995; Drahozal 1998; Posner 2010; Epstein and Knight 2012). Thus, judges will seek to build their reputations with the groups and networks within which they have been socialized and which they identify with or interact with regularly. The judicial interest in reputation-building creates the opportunity for institutions outside the judiciary to shape judicial preferences.

Institutional interlinkages are links to the internal rules and processes of the judiciary that allow other institutions to shape the internal structure and culture of the judiciary. There are two types of institutional inter-linkages crucial to this discussion: *utilitarian* and *normative* interlinkages.[3]

Where two institutions share utilitarian interlinkages, one institution is in a position to shape the material benefits offered to, and material costs imposed on, members of another institution. Those who appoint, sanction and remove judges at the lower rungs of the judiciary can significantly affect the political and jurisprudential leanings of those judges (Kapiszewski 2012). If the military or allied institutions and elites have a role in the appointments, promotions, transfers and disciplining of judges, I describe this as a utilitarian interlinkage with the judiciary. This utilitarian interlinkage will allow the military and allied elites to appoint, promote and materially benefit a judge who builds a reputation for making decisions in line with the preferences of the military.[4] These preferences include both policy preferences, regarding the political agenda of the military and the military's role in the political system, and legal preferences, regarding the appropriate role for the judiciary and the correct sources of legal authority and forms of legal interpretations.

The social and professional networks from which judges are recruited, and with which judges seek to build esteem, have normative interlinkages with the judiciary, as they set the norms with which judges have to comply in order to build a reputation and gain esteem. The idea that the social and professional networks from which judges are recruited, and with which they regularly interact, shape the values and ideals of these judges is well established among socio-legal

---

[3] The concept of institutional interlinkages is adapted from the study of interlinkages between international institutions in global governance that explain the transmission of global norms across international institutions. The literature on global climate governance and energy policy uses a typology for interlinkages including institutional interlinkages and utilitarian interlinkages which I adapt for this study (Stokke 2001; Goldthau 2013).

[4] This is, in some ways, similiar to the notion of the military being part of what Brinks and Blass (2018) call the 'Constitutional Governing Coalition.'

scholars (Ladinski 1965; Edelman 1992; Hirschl 2004).[5] The superior judiciary of any state is typically recruited from one or a combination of sections of the legal complex. The 'legal complex' describes the cluster of related legal actors related to each other in dynamic structures and is composed of the different legally trained or engaged occupations that belong to the legal and judicial institutions of a given society, and whose tasks are to create, elaborate, transmit and apply the law (Karpik and Halliday 2011). The legal complex includes private lawyers and prosecutors, judges (whether in a court system or in administrative and bureaucratic settings), governmental lawyers and prosecutors, legal academics, civil servants acting as appliers of regulation and legal advisers, whether to government institutions or to private enterprises. Scholars of the legal community have demonstrated the importance of legal professionals and associations as a key support structure for the judiciary, mobilizing to seek the implementation of its decisions and to protect it from executive retaliation (Epp 1998; Halliday et al. 2007, 2012; Moustafa 2007; Ghias 2010). In this study, I show that the legal community is both a support structure and an audience with which judges seek to craft reputations, which thus influences the internal culture and behaviour of the judiciary.[6] For each state the question is: which section(s) of the legal complex are judges recruited from, and what is the relationship of that section with the military?

In closed recruitment systems, judges are typically recruited from judicial bureaucracies, and in open recruitment systems, judges are recruited from outside the bureaucracy, typically from the legal profession (Epstein et al. 2001; Pompe 2005; Ginsburg and Garoupa 2009). It is through these networks that new ideas regarding policy and legal preferences diffuse to the judges (Hilbink 2007; Ocantos 2014). Woods (2009) highlights how the communities or networks in which judges are embedded shape the thinking of judges through processes of informal interactions. Judges train, work and socialize with these networks prior to being appointed and continue to be embedded within these networks even after being

---

[5] Edelman (1992) finds that the Israeli legal community and political leadership deemed it essential that judges were recruited from Israel's Jewish majority, since judges recruited from the Arab minority would not have the necessary traditional Judaic values. Hirschl (2004) argues that across South Africa, Israel, Canada and India, the elite background of judges helps explain their support for an increasingly neoliberal approach to managing the economies of these states.

[6] See also Moustafa 2007; Woods 2009; Ocantos 2014; Ocantos 2016.

appointed. These networks shape judges' perceptions of what are acceptable and unacceptable actions for judges to take. For example, networks of state bureaucrats that depend on regime support and are disconnected from civil society may be more inclined to endorse deference to executive institutions. Thus, we must pay attention to the social characteristics and legal and policy preferences of the section of the legal complex from which judges are recruited. If judges are recruited from sections of the legal complex that are tied to the military, or benefit from military supremacy, I describe this as the military's normative interlinkage with the judiciary. Normative interlinkages mean that only judges who make decisions in line with the preferences of the military gain the esteem of the pro-military sections of the legal complex from which judges are recruited. Thus, judges will seek to make decisions in line with the normalized pro-military preferences of the section of the legal complex in which they have been socialized, and which they identify with or interact with regularly, in order to gain the esteem of that section.[7]

Audiences that are salient in the processes of career and esteem building shape the institutional preferences of the judiciary. The networks judges are recruited from, and the authorities that judges are recruited and promoted by, both seek to ensure that their preferences are reproduced on the bench. When we ask which judge develops a reputation as an able judge, deserving of promotion and of professional esteem in a judicial system, the answer is: it depends on who the audience for that judge is. Therefore, judges who sincerely share the audiences' preferences, and judges who strategically endorse the audiences' preferences, will advance in their careers and build esteem. As this process of learning and selection repeats itself over time, and more and more judges who express these preferences enter and move upward in the judicial hierarchy and gain esteem as judges, the preferences of these audiences become normalized within the judicial system and form the institutional preferences of the judiciary. These preferences become codified within the judiciary and internalized by judges, thus serving as cognitive filters through which judges interpret their institutional environment and role within this environment (Hay 2006).

---

[7] While my focus here is on the military's interlinkages with the judiciary, this same argument applies to any institution, whether it be the military, a particular political party or a significant civil society organization. Any of these external actors can have normative or utilitarian interlinkages with the judiciary and be a crucial audience for the judiciary.

The audience-based approach addresses the limitations of the strategic approach, as it (1) expands the number of judicial interests and motivations to provide a more accurate understanding of judicial behaviour, (2) explains how societal groups can actually shape the norms and preferences of the judiciary when they serve as audiences for the judiciary and (3) explains high-risk judicial activism.[8] It also improves on current ideas-based explanations. Recognizing the fact that salient audiences lie at the heart of this process of preference formation also helps shed light on how external actors outside the judiciary shape the development of institutional legal and policy preferences. It also provides an explanation for how these preferences evolve and change over time. Simply put, when the salient audiences in the process of judicial recruitment and promotion change, the preferences that have been entrenched in the judicial system are contested and, over time, replaced. By examining the process by which the actors controlling judicial careers, and the networks within which judges seek to build esteem, change, we can understand how institutional preferences are reconstituted and trace how these new preferences affect changes in the judiciary's behaviour towards the military.

THE MILITARY AS JUDICIAL AUDIENCE

Militaries vary in the degree to which they sustain utilitarian and normative interlinkages with the judiciary. This variation determines the degree to which the military constitutes the dominant audience shaping the norms and preferences underlying judicial behaviour. Where the military and its allies constitute the dominant audiences, only judges who sincerely share or strategically endorse the preferences and values of the regime will advance their careers and enhance their esteem. Thus, the military can ensure that the legal and policy preferences underlying judicial behaviour align with the military's interests. In its decisions, the judiciary can support the military either by legitimizing the prerogatives and political agenda of the military, or by deferring to the military's actions and authority. Alternatively, it can act assertively

---

[8] Judges might advance their interests in career-building and esteem-building by behaving in accordance with the legal and policy preferences that have been normalized within the judiciary by the relevant audiences, even when adhering to these preferences carries a high risk of jeopardizing their interest in avoiding retaliation from powerful actors.

against the military by challenging the regime's agenda and authority in its decisions. To capture this variation in military–judicial interlinkages and its impact on judicial behaviour towards the regime, I propose a four-part typology. Each configuration of military–judicial interlinkages should result in a varied mix of judicial deference, legitimization and assertiveness, but with one form of judicial behaviour more common than the others.

There are two ways the military can go about creating a loyal judiciary: by creating a *controlled court* or by creating a *collaborative court*. Most military regimes will seek to combine features from both types of judiciaries to ensure loyalty. A controlled court is one that shares utilitarian interlinkages with the military or institutions and elites tied to, or allied with, the military, that is, the military is a key audience for the careers of judges. Each judge's career depends upon ensuring the continued support of the military or affiliated elites. Where the military and affiliated elites shape the career advancement of judges, they will recruit and promote judges who either support the military or are, at least, risk-averse and pliable enough to avoid challenging the military. Hence, a controlled court will be characterized primarily by a pattern of deferential support to the military where the judiciary reads its jurisdiction narrowly, avoiding taking up litigation challenging the military, and refraining from intervening in the actions of the military when it does. Where the military-led executive controls the appointment and promotion of judges it is relatively easy for the judiciary to be controlled. In Nigeria, during the military dictatorships of the 1970s and 1980s, judicial officers were appointed by the president of Nigeria and the state governors on the recommendations of their State Judicial Commissions which were appointed by the governors. The president and governors had both powers of appointment and removal of judges. Nigeria's military dictators frequently used these powers to remove judges who were hostile to their interests and ensured a silent, deferential judiciary (Oko 2005).

A collaborative court shares normative interlinkages with the military, that is, the judiciary comprises judges recruited from social and professional networks that benefit from, and are supportive of, the military. When the judiciary is recruited from, and embedded in, a professional network that is tied to, and supportive of, the military, we should see a collaborative judiciary, as judges are socialized to support the agenda of the military, and their esteem with these networks would suffer from challenging or delegitimizing the state. Hence, collaborative courts will be characterized by a pattern of legitimization of the military's agenda, where the judiciary will take up litigation challenging the military and rule in favour of the military, articulating a legal rationale that legitimizes the agenda of the regime. Through the 1960s, the Turkish superior judiciary was a collaborative court.[9] The military, bureaucracy, Republican Party, universities and judicial community comprised what Belge (2006) calls the Republican alliance. They adhered to the Kemalist republican principles of secular top-down modernization and sought to place limits on majoritarian institutions where left-wing and identity-based political parties could undermine this political project. Through a Kemalist legal education and the bureaucratic judicial structure, Kemalist norms and preferences were reproduced in the professional networks staffing the judiciary, and judges seeking to build esteem within these networks would adhere to these Kemalist norms (Benvenuti 2011). Accordingly, after the coup of 1960, when the military regime established the Turkish Constitutional Court, the court used its powers expansively as the guardian of the military's ideological agenda (Belge 2006; Shambayati and Kirdis 2009). Close normative interlinkages between the republican elites and the judiciary ensured the judiciary collaborated in upholding the military's Kemalist political agenda.

The *loyal court* is where the key audience(s) that control the career path of judges are aligned with or include the military, *and* the judges are recruited from a network that is aligned with the military. Therefore, judges seeking promotion or who are interested in building esteem are expected to endorse the institutional preferences that serve the military's interests, and over time, as more and more judges endorse these preferences, it becomes normalized within the judiciary. The loyal court's jurisprudence is characterized by deference to the authority of the military and legitimization of its agenda. The judiciary will read its own powers and jurisdiction narrowly to provide the military maximum autonomy, and where the judiciary takes up litigation, it will rule in the military's favour, legitimizing the military's actions and agenda. Under General Suharto's military-led regime, Indonesia's superior judiciary characterized a loyal court. This loyalty was a product of deep institutional interlinkages between the military and judiciary. Suharto's Ministry of Justice had direct control over judicial appointments and

---

[9] I provide further detail on this in Chapter 7, where I discuss the Turkish case in more detail.

promotions, and it used loyalty to the regime's integrationist ideology as a key criterion for promotions to attractive positions (Pompe 2005). Most judges were recruited from the close-knit Javanese bureaucratic elite – beneficiaries of Suharto's regime – and Suharto co-opted the Judges' Association, to which most judges belonged (Lev 1972). Thus, through close utilitarian and normative interlinkages, the regime became the primary audience shaping judicial norms and preferences. The result was a loyal judiciary that actively endorsed Suharto's integrationist ideology and granted the military regime almost unchecked power and authority.

The fourth is the *confrontational court*. In the confrontational court, neither the military nor its affiliates are in primary control of the appointment process, nor are the judges recruited from professional networks closely tied to the military. The military and the judiciary enjoy no institutional interlinkages and thus the military cannot shape preferences of the judiciary. I call this the confrontational court because this court will not see itself as subordinate to the military, nor necessarily subscribe to the military's ideological agenda, and will only support the military where the interests of the two institutions align. It is therefore less likely to read its powers narrowly to avoid challenging the military, or to uphold the agenda of the military. Where their interests clash, that is, where the prerogatives of the military clash with the interests and ambitions of the judiciary, the judiciary is more likely to confront and clash with the military. In the later years of General Franco's regime, the Spanish judiciary was a confrontational court, in which judges challenged the regime even at great personal and professional risk. Under Franco, regime control over the appointment process was limited, as the selection of new judges was largely entrusted to the judiciary itself (Taharia 1975). Further, in the 1960s, the legal community within Spain increasingly endorsed new norms of democracy and human rights. These norms diffused into the legal community through its ties to a liberalizing Catholic church, opposition parties within Spain and activist lawyers and judges in neighbouring democratic European states (Hilbink 2012). Thus, the regime's limited control of the judicial appointment process, and the growing support for democratic and human rights within the networks from which judges were recruited, led to the emergence of a confrontational court in Spain. In his survey of Spanish judges in the 1970s, Taharia (1975) found that a majority of judges had a perspective on state–society relations that was considerably at odds with the ideology of the

31

TABLE 1.1   A typology of judicial relationships with the military

		Normative interlinkages	
		Yes (Social and/or professional networks judges are recruited from are aligned with the military)	No (Social and/or professional network judges are recruited from are not aligned with the military)
Utilitarian interlinkages	Yes (Appointing authority(s) aligned with the military)	*Loyal court* (Support for the military's agenda and deference to military authority)	*Controlled court* (Deference to military authority)
	No (Appointing authority(s) independent from the military)	*Collaborative court* (Support for the military's agenda)	*Confrontational court* (Assertiveness against the military)

Franco regime. By the 1970s, a growing a number of judges belonging to the pro-democracy professional association, Justicia Democratia, took up important positions within the judiciary, and the judiciary became a site for high-risk assertiveness against the Franco regime (Hilbink 2012).

Three disclaimers are necessary. First, the categories in Table 1.1 represent ideal-types that approximate reality. The category that each state most closely approximates will depend on how dominant an audience the military is for the judiciary in that country, that is, how strong the normative and utilitarian interlinkages between the military and the judiciary are, in comparison to other external actors and the judiciary in that state. But it is unlikely that, in any state, the military will be the sole audience for the judiciary or, alternatively, will have no interlinkages with the judiciary. Thus, judiciaries in different states may share characteristics with multiple categories, but only one category will best approximate the judiciary–military interlinkages found in each state. Second, it is unlikely that a loyal court will produce no assertive jurisprudence that challenges the military, nor is it likely that a confrontational court will produce no jurisprudence that defers to, or legitimizes, military power. However, the pattern of judicial behaviour in a loyal court will, in aggregate, lean significantly more towards deferring to, or legitimizing, military power, than the pattern of judicial behaviour in a confrontational court. Third, just because a judiciary is more willing to confront military power does not mean it will be more supportive of an elected democratic constitutional order. The confrontational court's preferences regarding democracy promotion will depend on the preferences of the confrontational court's audiences.

The framework outlined here also explains the mechanism by which the judiciary's legal and policy preferences towards the military shift. Institutional preferences shift when the institutional arrangement under which these preferences gets entrenched and keeps reproducing itself is disrupted. This would happen when the judiciary shifts between the categories outlined in this chapter. The question is: how do institutional interlinkages between the military and the judiciary get disrupted? First, the pool from which judges are selected can change, or the values and ideas held within that network can change. Processes that can change the pool of judicial recruits could include an institutional shift in the source of recruitment to another section of the legal complex, such as increasingly recruiting judges from the judicial service or bureaucracy as opposed to a more autonomous bar of private lawyers. It could also include changes in the socio-economic background of the network, as, over time, an increasing number of lawyers in the bar may come from demographics that have not traditionally been allied with, or beneficiaries of, the military. Second, the appointment authority, or the values held by that appointing authority, can change over time as well. A shift in legal and policy preferences only begins once the place of new audiences in judicial career- and esteem-building processes is institutionalized, and it happens gradually as new audience preferences become hegemonic within the judiciary.

Thus, using the audience-based framework, this study develops a more holistic understanding of the judiciary's approach to decision-making in the complex institutional environment of military regimes and new democracies, where militaries remain independent political principals. This framework sheds light on the multiple motivations of judges, explains how the military can impact these motivations to shape judicial preferences towards the military and shows how judicial preferences vary depending upon the audiences implicated.

JUDICIAL–MILITARY RELATIONS IN PAKISTAN

In this book, I study variation in the judiciary's military jurisprudence over time, across different types of military prerogative. Pakistan's high courts and Supreme Court have issued judgments dealing with three broad categories of military prerogative. Therefore, any comprehensive account of judicial–military relations in Pakistan must account for both High Court and Supreme Court jurisprudence.

1. *Security prerogative judgments*. This includes judgments dealing with the military's control over formulating national security policy and carrying out security operations, and oversight and discipline of the forces involved in carrying out this security mission. These forces include the military, military and interservices intelligence and several associated paramilitary outfits that fall under the military's control, including the Frontier Corps, the Pakistan Rangers, the National Guard, the Anti-Narcotics Force and the Airport Security Force.[10]
2. *Economic prerogative judgments*. This includes judgments pertaining to the military's acquisition and administration of its economic assets and the regulation of its economic activities. Pakistan's military economy comprises three distinct segments: major public sector organizations controlled by the army; the commercial subsidiaries that ostensibly provide for the welfare of the army; and the vast real estate empire owned and administered by the army and a subordinate civilian bureaucracy.
3. *Political and policymaking prerogative judgments*. These judgments deal with the role the military plays in policymaking and political processes, unrelated to security. Thus, it covers the granting of non-security executive, legislative and judicial functions to the military. At the apex of the executive structure, this includes formal seizures of executive power through military coups, and informal interventions in the political process to favour allied political parties. Below high-level political interventions, military officers are also recruited

---

[10] Under Article 199(3) of the Constitution, the courts are barred from making orders on applications pertaining to members of the armed forces, in respect to any action that relates to his or service in the forces. High courts frequently had to determine what classes of civilian, military and paramilitary personnel fall into this category of armed forces, and what actions are covered by this article and therefore fall out of their jurisdiction.

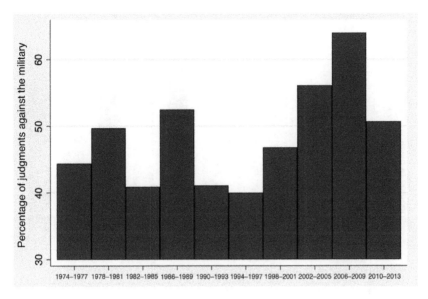

Figure 1.1 Judicial assertiveness against the military over time (1974–2013).
Note: (n=704).

laterally into civilian bureaucracies. Legislatively, military regimes seek to create news laws and amend the constitution. And judicially, summary military courts have also been established at different times to deal with criminal cases.

The military is likely to be more protective of its security and economic prerogatives as these are more crucial to maintaining its institutional autonomy. By institutional autonomy, I mean the military's discretion to organize, acquire resources and conduct operations that it deems necessary to carry out its mission to protect national security without external interventions (Pion-Berlin 1992; Croissant et al. 2010). Therefore, the military is most likely to retaliate against judicial challenges to these prerogatives, making judicial contestation of the military's economic and security prerogatives especially high risk (Kureshi 2021).

Figures 1.1 and 1.2 sum up military-related jurisprudence between 1974 and 2013.[11] Figure 1.1 shows that the judiciary grew more assertive

---

[11] I begin from 1974 because Pakistan's courts have been under the same 1973 Constitution since then.

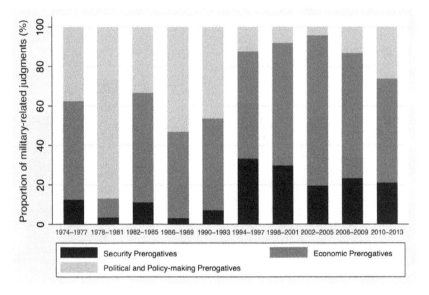

Figure 1.2 Judicial assertiveness against the military, by prerogative type (1974–2013)
Note: (n = 704).

towards the military, particularly after 2002, demonstrating that while 2007 clearly represented a high watermark in judicial assertiveness against the military, increased judicial assertiveness did not just begin in 2007, but built up in the preceding years.

Figure 1.2 differentiates assertive jurisprudence based on the military's three types of prerogative. The figure shows that over time, a growing proportion of rulings against the military dealt with economic and security prerogatives, making the increased judicial assertiveness against the military after 2002 shown in the figure above even riskier.

Taken together, the two figures provide preliminary evidence of the judiciary's increased willingness to act assertively against the military over time, at least up till 2013. Although the trajectory in the judiciary's assertive jurisprudence has not always followed an entirely linear pattern, a finding substantiated by scholars of the Pakistani judiciary, including Newberg (1995), Khan (2015) and Cheema (2018b, 2021), there is a gradual but marked increase in high-risk judicial assertiveness over time that merits explanation.

The relationship between the military and the judiciary in Pakistan has been the subject of much analysis over the years. In this section, I present possible explanations for the shift in judicial behaviour towards the military summarized earlier, as discussed in this literature, and argue that, while each of the factors discussed within this literature has had a significant impact on the jurisprudence of the judiciary towards the military, each of these explanations only partially explains the changes in the judiciary's relationship with the military. I then argue that a shift in judicial audiences away from the 'military establishment' played a critical role in explaining the increased judicial contestation of military prerogatives.

Legal Doctrines

A judge's professional understandings of the nature of the law and the tools of legal interpretation play an important role in shaping their decisions. Scholars who focus on the explanatory power of dominant paradigms of legal theory have noted that the prevalence of 'legal positivism', is an important feature of deferential courts in authoritarian regimes (Hilbink 2007; Ocantos 2016). Legal positivism is a legal theory that expects judges to adhere to, and implement, the law and legal procedures, regardless of how they enable the executive or constrain the judiciary. A shift from positivism to a natural rights–based discourse in many legal systems has been noted as a cause for judiciaries shifting from deferring, to contesting, powerful authoritarian regimes (Hilbink 2012; Ocantos 2016). The Pakistani judiciary has also, in recent years, shifted from articulating its decisions in the language of legal positivism, to demonstrating a greater inclination to relax procedure, discard legal standing requirements and strike down laws, acting in what it deems to be the 'public interest' (Khan 2015).

This turn in legal norms is important for understanding the judiciary's increased assertiveness towards other state institutions, including the military. However, we need to understand what motivated this shift in the judiciary away from a positivist commitment to legal norms and procedure and towards an emphasis on prioritizing a judicialized notion of the public interest. Further, a diminishing commitment to legal positivism is not enough to explain the shift in assertiveness, as even during the era of judicial collaboration with the military, judges did not always adopt a positivist approach. Judges were willing to bypass procedure, precedent and even the clear commands of the constitution, when called upon to adjudicate upon the legitimacy of military coups. Thus, while legal positivism was the dominant jurisprudential paradigm for much of Pakistan's history, the judiciary had shown a willingness to violate these jurisprudential norms when the outcome favoured the military in the civil–military balance. Therefore, a shift in legal norms from legal positivism to outcome-based activism is important, but, on its own, does not provide a complete explanation.

Attitudes and Policy Preferences

An attitudinal explanation would focus on the policy preferences of judges and consider how they shape the judiciary's behaviour (Segal 2008). In this view, the judiciary's past collaboration with the military reflects the preference of the judiciary for military policies. Similarly, the change in the judiciary's decision-making in recent years would be explained by a shift in judicial policy preferences. I find evidence of a preference for a strong executive and a disdain for democratic party politics from leading judges during the 1950s and 1960s, both in their judgments and in their off-bench speeches. Similarly, in recent years, judges, in their words, both on and off the bench, have exhibited greater opposition to an unconstrained military. However, while there is certainly evidence of an attitudinal shift in the judiciary away from a preference for upholding military supremacy, this explanation is incomplete for two reasons. First, we need to explain why the shift in judicial preferences happened. Second, Pakistani judges' new assertiveness is not simply a product of changing policy preferences, as judges also seem to be imbued with new legal preferences and a new conception of their role as powerful stakeholders in the political system, with an ambition to reshape both state and society. Third, my research showed that, during the Musharraf's regime (1999–2008), even when judges made decisions supporting an expansion of military authority, they sought to present themselves as acting independently of, and sometimes even in defiance of, the military. These concerns pertaining to reputation clearly informed judicial behaviour. Thus, the realization of policy preferences, the prime focus of the attitudinal approach, does not adequately explain the judiciary's confrontational turn.

Political Fragmentation

A strategic explanation would focus on the surrounding political environment, as courts act more assertively against other state institutions when the political system is weaker or more fragmented, raising the cost of repealing judicial decisions or reducing judicial authority for the other political actors (Chavez 2004; Ferejohn et al. 2007; Rios-Figueroa 2007). In this view, the historic deference shown towards the military was a product of the military's political dominance of the political system for much of this history, and the powers the military had to retaliate against adverse judicial decisions, particularly at the times when military rule was at its most unfettered (Newberg 1995; Kalhan 2013). Similarly, periods of relative judicial assertiveness could be explained by increased political fragmentation, either when weakening military regimes faced growing opposition, or during democratic intervals, when power was fragmented between elected political parties and an unelected military. During these periods of political fragmentation, the judiciary would likely have more space to act assertively (Cheema 2018b, 2021). Scholars including Newberg (1995), Siddique (2006), Kalhan (2013) and Cheema (2021) attribute the increased judicialization of politics during the 1990s and assertive decision-making to the increased fragmentation of authority during democratic rule. Similarly, Khan (2015) attributed increased assertiveness in the latter part of Zia's and Musharraf's regime to late-stage military regimes in decline, facing greater opposition and, thus, fragmentation.

Undoubtedly, judges in Pakistan are strategic actors carefully navigating an uncertain political environment, showing deference when necessary to avoid backlash and acting assertively when the political environment provides the opportunity to do so. However, the political environment only provides a partial explanation for both the manner and timing of the assertion of judicial authority. As I explain in subsequent chapters, Pakistan's courts engaged in high-risk judicial assertiveness, more often than perhaps these accounts give credit for. Whether it was during the early years of General Zia-ul-Haq's repressive dictatorship, or during the latter period of General Musharraf's dictatorship, the courts periodically acted assertively when it was risky, and paid the price for it. Further, as already shown, there is a steady increase in judicial contestation of the military over time that does not map neatly on to the variation in political fragmentation over this history. As Cheema (2018b, 2021) points out, there was a non-linear but clear expansion of judicial power over time, and this historic shift cannot be explained only by the waxing and waning of executive authority.

Further, the manner in which the courts exercised authority also mattered. As already shown, over time courts were increasingly willing to contest prerogatives they would not have disputed before. Also, as shown in subsequent chapters, the content of the decisions shows that over time the judiciary increasingly sought to play a different and more expansive and authoritative role in the political system. Thus, any explanation for the shift in the assertiveness of the judiciary, and the changes in the content of its jurisprudence, requires also paying attention to shifts occurring within judicial institutions, changes occurring in its relationship with state and society, and the impact these had on the values and preferences that emerged within judicial culture and shaped judicial decision-making.

The Media and Public Support

Another explanation is that the judiciary grew more willing to assert itself against the military when it benefitted from the growth of private media that provided favourable coverage to the judiciary when it asserted its authority, and helped it generate public support. Scholars of the strategic approach would highlight how judiciaries are more willing to act assertively when they are confident of public support. Constitutional courts around the world have been found to strategically avoid clashes with powerful actors in the early phase of the court's existence and cultivate favourable public perceptions over time, through decisions, so as to strategically enhance judicial authority over time (Ginsburg 2003; Vanberg 2005).

Since the early 2000s, Pakistan saw a private televised media boom. During multiple interviews, judges and lawyers spoke about how the proliferation of private news outlets connected judges with the public in a way that they had not been connected before. Ghias (2010) explains that favourable coverage from the media brought the judiciary public support, and this favourable coverage emboldened judges to assert themselves against state institutions, including the powerful military. The media's role is significant, but this explanation assumes that the judiciary's willingness to challenge the military was always there, and the support of media coverage provided the judiciary with the opportunity to act against the military. Yet the judiciary had historically not simply deferred to military pre-eminence but had actively played a role in enhancing and legitimizing military authority, indicating there had been a shift in the preferences of the judiciary, which could not have been prompted by the opportunities created by the media.

Instead, I argue that the proliferation of private electronic media had a more indirect role to play in increasing judicial willingness to contest state institutions. Electronic media closely connected the judiciary with audiences that judges cared about and gave these audiences a platform through which they could engage closely with, and form and express opinions about, judicial decisions. Judges coming from social networks were now especially concerned with how the media covered their decisions and shaped their reputation with their respective networks. Thus, I argue that the role of the media was to increase the importance of the judicial motivation to build reputations with the social networks with which these judges identified, by reducing the distance between the judges and their social and professional networks, and this impacted judicial decision-making. However, the question remains: why did the audiences that affected judicial reputation prefer an assertive judiciary challenging other state institutions?

The Chief Justice

Chief justices can play a critical role within the institutional setting of the judiciary to shape the behaviour of the judiciary, through their powers to assign benches for cases, circulate judges, select judges to write opinions and set the agenda and norms of the court, (Epstein and Knight 1998; Davis 1999; Dyevre 2010; Abeyratne and Porat 2021). Pakistan's chief justices wield considerable power in appointing and elevating judges, selecting judges for benches and determining the extent of the original jurisdiction of the Supreme Court. Further, the rise in judicial activism and the confrontation between the judiciary and the military was most closely associated with one chief justice: Iftikhar Chaudhry. The period during which Chaudhry was chief justice saw the superior judiciary's activism and assertiveness reach unprecedented levels (Gilani and Cheema 2015; Siddique 2015). Chaudhry's tenure as chief justice was certainly a critical juncture in Pakistan's judicial history. But Chaudhry was not alone in asserting the Court's authority. Chaudhry's assertive approach would have had limited impact if it did not have the support and sympathies of sections of Pakistan's legal complex, including other judges and bar association leaders. Thus, Chaudhry could not have resisted Musharraf's military dictatorship in isolation, and the question arises as to what conditions developed within the judiciary that made Chaudhry's assertive tenure possible.

All these explanations provide some important insights into why the judiciary started contesting military prerogatives with increased frequency. But what is needed is an explanation for why the superior judiciary entered a phase of assertive decision-making that (1) continued during periods of direct military control and democratic transition, (2) deviated significantly from past precedent and jurisprudential norms and (3) did not significantly diminish after Justice Chaudhry's term ended.

The Audience Explanation

I argue that the Pakistani judiciary's turn towards increased contestation of military prerogatives is best explained by a shift in the authorities managing judicial careers and in the networks from which judges are recruited, towards authorities and networks not aligned with or dependent on the military.

As I detail in subsequent chapters, the Pakistani judiciary shifted from being a *loyal court* in Pakistan's early years, actively upholding military interests through its decision-making, to being a *confrontational court*, seeking to establish its role as an independent power centre in Pakistan's political system. The judiciary aligned with the military when it suited the interests of the judiciary, but confronted and clashed with the military when their interests clashed.

At the outset, after Pakistan's independence the Pakistan superior judiciary fit all the characteristics of a loyal judiciary. At the time of Pakistan's first military coup, soon after Pakistan's independence, the primary appointing authority was the military-led executive. Even as new judges were often nominated by serving judges, the final decision lay with the executive branch, and judges were often personally interviewed by Pakistan's military dictator, Ayub Khan. Therefore, professional success was linked to pleasing the military rulers and their political and bureaucratic allies. Upward mobility within the superior judiciary depended upon endorsing a strong military-led executive.

Superior court judges at the time were recruited from the executive-run lower judiciary, the civil service and the bar of private lawyers. Thus, at least half of the judges came from government services subordinate to the military-run executive branch, and the remainder came from the lawyer's community. Most leading lawyers at the time belonged to Pakistan' post-colonial elite, educated and trained in the United Kingdom, with strong ties to the bureaucratic and military officers' elite that emerged from the same network. The military regime actively sought to preserve the privileges of these elite networks. These lawyers and bureaucrats were trained and socialized in networks that sought to reproduce the British colonial system that institutionalized a powerful executive branch, which preserved elite privileges and kept mass society at a distance (Jalal 1990). Thus, Pakistan's judicial elite was appointed directly by the military regime and came from Pakistan's bureaucrats and post-colonial elite lawyers, both networks that shared close ties with military officers. This system ensured that both the key audiences for career advancement and esteem building had an interest in promoting the military's authority, thus constructing institutional preferences favouring collaboration with, and deference to, the military, in advancing its political agenda and interests.

However, three key transitions in Pakistan's judicial structure and recruitment pool led to a change in the key audiences shaping the judiciary's legal and policy preferences:

1- The *indigenization* of the Pakistani judiciary. Over the next few decades fewer and fewer judges emerged from Pakistan's Western-educated post-colonial elite, as an increasing number of judges came from locally educated middle-class backgrounds. As the rewards for being private commercial lawyers increasingly outweighed the rewards for joining the judiciary, a growing proportion of elite lawyers gravitated towards private commercial law, while the judiciary became more appealing to locally educated middle-class lawyers seeking the upward mobility and respect promised by being members of the judicial elite. Thus, the composition of the network from which judges were primarily recruited changed from a foreign-educated and -trained elite disconnected from mass politics and closely aligned with the military elite, to a locally educated middle-class network engaged with mass politics and less tied to future military rulers. These locally educated lawyers were also less focused on positivist legal and constitutional doctrines. This had a counterintuitive effect. Judges were less restricted by formal legal requirements and paid more attention to providing judgments that would win the praise of the middle-class lawyers' community. The indigenization of the judiciary meant: (1) that the judiciary was no longer embedded in Pakistan's post-colonial elite, but in Pakistan's middle class; and (2) that building esteem with this network meant paying less attention to procedure and more attention to popular outcomes.

2- The *politicization* of the Pakistani legal complex. In the years after Pakistan's independence the Pakistani lawyers' community was still very small and politically relatively inert, and Pakistan's prominent bar associations focused primarily on professional concerns. However, towards the late 1960s and 1970s, the lawyers' community became increasingly involved with the tumultuous political events reshaping Pakistan's political order at the time. These events ended the monopoly certain elite groups had over the state's politics, as mass society, including the legal networks, grew increasingly politically aware and engaged. However, the critical juncture for Pakistan's lawyers' community was the dictatorship of General Zia-ul-Haq, which sought to suppress all sites for mass politics in the country. One of the first and only venues General Zia permitted to continue with electoral traditions was the bar (for reasons that are explained in subsequent chapters), and the result was that bar associations were among the few spaces available for political activity. Soon this attracted political workers and political party members to the bar associations, and the bar became a site for the development of an oppositional politics that challenged the military regime. An anti-establishment politics favouring judicial activism and confrontation with military and political party elites emerged in Pakistan's bar, the key recruiting site for Pakistan's judges, and judges increasingly had to at least pay lip service to this growing norm of activism in order to maintain a reputation within the bar. This is not to say that many lawyers and judges were not still willing to work and cooperate with the military, but presenting one's self as independent from military and political party elites became increasingly important for gaining the esteem of the most relevant sections of the legal complex.

3- The *separation* of the judiciary from the executive. The Constitution of 1973, promulgated during Pakistan's first brief period of democratic rule, established the principle that the judiciary and the executive branch had to be separated. Over a series of steps this separation was formally completed. First, the practice of appointing judges from the civil service came to an end, and at least two-thirds of superior court judges came from the bar, while only a third came from the lower courts. Second, the judiciary was able to assume control of its own budget and financial resources. Third, and most crucially, the judiciary made a more decisive break from the executive, when the judiciary asserted greater control over the judicial appointment process. In the consequential *Al-Jehad Trust* case in 1996, the Supreme Court reduced the executive branch's discretion in appointments, and in 2010 it further reduced executive control, with the establishment of a Judicial Commission to manage judicial appointments .[12] This had two important effects. First, the path to judicial

---

[12] These reforms happened during Pakistan's periods of civilian democratic rule, although the military remained the most powerful state institution.

selection did not necessarily require establishing a reputation with the executive branch, diminishing the role of executive institutions in career advancement. Second, as the voice and role of the executive branch diminished in the process of appointments, the role of the bar increased. Judges, being former lawyers themselves, increasingly consulted and relied on the advice of their fellow lawyers from their respective law firms and bars in making appointments. Thus, alongside reputation with chief justices, reputation within the lawyers' community became an increasingly important consideration in the process of judicial appointments and promotions.

By the late 1990s, the institutional environment of the Pakistani judiciary had been completely rearranged, and the audiences shaping judicial preferences in the 1960s had been largely altered as a consequence of these three processes. In particular: (1) the military, as the primary executive institution, and affiliated elites lost pre-eminence in the judicial appointment process, while judges and bar leaders became more consequential audiences in this process; and (2) judicial recruitment shifted from a section of the legal complex that was more aligned with the military to one that was more independent from and, on certain issues, oppositional to the military. Thus, I argue that when the audiences salient for career advancement and esteem building within the judicial system shifted towards authorities and networks that were not closely aligned with the military, the Pakistani judiciary shifted from a *loyal court* to a more ambitious *confrontational court* that was more willing to contest military prerogatives when interests and ambitions clashed. Figure 1.3 charts the evolution of the judiciary from a loyal to a confrontational judiciary.

Thus, the Pakistani case illuminates the key features of judicial–military relationships in authoritarian and post-authoritarian states. The Pakistani judiciary grew more willing to contest the military's prerogatives over time, as the military played a diminished role in appointments and judges were appointed from a bar that was not aligned with the military, taking the judiciary in a direction of greater independence from and confrontation with the military. Three key disclaimers are crucial here. First, this does not mean that the judiciary did not respond strategically to the political environment, and the relative deference towards the military's security prerogative and restraint during the initial years of military rule can be explained by strategic deference. Second, the military's role in the process of judicial appointments had diminished,

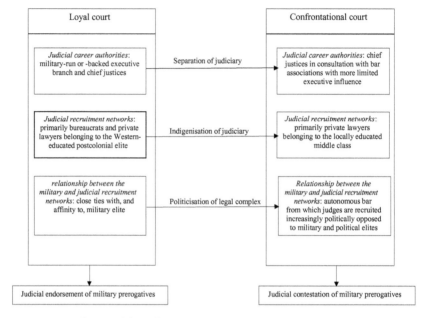

Figure 1.3 Evolution of the Pakistani judiciary.

but was not entirely eliminated, and the military retained informal and indirect links to the judicial appointment process. Third, just because a judiciary is more independent-minded and ambitious, and thus more willing to confront military supremacy, does not mean this judiciary will necessarily embrace elected civilian supremacy. As I show in Chapter 5, the confrontational court that emerged in Pakistan challenged both military regimes and elected civilian governments, with mixed consequences for Pakistan's democratic future.

CONCLUSION

The central claim of this study is that, when explaining judicial–military interactions in authoritarian and post-authoritarian states, where the military acts as an autonomous political principal, the willingness of the judiciary to contest military prerogatives depends on whether the authorities and networks shaping the judiciary's legal and policy preferences are aligned with the military or not. The study develops an 'audience-based approach' to show that judges have motivations beyond policy maximization, including career advancement and esteem building, and that these motivations make different audiences consequential, as these audiences will shape the legal and policy preferences underlying judicial behaviour. Further, this audience-based approach explains how institutional preferences shift. Thus, this approach borrows from both the ideas-based and interest-based frameworks to provide a holistic and unifying framework for explaining variation in the judicial contestation of military prerogatives in authoritarian and post-authoritarian states. In the case of Pakistan, I demonstrate the utility of this theoretical framework in subsequent chapters.

CHAPTER TWO

THE LOYAL COURT (1947–1977)

The Entrenchment of a Judicial–Military Partnership

INTRODUCTION

The Pakistani judiciary, in its institutional structure, developed during the British colonial era. After Pakistan gained its independence in 1947, the judiciary became an important pillar of the military-bureaucratic nexus that consolidated its control over the political order of the state. Between 1958 and 1971, the state was directly ruled by a military regime. Why did the judiciary support the military's rise to power and pre-eminence?

This chapter answers this question by offering a brief history of the institutional development and jurisprudence of the high courts during this period. I first explore the political developments of this period, and then describe how the jurisprudence of this era helped consolidate and legitimize military rule and furthered its agenda and discretion. I show that the judiciary actively collaborated with the military because the military and judiciary developed close institutional interlinkages during this period, ensuring the military was a critical audience shaping the judiciary's internal norms and preferences. Under British rule, the judiciary was constructed as part of a set of institutions wedded to the purpose of upholding the discretion of the British executive institutions to maintain order and stability. Judges were appointed by the British executive and were recruited from the same pool of British-trained elite bureaucrats and barristers. After independence, the civil–military bureaucracy continued to control the appointment process, and judges continued to be nominated from the same pool of British-trained lawyers and bureaucrats, who belonged to the same social and professional networks as bureaucratic and military elites. Those seeking to further their judicial careers and reputations had neither the professional understanding nor incentives to challenge the discretion and ambitions of the military. Thus, the judiciary became an active collaborator in upholding and legitimizing military dominance in Pakistan's political order, because an institutional norm of collaboration with the military was entrenched during this period.

In the final part of this chapter, I discuss Pakistan's first period of constitutional democratic rule between 1973 and 1977, and outline the beginning of the judiciary's separation from the military, exploring how a new democratic constitutional order, and the changing roles of the military and the judiciary, began to slowly disrupt the internal culture of the judiciary.

Thus, this chapter outlines the heyday of judicial–military collaboration, explains how this collaboration was sustained for such a long period and shows how the judiciary started evolving into a more autonomous institution.

PAKISTAN AFTER INDEPENDENCE (1947–1970)

Military and Bureaucratic Ascendance after Independence

When the Pakistani state was formally established, it was little more than a state on paper. The state was composed of five provinces that had seceded out of the political structure of colonial India, and had no established governing institutions bringing these provinces together under a single administrative umbrella. Pakistan was composed of one large province, East Bengal, on the eastern edge of the Indian subcontinent (which gained its independence from Pakistan in 1971 and is now known as Bangladesh), and four smaller provinces (West Punjab, Sindh, Balochistan and the North-West Frontier Province) on the opposite end of the subcontinent in the north-west.[1] The Muslim League, the founding political party of Pakistan, was a loose coalition of interests with little organizational thickness to manage the task of integrating the new state, unlike its counterpart in India, the Indian National Congress (Tudor 2013). In the absence of centralized administrative arrangements, a founding party with insufficient organizational

---

[1] These were the provinces that were identified as Muslim majority provinces within British India.

machinery, a financial crisis, a massive demographic change and refugee crisis, and unsettled borders with a looming threat from India, Pakistan faced an acute existential crisis.

In the absence of a new constitution, the state continued to be regulated under the legal instruments of British India – the Government of India Act of 1935 and the Indian Independence Act of 1947 – which together functioned as a provisional constitution.[2] The Government of India Act was the blueprint for British rule, and had created only partial self-rule, establishing elected provincial assemblies, but placing primary authority in the hands of a set of paternalistic executive institutions tasked with maintaining order, stability and control over the colonies. At the apex of this administration was the vice regal office of the governor-general which represented the British Crown and could dismiss provincial governments at will. The governor-general was assisted by an administrative bureaucracy with its organized hierarchical structure of command and control, and coercive institutions, including a military, which had a significant role and presence in the north-western regions bordering Afghanistan. The Indian Independence Act in 1947 provided for the creation of an indirectly elected Constituent Assembly with the task of drafting a new constitution, but maintained the unelected governor-general's role.

At the outset, the provincial arenas served as the main centres of political activity, while at the level of the central government there were two types of leaders: indirectly elected politicians with few identifiable bases of support, and civil and military bureaucrats who were well versed in the traditions of British Indian administration (Jalal 1990). The federal politicians of the Muslim League did not have the support nor connections to organizationally link the districts and provinces to the state, and after Jinnah (the party's leader and founder of Pakistan) died in 1948, the party was in organizational disarray. Jalal argues that a 'superiority syndrome' quickly developed within the bureaucracies who viewed politicians with 'condescension and suspicion' (Jalal 1990: 70). With unsettled borders, internal discord and war with India in 1948, the rapid expansion of the military also became a priority. Given Pakistan's dire financial situation, the country turned to the USA for aid; the USA saw the new state as a Cold War ally, and focused its aid

---

[2] Indirect elections meant that the directly elected provincial assemblies voted on the candidates for the Constituent Assembly, as opposed to the general population. See Government of India Act 1935; Indian Independence Act 1947.

and assistance on the army, which soon bypassed the political government to develop independent relations with the USA for the purpose
of arms procurement (Jalal 1990). Thus, by 1951, power had shifted
from the political founders of the state to the civil and military bureaucracy, which was made most apparent when a civil bureaucrat, Malik
Ghulam Muhammad, known for his 'impatience with politicians' and
close ties with the military, assumed the powerful position of governor-
general (Jalal 1990: 136).

Developing a constitution for the new state was also proving particularly difficult as the military and civil service leadership, primarily
recruited from West Pakistan, resisted a representative constitutional
arrangement that gave East Pakistan (the name given to East Bengal
after 1955), which constituted a majority of the population, greater
political authority and autonomy. By 1954, the impasse between the
indirectly elected Constituent Assembly and the alliance of the bureaucrat governor-general, the commander in chief of the military and
senior civil servants reached its height, and Ghulam Muhammad
declared an emergency and unilaterally dissolved the Constituent
Assembly, the first in a long series of interventions by unelected civil
and military bureaucrats seeking to consolidate power.[3]

The Judiciary in the Early Years after Independence
Where did the judiciary fit into this picture of growing bureaucratic and
military control?

During British rule, the Government of India Act 1935 established a
judicial system with a set of high courts and chief courts across India.
The judiciary had little institutional independence, as it was constructed, 'not as a check on the executive', but as part of the civil
service administration (Siddique 2013: 87). Judges of the high courts
did not have a fixed tenure, as they were appointed and could be
removed by the Crown, that is, by the governor-general, on condition
of their 'good behaviour', and there were several British judges who
were retained after independence (Sidhwa 1989, 17).

---

[3] As the *Dawn* newspaper subsequently noted on the governor-general's dissolution,
'[t]here have indeed been times – such as that October night in 1954 – when, a
general to the right of him and a general to the left of him, a half-mad Governor
General imposed upon a captured Prime Minister the dissolution of the Constituent
Assembly and the virtual setting up of a semi-dictatorial executive'. 'Revolution',
Dawn, 11 August 1957.

After independence, Pakistan's Federal Court was established in 1948 at the apex of the judicial system. Sir Mian Abdur Rashid was the first chief justice of Pakistan's Federal Court, and the courts continued to be run in accordance with the Government of India Act 1935.[4] However, in 1954, the Government of India Act was amended to grant the courts writ jurisdiction. Writs are legal instruments developed in British common law, and refer to official orders directing the behaviour of another state institution such as an executive agency or lower courts, and give high courts the authority to check the actions of other government institutions.[5] From the start, Newberg (1995: 49) writes, the courts became an important forum, as participants in the political arena used the courts to 'air their views, and challenge their opponents' and it provided the only bridge between the discordant political and administrative systems at the time.

So what role did the judiciary play in this period? The judiciary was put to the test in 1955, in the historic *Maulvi Tamizuddin* case.[6] A Bengali politician, Maulvi Tamizuddin, petitioned to the Sindh High Court, challenging the governor-general's dissolution action. In determining the legality of the governor-general's actions, the judiciary was called upon to determine the balance of power between the governor-general and the Constituent Assembly. The Sindh High Court ruled in favour of the Constituent Assembly, arguing that the power of dissolution was limited and deciding in favour of legislative supremacy and a restrained executive. The governor-general then appealed this decision, contesting the judiciary's authority to review the governor-general's actions in the Federal Court (the Supreme Court after 1956).

By 1954, Justice Abdur Rashid had been replaced by Justice Munir as the chief justice. Justice Munir's assumption of the chief justiceship was in itself a product of executive manipulation within the judiciary. Several judges were senior to Justice Munir in the Supreme Court, but the machinations of Governor-General Ghulam Muhammad

---

[4] Under this arrangement, each major province had a Chief Court or a High Court, and the decisions of the High Court could be appealed to the Federal Court.

[5] For more details on the structure and writ jurisdiction of Pakistan's superior judiciary, see Appendix.

[6] See *Federation of Pakistan* v. *Maulvi Tamizuddin Khan*, PLD 1955 FC 240.

helped bring Justice Munir to the helm (Khan 2016).[7] Justice Munir had already developed a reputation for favouring executive power during his time as chief justice of the Lahore High Court. More significantly, Ghulam Muhammad took the chief justice into consultation before dissolving the Constituent Assembly (Jalal 1990). Under the circumstances, given the close ties between Justice Munir and Ghulam Muhammad, and his prior involvement with the decision to dissolve the assemblies, it comes as little surprise that Munir and the Federal Court upheld the order of dissolution.

The Court ruled that the Sindh High Court simply did not have the jurisdiction to question the dissolution decision by the governor-general because the statute that had granted the judiciary the power to accept writs against the governor-general had not received the assent of the governor-general. In this historic decision, Newberg (1995: 47) writes that 'defining constitutionalism as a limit on the legislature, Munir set the groundwork for executive supremacy and intervention'. Munir described the governor-general's exercising of powers of dissolution as a necessity to avert a disastrous outcome, and his judgment faulted the politicians of the Constituency Assembly, stating that 'if the result is disaster, it will merely be another instance of how thoughtlessly the Constituent Assembly proceeded with its business'.

In a subsequent decision that emanated from the fallout from the governor-general's dissolution action, the Court revisited these questions, and the governor-general's powers of assent and dissolution.[8] This time the Court formalized the logic outlined in the *Tamizuddin* decision, articulating the doctrine that came to be known as the 'doctrine of necessity'. Justice Munir held that the actions taken by the governor-general lay outside the Acts of 1935 and 1947 but were necessary to 'prevent the State from dissolution and the constitutional and administrative machinery from breaking down', and said 'an act which would otherwise be illegal becomes legal if it is done *bona fide* under the stress of necessity'.[9] Notably, the Court also limited the

---

[7] Khan (2016) writes that Justice Akram was supposed to be appointed chief justice, but the governor-general told him that he was inclined to appoint a British judge over a Pakistani judge as chief justice, unless Justice Akram agreed to forego the position. Justice Akram was forced to accept this or face the possibility of forcing the return of an English judge at the helm of the judiciary.

[8] See *Reference by His Excellency Governor-General* 1955 PLD FC 435.

[9] Reference by H.E. The Governor General, PLD 1955 FC 435.

governor-general's *legal* powers by saying that the governor-general did not have the legal authorization to carry out this dissolution, and thus also had no power to appoint members to the new Constituent Assembly (Aziz and Cheema 2021) But the Court justified the extra-legal actions of the governor-general as a necessity to save the state. The doctrine of necessity became the legal foundation for extra-constitutional interventions through Pakistan's history. Thus in 1955, the Federal Court played an important role in consolidating the control of the civil–military bureaucratic axis over the political order.

Justice Munir said in a speech some years later, after retiring, that the decisions he made in 1955 were necessary as there would have been 'chaos in the country and a revolution that would have been formally enacted possibly by bloodshed' (Chaudhry 1973). Munir claimed he saved the country from revolution. A lawyer who personally knew Justice Munir said that Munir privately claimed that if the judiciary did not decide in favour of the governor-general, 'there was a real possibility of a coup d'état, and the military would take over'.[10] Yet, Justice Munir's public claim to be forestalling a revolution and private claim to be holding back a military takeover were contradicted by his subsequent judgments regarding the military takeover in 1958.

Martial Law in Pakistan: 1958–1969
Pakistan's first Constitution was established in 1956 after a new and weaker Constituent Assembly agreed to meet a key demand of the bureaucracies that four provinces of West Pakistan were integrated into one unit. The One-Unit policy, implemented in 1955, gave the civil service greater control over the integrated region, and developed parity between West Pakistan and East Pakistan, undercutting the Bengali electoral majority. The new president, Iskander Mirza, was himself a major general integrated into the civil bureaucracy, indicating how the alliance of civil and military bureaucrats had ascended to the helm of the political system. Shah (2014a) writes that the military officers held politicians in contempt, and believed that centralized government, unmediated by populist pressures, was a prerequisite for national security. This prejudice was reaffirmed by the rapid development and profession-alization of the military with the assistance of US aid and training, while the political government continued to be paralysed by deadlock.

[10] Interview No. L-51, 20 April 2017.

The new constitutional arrangement did little to resolve tensions between East and West Pakistan, and the military and civil service feared that the Bengali majority would win in the upcoming elections and demand a real decentralization of power. After four governments fell in quick succession, because of an inability to bring the executive and the legislature together on core questions of the federation, and a growing economic crisis, the military directly intervened and took over in a military coup in October 1958. The military cited internal strife, partisan bickering, provincialism and economic degradation threatening national security, as reasons necessitating intervention (Jalal 1990). The Constitution was suspended only two years after its proclamation, the assemblies were all dissolved, political parties were banned and elections were postponed indefinitely. At the helm was a 'diumvirate' of President Iskander Mirza and the commander in chief of the army, Ayub Khan. Ayub Khan, in a diatribe against the political class, said there was no limit to the depth of their [politicians'] baseness, chicanery, deceit and degredation'.[11] Mirza called this a 'peaceful revolution', stating: 'My authority is revolution ... I have no sanction in law or Constitution.'[12] Within a month, Ayub Khan and a group of generals in the central cabinet decided to remove Mirza and assume complete control of the state.

Ayub Khan's regime ruled Pakistan from 1958 to 1969. Until 1962 the state was run under the Laws (Continuance in Force) Order of 1958, which maintained the basic legal framework of the 1956 Constitution but provided the executive with unfettered powers. During its early years, the regime had two primary guiding principles of governance: 'administrative efficiency and the negating of politics' (Newberg 1995: 79). Ayub Khan carried out a series of reforms and reorganization efforts pushed through via executive ordinances, and his regime was characterized by a close partnership between the military and the civil service bureaucracy. Executive orders including the 1959 Public Offices (Disqualification) Order and the 1959 Elective Bodies (Disqualification) Order were used to purge thousands of politicians. Repressive measures were also used against public protests and strikes, as well as media publications. In 1959, Ayub Khan established the Basic Democracies Order, a radical revision of Pakistan's electoral system, creating a system of limited representation, simultaneously devolving political power to the local level, and increasing the power

[11] 'Democracy Is the Ultimate Aim', CMG, 9 October 1958.
[12] '2-Man Regime Described', CMG, 10 October 1958.

of the central government and bureaucracy, undercutting the provincial tier of government on which most political parties were organized.

In 1962, Ayub Khan introduced a new Constitution that formalized the Basic Democracies System and turned Pakistan from a parliamentary to a presidential system, with Ayub Khan as president. The new Constitution brought a formal end to martial law but placed the military leader firmly at the helm of a centralized and largely undemocratic and unrepresentative political system. He also introduced the Political Parties Act that permitted the reintroduction of political parties in the political system but regulated them. Finally, in 1964, in the 1st Amendment to the Constitution, fundamental rights were reintroduced, thus restoring the civilian courts as venues for challenging the military's rights violations. Ayub Khan then ran for presidential election in 1965 and won, in a new constitutional framework, with limited representation, and a powerful president-led executive.

The Judiciary under Ayub's Military Regime
On the same day that Ayub Khan took full control of the state, the Supreme Court upheld usurpation of power by the military.[13] A suit had been issued regarding the Frontier Crimes Regulations, the regulatory framework for Pakistan's tribal frontier that fell outside the regular legal framework, to determine whether writs against the Frontier Crimes Regulations were valid once that Constitution had been abrogated. The petition before the Court only pertained to the validity of writs in the absence of the Constitution and was not framed to challenge the legality of the abrogation of the Constitution in the military coup. But the Court, in a far-reaching decision, went far beyond the question posed by the petition to rule on the legality of the coup itself, and 'seized this opportunity to provide the regime with validity'.[14] Within a month of the coup, Justice Munir announced his theory of revolutionary legality, building on a misreading of Hans Kelsen's theory, and held 'the decisive criterion of a revolution is that the order in force is overthrown and replaced by a new order in which the former had not itself anticipated'. He argued that a victorious revolution was simply an internationally recognized legal method of altering a constitutional order, and since this revolution was victorious it must be accepted as legal. In short, Munir argued that if the coup d'état is successful, it is lawful.

[13] *State* v. *Dosso* 1958 PLD SC 533.
[14] Interview No. L-71.

Thus, Munir validated the proclamation of martial law, including the consequent restrictions on the judiciary, as the new regime created parallel military courts outside the jurisdiction of the civil courts, and banned any writs against the new government, under the Laws (Continuance in Force) Order of 1958. The *Dosso* case negates the earlier claims made by Justice Munir that he was holding back revolution and a military coup, since in this judgment he endorsed a military coup on the grounds that it was a successful revolution. The Court continued to uphold the new political order, and in *Mehdi Ali Khan* (1959), it held that any executive order passed under the Order of 1958 was not void if it came into conflict with fundamental rights, and thus superseded fundamental rights.[15] In short, Munir and the Federal/Supreme Court helped establish and legitimize a new military government with vast executive discretion.

Justice Munir retired as chief justice in 1960 and was soon replaced by Justice Cornelius. Cornelius had dissented in the famous 1955 decisions that upheld the dissolution of the assemblies, and, while concurring in the *Dosso* decision, he did not address the question of validating martial law in the decision but opined that fundamental rights 'being natural rights' were not undone by the abrogation of the Constitution and existed even in the absence of a legal framework.

Under Cornelius, the Court created a space for fundamental rights and a role for the judiciary within the new military regime system. The judiciary became an important venue for scrutinizing the actions of the lower rungs of the bureaucracies, including promotions, transfers and service structures, a role that the military regime tolerated as a way to manage the different echelons of the state's bureaucratic structure (Cheema 2021).[16] Between 1964 and 1969, judges also disagreed with the regime over the role and functioning of political parties, and the limits on executive power of the military regime to suppress opposing political parties and political expression. Even after legalizing political parties, the regime continued to dissolve them on the grounds that political parties violated public order. The judiciary resisted the unilateral dissolution of parties in *Maudoodi* v. *West Pakistan* (1963), where the Supreme Court upheld the rights of the Islamist political party, Jamaat e Islami and its

---

[15] *The Province of East Pakistan* v. *Md. Mehdi Ali Khan Panni*, PLD 1959 SC 387.

[16] *Mohammad Ali Akhtar* v. *Pakistan*, PLD 1963 (WP) Karachi 375.

members.[17] After 1965, as political opposition against Ayub Khan grew, a slew of *habeas corpus* petitions came before the courts, from politicians and political activists who had been placed in preventive detention by the regime.[18] In 1966, when opposition parties convened a conference criticizing the government, in violation of Section 144 of the Pakistan Criminal Procedure Code, which prohibited such assemblies, speakers spoke concerning the need to bring about change in the political system. Political leaders who spoke at the conference were arrested for allegedly instigating riots and violating public order. When the High Court upheld the detention orders, the Supreme Court, on appeal, chastised the court for deferring to the executive, saying that 'determining reasonable grounds for detention is a judicial function', and it set judicial standards for determining if preventive detention actions by the regime were indeed lawful.[19] Cornelius' court expanded the writ jurisdiction of the judiciary and upheld fundamental rights, in a series of thoughtful judgments.

Yet, as Newberg (1995) and Azeem (2017) point out, the judiciary during Ayub Khan's regime carved out a space for itself within the military regime, but ultimately did not challenge the contours of the garrison state. The Court's defence of the Jamaat e Islami's political activity was not extended to rights petitions by left-wing socialist, communist and nationalist political parties who were viewed as a greater threat. In *Mian Iftikharuddin* (1961), the Court upheld the government's dissolution of a publication house tied to left-wing political parties without providing any compensation.[20] In *Siraj Patwary* (1966), the Court upheld Ayub Khan's Basic Democracies system, articulating and upholding its principles and practices, and also sided with the regime in a question over the division of power between the provinces (namely East Pakistan) and the centre.[21] The Court set a

---

[17] *Saiyyid Abul A la Maudoodi, et al. v. The Government of West Pakistan and the Government of Pakistan*, PLD 1964 SC 673.

[18] *Government of East Pakistan v. Mrs Rowshan Shaukat Ali Khan*, PLD 1966 SC 286.

[19] *Malik Ghulam Jilani v. Government of West Pakistan*, PLD 1967 SC 33.

[20] Justice Dorab Patel, a future Supreme Court judge, condemned this decision, saying 'it would be extremely difficult to find a case during our Martial Laws in which the Martial Law authorities had acted in a manner as shocking as in Iftikharuddin's appeal' (Patel 2000: 78). See *Mian Iftikharuddin and Arif Iftikhar v. the Government of Pakistan*, PLD 1961 SC 585.

[21] *Province of East Pakistan et al. v. Sirajul Huq Putwari and others*, PLD 1966 SC 854.

lenient standard for legislation, arguing that as long as a law is made in its proper form, that is, followed a procedurally correct format, then it must be upheld, regardless of its content.[22] Thus, on the question of delegation of powers to the provinces, as long as the law limiting this delegation of powers was properly passed, it was legal. Similarly, on the question of preventive detention of politicians, the Court largely sided with the regime on its determinations of the public order. The Court had articulated a judicial standard for preventive detentions, but ultimately, based on this standard, continued to uphold the government's decision to detain political leaders in most cases.[23]

In short, during Ayub's military regime, the high courts did not challenge the military regime's priorities and prerogatives, but merely sought to create a system where these priorities and prerogatives followed a set of procedures that were built into the Constitution and upheld by the judiciary. As long as laws were properly passed, or executive actions were properly carried out, the judiciary was likely to uphold the actions of the military regime, even as they perpetuated the repression of politicians, activists, trade unions and political parties, and advanced the authority of the central government over the provinces.

The Judicial Role in the Era of Military-Bureaucratic Supremacy
It should be clear from the preceding account that during this period of military and bureaucratic dominance of the political system, the judiciary threw its support squarely behind the military regime, while carving out a continuing role and relevance for itself. In so doing, the judiciary gained a reputation for collaborating with the regime. Rahman writes: 'What emerges is a litany with few but notable exceptions, of ... decisions of dubious constitutional and legal validity by the high courts of the land ... that brought grist to the mill of military and bureaucratic adventurers.'[24] How do we explain this track record of support for the military?

---

[22] It 'evinced remarkable faith in the government's pursuit of the common good' (Newberg 1995: 100).
[23] In *Malik Jilani* (1967), the Court upheld most of the detention orders for speeches given criticizing Ayub Khan and his Constitution, stating freedom of speech was not a 'justification for politicians to play with fire in the hope that they will eventually be able to subdue the conflagration they caused'.
[24] Rashed Rahman, 'Judiciary's Role in Pakistan', *News*, 7 January 1993.

One argument made is that the judiciary was guided by political realism: surviving in a time of military-bureaucratic dominance meant acquiescing to military authority or risking military disobedience and retaliation. In a later speech, Justice Munir indicated that, in the *Maulvi Tamizuddin*(1955) decision, he was acting strategically because real power lay with the military-backed governor-general, saying, 'who could say that on 9th February, the coercive power of the state was at the service of the court and not the governor-general?' (Chaudhry 1973: 21–2). If the Court made decisions against the governor-general, 'who was to enforce them and was the court itself in a position to punish the contempt committed by disobedience?' (Chaudhry 1973).

However, the judiciary's choices were not only motivated by strategic concerns about the risks of challenging a powerful military. Judges seeking to avoid a confrontation with the military had options other than upholding military authority. The high courts and Supreme Court had considerable discretion in selecting cases for adjudication, and the Supreme Court had even more discretion in selecting cases for appeal.[25] The courts also had the discretion to select and frame the legal questions they took up for appeal. This discretionary authority allowed the high courts to avoid taking up cases regarding military authority, or avoid taking up legal questions that directly affected the military's authority. *Dosso* (1958) was simply a case of murder committed in a region that fell under the jurisdiction of an exceptional set of laws. The case did not deal directly with the legality of the military regime. Therefore, the Supreme Court could have avoided dealing with the question of the validity of the regime (as Justice Cornelius did in his concurring opinion), or it could have simply not taken up the appeal petition, thus neither challenging the regime nor giving it validation. Instead, the Court went much further, taking up the petition and using it as a vehicle for legitimizing the coup. *Dosso* typified the approach taken in a series of decisions by the judiciary where the courts did not simply uphold the policies and discretion of the military regime, but also provided detailed discussion of the merits, principles and necessity of these policies. On the other hand, in *Mehdi Ali Khan*, where the Court was pushed to review its decisions upholding military rule, it declined to carry out such a review, reading its own powers narrowly. Thus, the judiciary used its discretion selectively both to provide the military regime with legal legitimacy and

[25] See Article 160 of the Constitution of 1956.

to limit legal challenges to this granted legitimacy. The manner in which the judiciary used its powers and discretion indicates that strategic caution was not the only motivation for upholding the military regime's authority and legitimacy.

The judiciary's deference to the military could also be explained by the absence of a legal framework that provided them with the tools to muster meaningful challenges or restrictions on the regime. Authoritarian regimes often create new constitutional frameworks that limit the ability of judiciaries to uphold rights in the presence of an autocratic centralization of power (Barros 2008). In the absence of a constitutional framework providing fundamental rights and judicial review till 1962, and limited jurisdiction provided after 1962, the argument goes that the judiciary simply did not have the legal means to challenge the actions of the regime (Newberg 1995). When the Lahore High Court ruled, for example, that the high courts had jurisdiction over certain orders of summary military courts, the martial law authorities simply passed a new law removing that jurisdiction, taking away the judiciary's legal authority to challenge the military (Newberg 1995).

However, while it is clear that the absence of a constitutional framework did limit judicial assertiveness in the early years of Ayub's regime, the judiciary's jurisprudence demonstrated that, when it came to validating military power, it was also willing to step outside legal norms and constitutional frameworks. In *Dosso*, when Justice Munir upheld Ayub Khan's coup, he developed a theory of revolutionary legality that bore little relation to the past precedents or the state's constitutional framework. When upholding the military coup, he stated that 'public law is not to be found in the books, it lies elsewhere in the events that have happened' (Chaudhry 1973: 22). But when the judiciary was presented with opportunities to apply the previous constitution (that, while abrogated, still operated in certain spheres), or natural rights, to define limits on the military-led executive, and permit the continued operation of some fundamental rights, it chose not to. In *Mehdi Ali Khan* (1959), the Court upheld the absence of justiciable rights, and permitted the military to extend its control further. Thus, the judiciary was not simply constrained by a formalistic approach to law that restricted the judges to the texts of the constitutions and laws, and that kept the judiciary silent in their absence. The judiciary *chose* to find extra-legal rationales for validating the military-run political system but *chose* to avoid reading fundamental rights into the new system, on the basis that the present legal framework placed constraints on it. As Justice Kaikaus stated, in an effort to legitimize Ayub Khan's actions against fundamental rights, '[t]he Fundamental Rights should not stand in the way of the present government', and went on to reassure the readers of his judgment that Ayub Khan believed strongly in the importance of fundamental rights, recounting the army chief's past speeches, and declaring that we cannot 'impute to such a person the intention of destroying fundamental rights'. Therefore, the legal framework under martial law did place constraints on the judiciary, but how far these constraints actually limited the judiciary's ability to contest the military depended on how the judiciary chose to interpret these limitations.

Outside the courts, there is also evidence that judges did not simply acquiesce to the authority of the regime but were integrated into the regime structure. Justice Munir was also one of the architects of the Laws (Continuance in Force) Order of 1958 that gave Ayub Khan unbridled executive power, and he was an adviser on the drafting of the 1962 Constitution that provided the president with unlimited power, of which Justice Manzoor Qadir of the West Pakistan High Court was the primary architect.[26] Justice Shahabuddin served on the Constitutional Commission that Ayub Khan had put together to help draft a constitution (Khan 2016), and Justice Cornelius served as legal adviser to Ayub Khan's military successor, General Yahya Khan (Azeem 2017).[27] This was not simply a case of judicial deference in recognition of the authority of the military, as judges actively assisted the military in constructing the legal framework that legitimized and expanded the military regime's powers.

The courts were willing enablers of the expansion of military power and were not merely constrained by an asymmetry in power, or a lack of formal legal checks on executive power. So why were these highly respected and capable judges willing to collaborate in upholding the powers of the military regime?

The argument I offer, is that the pro-military inclination of the judiciary during this period is best explained by the institutional preferences of the judiciary, shaped by its institutional interlinkages with the military and political and bureaucratic elites affiliated and aligned with the military. The institutional interlinkages between the civil–military bureaucracy and the judiciary ensured that the military and

---

[26] Rahman, 'Judiciary's Role in Pakistan'.
[27] Justice Cornelius also chaired administrative committees including the Pakistan Cricket Control Board.

affiliated elites were critical audiences in shaping the legal and policy preferences of the judiciary, and served to reproduce a pro-military inclination within the high courts.

The first institutional interlinkage is the military's utilitarian interlinkage with the institutional hierarchy of the judiciary, determining appointments, promotions and case selection. After independence, Pakistan retained the same judicial appointment system established by the British, under which the governor-general, and later the president (once a constitution was established), assumed the same power over the appointment process. Under the Constitutions of 1956 and 1962, the chief justice of the Supreme Court was selected by the president, and the judges of the high courts were appointed by the president in consultation with the chief justice of Pakistan and the chief justice of the High Court. What this ideally meant was that the chief justice of the High Court initiated the appointment process by preparing a list of names consisting of leading advocates and senior judicial officers from the subordinate judicial bureaucracy whom he recommended for appointment as judges. The file was then forwarded to the governor of the province who was appointed by the president, and he added his comments and recommendations. Then it was sent to the Federal Law Ministry from where it went to the chief justice of Pakistan. The chief justice added his own comments and recommendations, and then it was passed on to the prime minister's office which made its own recommendations, before it finally went to the president. Ideally, therefore, there were several tiers of comments and recommendations before a final decision was made, but ultimately the final decision remained with the president and the president had the discretion to reject all the recommendations and choose someone himself. Realistically, this meant that the high courts were unlikely to recommend someone who the president and his law minister were likely to reject, and the president could bypass this process by selecting candidates on his own, often directly from the civil service bureaucracy.[28]

Ayub Khan and his Law Ministry frequently abused this process to push forward their favourites.[29] Ayub Khan appointed one member of

---

[28] Multiple interviewees told me that, during Ayub Khan's regime, the practice of *consultation* sometimes simply involved informing the chief justice of the president's choice beforehand. Interview No. L-10, 10 April 2017; Interview No. L-30, 9 February 2021.

[29] Hamid Khan, 'Judiciary – Institution in Decay – I', *Dawn*, 14 October 1994.

his parliament as a High Court judge, in exchange for his vote for an important legislative act, and also appointed the brother of a prominent politician who had helped him win his presidential election in 1965. Given the small number of judicial appointees during this period, Ayub Khan personally invited candidates short listed for High Court appointments for interviews during his regime and rejected candidates for arbitrary reasons.[30] Another future justice of the Supreme Court was approved to become a High Court judge when his name came before Ayub Khan for interview; Ayub Khan said 'I know his father' and approved him on the basis of this personal connection.[31] This meant that the military-run executive selected several judges for appointment, and the judges involved in the selection process were unlikely to nominate judges that the president or his law minister may have rejected. Thus, both directly and indirectly, the military-led executive exercised significant control over judicial appointments

The same executive practices applied to promotions. The president was expected to consult with the chief justice before promoting judges to the Supreme Court, and when appointing the chief justice, he was expected to respect seniority. However, the president frequently violated this process to promote his favourites. When Justice Munir became chief justice, he was handpicked by Governor-General Ghulam Muhammad, bypassing three senior judges who had been on the Supreme Court bench for a longer period. Similarly, Justice M. R. Kayani, a prominent judge of the West Pakistan High Court and a critic of the military regime, who had encouraged the regime to be open to 'healthy criticism', was denied promotion until he finally retired from the bench. Thus, in this system, the executive branch, run primarily by the military and military-affiliated civil service, played the primary role in judicial appointments and promotions, and could ensure that the judges who were appointed and rose up the ranks were those who were expected to decide in support of the military:

> There was no real gap between the judiciary and the military. To become a judge, you spent your time ingratiating yourself to the establishment [a popular term for the nexus of the military and civilian

---

[30] Interview No. L-30. Also see *Al-Jihad Trust* v. *Federation of Pakistan* (PLD 1996 SC 234). Khan writes that Ayub Khan had rejected candidates during interviews for cosmetic reasons such as poorly matched clothes, and regional affiliations. Khan, 'Judiciary – Institution in Decay – I'.

[31] Interview No. L-9, 10 April 2017.

bureaucratic leadership]. Very few lawyers, seeking judicial appointments would be out there agitating against the regime.[32]

Thus, the military and affiliated bureaucratic and political elites were important audiences for the judiciary, shaping its internal norms, as the system and its hierarchy incentivized granting discretion to the executive branch, limiting relief to oppositional political parties, and upholding the prerogatives of the military regime.

The second institutional interlinkage with the military was the pool from which judges were recruited. The social and professional network the judges came from and were socialized in, played a big role in shaping their worldview, and was also the network with which judges sought to build a reputation. The judiciary arrived in three streams – from the federal civil service of Pakistan trained in the British-run civil service before independence, from the judicial services of the subordinate judiciary that was also fused with the provincial executive bureaucracies and from lawyers and barristers, often trained in the United Kingdom.[33] Between 1949 and 1966, a majority of Supreme Court judges (55 per cent) were appointed from executive-run bureaucracies, and gained educational and professional experience in the UK, indicating they belonged to elite networks that had access to a British education.[34]

A majority of judges were coming from the bureaucracies: the judicial services of the lower courts that were fused with the provincial civil services, and the federal civil service of Pakistan, and thus belonged to the social and professional network of bureaucrats. The civil service bureaucracies had been the primary cadre of administrators under the British, and the British had paid the closest attention to their grooming and training. Those recruited for the civil service by the British 'usually came from families of some distinction or status derived either from wealth, learning or hereditary tribal leadership' (Braibanti and LaPalombara 1967: 378). British bureaucrat officers remained in the high courts after independence, right till the 1960s, with nine British judges in 1947, falling to two British judges by 1961. British officers espoused the 'values of an elitist cadre', and this disposition and these

---

[32] Interview No. L-3, 22 May 2017.

[33] The lower courts of the subordinate judiciary were staffed by officers from the judicial service, a provincial bureaucracy.

[34] Foreign education is a reliable indicator of elite socio-economic status in a country where the majority did not have access to foreign education.

values were shared by Pakistani members who were also educated at Oxford and Cambridge (Braibanti and LaPalombara 1967: 386). Thus, in the early years, members of Pakistan's federal civil service bureaucra-cies, who typically began their careers in the Indian civil service before independence, were usually from elite families, educated abroad and trained with the values and ruling practices of British colonial rule: executive discretion with limited accountability.

The experience of these judges within the civil services or within the subordinate judicial service made them more deferential to executive authority. Justice Cornelius described this training as follows:

> [I]n the last years of British rule, there was much political agitation with its crop of detention and arrests, followed by petitions in the nature of habeas corpus . . . in nearly all cases the question was reduced to whether or not there had been compliance with the Defence of India Act (a repressive statute designed to maintain law and order and suppress political agitation) . . . and no concept of human rights. (Cornelius and Haider 1981: 185)

This pro-executive training for judges from the bureaucracies was not unique to just British rule, as one former judge explained to me, but has persisted through Pakistan's history in the judiciary bureaucracy of the lower courts:

> Civil judges spend 20–25 years in the judicial services before being appointed to the High Courts, dealing with very petty complaints, and when they are promoted to the High Court they maintain their mindset as district bureaucrats, and when dealing with constitutional claims, they don't trust litigants, deny relief, and side with the state a lot more.[35]

Thus, judges from the bureaucracies worked and trained in a social and professional network that favoured executive discretion and was disdainful of populism and partisan politics. Justice Cornelius exempli-fied this cadre of civil judges, and his speeches give us indications about the attitudes and preferences of these judges. He stated in a speech that 'the price of democracy is partisan politics and the citizen must develop immunity to that insidious poison' (Braibanti 1999: 250). Similarly, in his description of British imperial rule, he stated that 'the Foreign officers in the (British) administration, from the governor-general

---

[35] Interview No. J-19, 23 April 2017.

down, acted for the most part with due regard for the general good and the requirement of justice' (Braibanti 1999: 210).

Cornelius, in his conception of the benevolence of British imperial rule, and his disdain for popular democracy, exemplified the values upheld by the bureaucratic elite, which actively supported the military as it rose to power and forced political parties out of the system.[36]

The other stream of judges were the lawyers. The legal community was organized into active but small bar associations, and the most prominent urban High Court bar associations were primarily led by Western-trained lawyers seeking to become judges:

> Historically the bar has not been homogenous in the sense that you could place lawyers in three categories. First the 'professionals of first choice'. These were elite lawyers who had the privilege to choose the legal profession for reasons other than material concerns, and they controlled constitutional litigation. They were built up with the colonial mentality. This was a product of education but more a product of the mindset presiding in their community. The second category were the 'have-nots' for whom law was not a profession of first choice, but one by default. They were compelled to work hard on real cases of litigation, including recovery suits and labour cases. The third were the 'absentee lawyers' whose real vocation was politics. But they could bring political cases to the court. So this was not a vocation for them but an extension of politics. Earlier on [in Pakistan's history], the 'professionals of first choice' were the most influential within the bar associations.[37]

Another senior lawyer and bar association leader explained to me that during the 1950s and 1960s:

> It was a very small bar at the time. It was understood that the bar has nothing to do with politics. The earlier tradition was that bars should have people of all political leanings. By and large, the bar had some prominent political figures, but the bar platform was not used for political purposes. We proposed a resolution in the Lahore High Court Bar Association condemning the martial law in 1958. Martial law sabotaged the constitution so it directly concerned the bar. But it was quite difficult to get the bar involved. The president of the bar at the time was a reluctant leader of the bar. The leaders were people willing to

---

[36] In his writings Cornelius also praised the Basic Democracies System, Ayub Khan's presidential system under the 1962 Constitution, and presidential discretion in judicial appointments (Braibanti 1999).

[37] Interview No. L-42, 1 April 2017.

work with the government, and the leadership was pro-establishment. We did not have a cadre for democratic activism at the time.[38]

These two accounts provide insights into the legal profession at the time, and the motives and mindsets of the lawyers who went on to become judges. Much like their counterparts from the bureaucracy, they also belonged to the established elite. The lawyers' community was probably the 'most powerful elite group, outside government service', and the most accomplished elite lawyers who were most likely to be nominated as judges were barristers trained in the Inns of Court in Britain, or lawyers who had served as prosecutors for the colonial government (Braibanti 1999: 113). These elite lawyers came from the same elite social networks that included the bureaucratic and military elite of the time, and often shared a similar colonial training and worldview.

Justice Munir was an advocate general for the British government before being appointed as a High Court judge. In his writings after retirement, Munir exclusively blamed the politicians for the end of civilian rule in 1958, stating 'thus was destroyed the common man's faith in the efficacy and suitability of parliamentary democracy and the warring and self-seeking politicians were digging the grave in which they and the nation were about to be buried (Munir 1978: 91). He praised Ayub Khan for saving the state, writing that during the four years of martial law, '[t]he general rot that had set in was arrested and many a reform ... was introduced' (Munir 1978: 92). His own writings and actions outside the judiciary indicated that he sincerely shared the same values as the military and bureaucratic elite, including disdain for politicians and support for Ayub Khan's dictatorship. All in all, the elite of Pakistan's legal community came from the same cluster of elite social networks of beneficiaries from the latter years of colonial rule and were at the forefront of a professional network that continued to imbibe colonial norms and preferences and reject mass politics.

Both the bureaucratic and legal elite emerged from pre-existing established elite networks that were also the primary beneficiaries of military and bureaucratic rule. Thus, the judiciary and the military continued to share strong normative interlinkages during this period. Jalal writes that the system of rule and policymaking under Ayub Khan

---

[38] Interview No. L-9, 4 December 2016.

was designed to 'disenfranchise the more volatile sections of urban society – industrial labour and the intelligentsia especially' and grant political privilege to 'sections of already dominant socio-economic groups' who did not have provincial bases of support (thus excluding nationalist politicians) (Jalal 1990: 296). Thus, opposition and resistance to military rule was muted from these quarters.

These were the authorities and social and professional networks that formed the key audiences for judges seeking to build a career and esteem: the military and military-appointed chief justices, the Western-educated bureaucratic elite of the civil services and the Western-trained legal elite. Under this system, anti-military judicial activism could hardly be expected or condoned. Those who desired to be appointed or promoted had to have the approval of the military and allied elites, and those who desired to build esteem as judges within the legal and bureaucratic elite had to present their distance from partisanship and redistributive politics and support for the maintenance of law and order:

> These judges and lawyers were the new colonial masters. For them the role of the court was a carry-over of the British court. More of a court that stressed law and order and stability, like a colonial judge. The judge of the superior courts thought the executive and state were synonyms. The principle of the separation of powers was not present in the mindset of the judge. Even after the enactment of the constitution, the courts represented the interests of the military class.[39]

Justice Cornelius, in a speech on the rule of law, emphasized this pro-executive deference, stating that '[t]he courses of justice run like the veins in a well ordered human organism. In that organism, a strong executive ... holds the first place.'[40]

The revolving door between the judiciary and the executive during this period demonstrated the lack of any meaningful separation between the two branches of government. Justice Amiruddin Ahmed served as governor of East Pakistan while a High Court judge. Justice S. A. Rehman held a string of important administrative and judicial appointments.[41] Justice Munir served briefly as Ayub Khan's law minister after the promulgation of martial law (Munir 1978).

---

[39] Interview No. L-42.
[40] 'Justice Cornelius Explains the Rule of Law', *Dawn*, 5 June 1962.
[41] 'SHC's Court Reference for Justice Rahman', *Morning News*, 13 February 1979.

Perhaps Justice Manzoor Qadir epitomized the nexus between the military and judicial elite and this revolving door. Educated in Britain, with a knighted father, Manzoor Qadir went on to serve as Ayub Khan's foreign minister from 1958 to 1962, after which he was directly appointed by Ayub Khan to the West Pakistan High Court and served as the chief justice of the West Pakistan High Court under the 1962 Constitution, which he himself had helped to design.[42]

Thus, the military and military allies, thanks to close utilitarian and normative interlinkages with the judiciary, were critical audiences in shaping the legal and policy preferences of the judiciary. Judges were recruited by the military and its allies and were recruited from social and professional networks affiliated with and supportive of the military regime and its priorities. For this reason, this was the era of the loyal court, as the judiciary developed institutional preferences that were supportive of the military.

There were certainly some dissident judges, such as Justice M. R. Kayani, who were more critical of the regime, and judges did not entirely approve of the repressive nature of the regime, and the limitations on their jurisdiction and formal legal authority between 1958 and 1962. Judges were also certainly weary of the power of the military in the political system and the risks associated with challenging the military. But, by and large, the internal consensus was that the judiciary would collaborate with the military regime, and consolidate its executive authority, while carving out a place for the judiciary within the political order as a venue for upholding procedural rights. It was this consensus that primarily explained the judiciary's decision-making that did not just acquiesce to military dominance but served to legitimize and sustain it.

In 1968, when Ayub Khan celebrated his 'decade of development and progress in law' amid widespread protests about rampant inequality and the repressive nature of his regime, the elites in attendance were bureaucrats and judges who lauded his regime.[43] These judges thus were part of the alliance of interests collaborating to uphold the regime. 'These judges did not have to be pressured to support the military ... they were independent-minded but colonial judges.'[44]

---

[42] 'Manzoor Qadir: An Obituary', *Dawn*, 13 October 1974.

[43] Bar associations took exception to the participation of the honourable judges in the celebrations as mass opposition grew against the regime at the time (Sidhwa 1989).

[44] Interview No. L-94, 18 March 2017.

PAKISTAN'S DEMOCRATIC INTERLUDE (1973–1977)

From Military to Civilian Rule

After 1965, an opposition movement started developing against Ayub Khan, and by 1968 these opposition parties had taken to the streets as frustrations grew. Clashes between activists and police, student unrest, labour unrest and political party mobilization rose, and ultimately Ayub was unable to suppress the movement against him and he opted to step down (Shah 2014a). The movement against Ayub Khan was primarily started by students, and then pushed further by two major political parties, the Awami League that represented the interests of the especially disgruntled population of East Pakistan, and the newly formed Pakistan Peoples Party (PPP), a left-leaning populist party recently formed in West Pakistan. Young junior lawyers in the bar associations got involved in the opposition movement, attending protest rallies in support of the political and student activists who had mobilized and faced the repression of the regime. 'The Bar did not involve itself initially in the protests against Ayub Khan. We did not take to the streets as an institution, but groups of young lawyers did engage in the protests.'[45] The pro-democracy movement against Ayub Khan was a first taste of political activism for many young lawyers in Pakistan at the time. This increased political activism and willingness to join street protests greatly divided the bar, and senior lawyers deplored the entrance of 'politics into the barroom', while retired judges labelled these protests 'hooliganism', urging for them to be stopped.[46] The events highlighted the opening of a generational divide within the legal community, regarding the legal community's role in political activity.

Ayub Khan was replaced by Yahya Khan, another general, who instituted an even more repressive martial law in order to bring stability to the state, but his regime had a time limit since he announced plans for a new election. Between 1969 and 1971, Yahya Khan abrogated the 1962 Constitution and ruled under a repressive Legal Framework Order but received little opposition from the judiciary or from the bar (Patel 2000).[47] The elections, the first free and fair elections in Pakistan's history, proved to be explosive, as the Awami League,

---

[45] Interview No. L-9.
[46] 'Use of Bar Rooms as Political Platforms Condemned', *Dawn*, 21 March 1977.
[47] 'President's Resolve to Defend Ideology Lauded: Lawyers Ready to Help Find Solutions to National Issues', *Dawn*, 21 August 1969.

demanding autonomy for the Bengali province of East Pakistan, swept all elections across the province, winning the largest number of seats overall, while the PPP swept most of the seats in West Pakistan. The military government was unwilling to accept a Bengali nationalist party taking power at the centre, and violent confrontations broke out between the centre and the Bengali province, which escalated into civil war in East Pakistan, as the disgruntled Bengali population demanded independence. The tragic war in East Pakistan was especially brutal and ended with the secession of East Pakistan (now Bangladesh), and the surrender and humiliation of the Pakistan army, which not only lost the war, but lost many soldiers who were taken as prisoners of war. By the end of the war, Yahya Khan stepped down, and Zulfiqar Ali Bhutto, the leader of the PPP, became the president and civilian martial law administrator, before the promulgation of the 1973 Constitution, a new constitution for a state undergoing reconstruction and reorganization. Bhutto took over as prime minister, as the first elected civilian leader of Pakistan. After the war, there was widespread disillusionment with the era of military rule that had produced such a disastrous outcome (Shah 2014a).

In 1973, the elected national and provincial assemblies passed a new constitution that has remained Pakistan's operational constitution since then, although it has gone through a series of suspensions and amendments. Under the 1973 Constitution, Pakistan was made a parliamentary republic, and the status of the president was diminished to largely a figurehead role, while the elected prime minister became the primary executive post. The Constitution articulated a list of protected fundamental rights and Article 8 of the Constitution also declared void all laws contrary to fundamental rights.

The military during this period went through an important transition. The military's resounding defeat during the war and Bhutto's overwhelming electoral victory in West Pakistan (now Pakistan) gave the PPP an opportunity to finally establish civilian control over the armed forces and reduce its political clout. The military continued to protect its institutional autonomy and the chief of army staff displayed 'thinly veiled contempt for Bhutto and his ministers', and often resisted Bhutto's orders (Shah 2014a: 121). After Bhutto learned of a potential coup conspiracy within the military, Bhutto publicly sacked and denounced the officers involved, and then purged the military of thirty senior officers. Under the new Constitution the military ostensibly fell under the Ministry of Defence, in an attempt to build civilian control over the military (Shah 2014a). Bhutto also created a special civilian arms organization, the Federal Security Force, that gained notoriety for pursuing his political opponents, and ran parallel to the military. The purges, public denouncing and parallel institutions all created resentment within the military towards the PPP government. At the same time, as Bhutto pursued his political opponents, he came to increasingly rely on the military, particularly as an insurgency grew in the province of Balochistan after Bhutto dissolved the opposition-led provincial government there. Far from cutting the military's powers and bringing it under civilian oversight, the government allowed the military to recover its autonomy and involvement in internal affairs and politics.

The Judiciary under the 1973 Constitution

Prior to the promulgation of the Constitution in 1973, the Supreme Court made two critical decisions. The first major decision was *Asma Jilani* (1972), after Bhutto took power, where the Supreme Court had to revisit the revolutionary legality doctrine used to bestow validity on Ayub Khan's coup and decide whether it applied to Yahya Khan's assumption of power in 1969 and his legal framework. The Court returned with a decisive verdict against Yahya Khan, determining that he had usurped power and that his action was not justified by the revolutionary legality doctrine, and therefore his regime had been illegal.[48] The judges shared the popular disillusionment with military rule at the time; Justice Yaqub Ali stated that 'the history of the constitutional mishaps which befell Pakistan between 1953 and 1969 bringing ruination ... forms the overcast background against which the court is required to answer the questions'. Yaqub Ali went further to state that the secession of East Pakistan was directly attributable to the assumption of martial law by the military, and Chief Justice Hamood-ur-Rehman declared that the doctrines of necessity and revolutionary legality could not be used to justify Yahya Khan's usurpation of power. The *Asma Jilani* decision gave the Court an opportunity to reflect on its past collaboration with the military and claim its separation from a humiliated military at a time when government by political party was in ascendance. However, the Court refused to bury the doctrine of necessity.[49]

---

[48] *Miss Asma Jilani* v. *The Government of the Punjab and another* and *Mrs Zarina Gauhar* v. *the Province of Sind and two others*, PLD 1972 SC 139.

[49] Even as the Court determined that Yahya Khan's usurpation of power did not meet the standards of 'necessity', they did not reject 'necessity' as a potential justification for interventions.

Further, its support for executive discretion persisted. In the landmark *Zia-ur-Rahman* (1972) decision, the Court had to decide the validity of the arrest and trial of journalists and political workers who had demonstrated against Yahya Khan's martial law, before a specialized court, out of the High Court's jurisdiction.[50] The Court ruled that since the order had been passed under the provisional constitution of the time, it remained valid, as the same provisional constitution had also provided for free and fair elections, and further the Court said that this arrest and trial order 'could be condoned on the basis of necessity'. Thus, even while declaring Yahya Khan's takeover illegal, the Court upheld his provisional constitution and his actions on the grounds of necessity. Justice Hamood-ur-Rehman stated that it was not the jurisdiction of the judiciary to examine the politics of the legislation passing the law under question that created the specialized courts, because that would take the judiciary into the arena of politics and policy. He argued that the role of the judiciary is simply accountability: to examine whether the executive is abiding by governing laws, but not questioning the laws themselves. Thus, the judiciary continued to act cautiously in dealing with executive power, invalidating the regime of Yahya Khan once Yahya Khan's regime was already disgraced and out of power, but still maintaining a space for the 'doctrine of necessity', and limiting the scope of its own power to deal only with executive actions that transgressed the executive's self-determined authority.

The 1973 Constitution provided the judiciary with its first experience of democratic constitutionalism. The new Constitution recognized the autonomy of the judiciary and authorized the separation of the executive from the judiciary. This meant that now federal civil servants could not be made judges, a key demand of the lawyers' community for some time, who saw it as essential to ensuring the judicial independence from the executive.[51] From now on, judges either came from the lawyers' bar or from the subordinate judiciary. The subordinate judiciary was also meant to be separated from the executive and brought under the exclusive control of the high courts, as part of the process of separating the two institutions, but this process

---

[50] *The State* v. *Zia-ur-Rahman and others*, PLD 1973 SC 49.

[51] The Executive Committee of the High Court Bar Association had called upon the government to drop the proposal for an increase of the CSPs share in the posts of the High Court judges, 'Appointment of More CSPs as Judges: Lawyers Urge Government to Drop Proposal', *Dawn*, 4 July 1969.

remained incomplete until the 1990s.[52] Nevertheless, the norm now became that about two-thirds of judicial appointees to the High Court came from the bar, and a third from the subordinate judicial service, and the proportion of civil servants remaining in the high courts was set to decline.[53] The appointment process still remained tilted towards the executive branch, and judges appointed from the bar were those who could be expected to defer to or uphold executive interests, but the pool from which judges were being recruited was changing, and this changing professional network of the judges would have important effects that are discussed in more detail in Chapter 4.

The judiciary's jurisdiction also expanded. Alongside the writ jurisdiction of the courts, under Article 199 the high courts were now also given the jurisdiction to enforce the observance of fundamental rights by the government. Finally, the Supreme Court's original jurisdiction was expanded, as, under the Article 184 (3), the Court had the power to make orders on questions that it deemed of public importance with reference to the enforcement of fundamental rights. The Constitution substantially expanded the role of the superior judiciary in the enforcement of fundamental rights. The era of democratic rule in the 1970s placed the judiciary in a position to arbitrate the contradiction between the promise of constitutional democratic rule and the quasi-authoritarian limitations on constitutional rights perpetuated by Bhutto's PPP government to pursue its ambitions through a strong, unchecked executive branch.

However, Bhutto did little to ingratiate himself with the judiciary and the legal community. Just as the Constitution provided the judiciary with an expanded new role in the political system, the PPP government sought to quickly amend the new constitutional and legal framework to weaken the judiciary and limit its constitutionally mandated role.[54] The government maintained a state of emergency, under which the government continued to curtail fundamental rights, including widening the scope of preventive detention. Under the 4th Amendment the government restricted the power of the courts to grant

---

[52] 'Executive-Judiciary Separation: Extension of Time-Limit Recommended', *Dawn*, 29 June 1976.

[53] Interview No. J-19; 'Certainly Not a Bureaucrat-Dominated Judiciary', *Leader*, 30 September 1995.

[54] 'Separate High Courts for Sind and Balochistan: 5th Amendment Moved in N.A. Emergency Orders above Challenge in Court', *Dawn*, 1 September 1976.

interim relief to detainees. The 5th Amendment declared all laws passed pursuant to the emergency proclamation to be validly made and thus not subject to judicial scrutiny. The government also created special tribunals with exclusive jurisdiction over offences punishable under the Defence of Pakistan Rules. Thus, Bhutto's government raised the expectations of the judiciary and legal community, by separating the judiciary, guaranteeing fundamental rights and expanding the role of the judiciary, and then disappointed these raised expectations by expanding the powers of the executive branch, and undermining the newly granted rights and judicial review, in order to deal with his political opponents.

Bhutto also took a high-handed approach with the judiciary and legal community more generally. Typically, judges to the high courts were appointed initially for a probationary period as ad hoc judges before their tenure was confirmed as permanent judges. Bhutto picked his favourites among judges for promotion and tried to abuse the ad hoc system by appointing judges to the high courts on an ad hoc basis and refusing to confirm their tenure in a timely manner so they remained deferential as their tenure remained unconfirmed and dependent upon his discretion.[55] This irked the judiciary and the legal community that had come to expect differently from a democratic constitutional government.[56] The bar associations were also frustrated by the perpetuation of the state of emergency given its impact on their work as litigators in fundamental right cases.[57] But Bhutto treated their concerns with derision. In a speech to the bar associations, Bhutto bluntly accused them of undermining the security interests of the country, stating:

> Are you then suggesting that, contrary to my deepest and most sincere conviction, I play straight into the hands of the enemies of the State by withdrawing this effective deterrent which the Constitution has provided my Government with? Do you think it preferable to endanger the country rather than extend the state of emergency?[58]

Thus, Bhutto made few allies within the community of judges and senior lawyers.

---

[55] Hamid Khan, 'Judiciary – Institution in Decay – I', *Dawn*, 14 October 1994.
[56] 'Government to Solve Problems of Lawyers – Jatoi', *Dawn*, 10 July 1974.
[57] Ibid.
[58] 'Govt. Doing All to Foster Growth of Legal Profession', *Pakistan Times*, 1 April 1974.

Judicial–Military Interactions during Democratic Rule

Bhutto's government started by curbing the role of the military before expanding it and, similarly, by expanding the role of the judiciary before curbing it. Both strategies ensured that Bhutto did not enjoy good relations with either institution. During Bhutto's regime, the high courts were still populated by judges appointed during the period of judicial–military collaboration in the 1950s and 1960s, thus the judiciary still retained the institutional preferences that had developed during that period. However, over the course of the 1970s, the number of bureaucrats in the judiciary steadily declined as civil service judges retired and no new judges replaced them, and the judiciary had been granted jurisdiction over fundamental rights. Thus, the judiciary was starting to separate itself from the executive and executive institutions, including the military, but this separation was gradual, and the norm of loyalty to the military still remained entrenched in the upper echelons of the judiciary. This provides the necessary context in which to understand the judiciary's military-related jurisprudence.

Between 1973 and July 1977, there were only thirty-one reported judgments from the high courts that dealt with military prerogatives, as the high courts reported few military-related cases during this period. Table 2.1 shows that in the first two years after the introduction of the new Constitution the judiciary challenged the military's prerogatives in a greater proportion of reported judgments, but in the last two years of the regime this proportion decreased. Initially, as the judiciary was exercising its new powers, it was more willing to check the actions of executive institutions including the military, but after those initial two years, as the government restricted the powers and jurisdiction of the judiciary, the courts were less willing to challenge the military.

These data only tell us about the downward trajectory in judicial decisions against the military. I also discuss three military-related

TABLE 2.1 Summary of decisions in military prerogative cases, 1973–1977

	1973–1975	1976–1977
Proportion of decisions against the military (%)	55	40

Note: (n=31).

decisions that directly concern questions about the judiciary's relationship with and jurisdiction over the actions of the military.

The first and most influential decision in defining the separate
spheres of civil and military jurisprudence under the new constitutional
framework was the foundational judgment, F.B. Ali v. The State
(1975).[59] Under Article 199(3), the jurisdiction of the courts was
ousted for a member of the armed forces 'in respect of his terms and
conditions of service, in respect of any matter arising out of his service,
or in respect of any action taken in relation to him as a member of the
Armed Forces'.[60] For such offences, members of the armed forces were
subject to the court martial proceedings of the military itself as instituted under the Army Act. In this case, retired military officers were
accused of fomenting a conspiracy against the state, by seeking to
seduce current members of the armed forces from their allegiance to
the military. They were tried by the military court martial, and they
filed a writ petition in the High Court challenging court martial
proceedings against them, given that they were retired, and hence
civilians. The Court had to decide whether civilians who have retired
or been dismissed from the army could be held liable for crimes under
the Army Act, thus ousting the jurisdiction of the civilian courts.[61]

The Court ruled in favour of the military, arguing that 'it does not
matter if those who have been accused have no nexus with the army as
long as their activity sought interference with the army'. Where this
was the case, the military had the discretion to decide which forum the
accused would be tried in: civilian courts or military court martial
proceedings. Further, these decisions could not be appealed to the
civilian courts on procedural grounds. The Court was clear in reiterat-
ing the nature and extent of the jurisdiction of the civilian courts,
including its responsibility to examine the constitutionality of laws. But
once it decided that the Army Act was constitutional, it interpreted
that the Act extended not just to military offences, but to certain types
of civilian offences. Thus, the judiciary set an important precedent in
allowing the extension of military court martials to civilians, and
ousting its own jurisdiction.

---

[59] F.B. Ali v. The State, PLD 1975 SC 506.
[60] Jurisdiction of the High Courts, Article 199, Constitution of 1973.
[61] The Army Act is the governing legislation for the army's organization and procedures, including the rules governing court martial procedures.

In another salient decision, *Sh. Karamat Ali* v. *State* (1975), the Court upheld the decisions made by military courts during the martial law era.[62] During the martial law era, military courts dealt with a wide range of civilian criminal offences.[63] The Court had to decide in this case, whether a case that had been decided by military courts during the martial law, but for which sentencing and confirmation had not been carried out, could now be challenged in civilian courts. The Court determined that unless it was clear that the military courts had acted out of jurisdiction or their intentions were *malafide*, the decision could not be challenged. Thus, even though the judiciary had ruled against the invocation of martial law by Yahya Khan, the courts were reluctant to revisit decisions and actions taken by the military courts and martial law administration during this period.

In 1977, Bhutto decided to call an early election to reaffirm his political standing and mandate. In response, nine political parties opposing Bhutto gathered together to form the Pakistan National Alliance (PNA). The PNA generated an unexpected level of support among those disgruntled with Bhutto's policies. The PPP won the elections comfortably, but allegations grew that Bhutto rigged the elections. In response, the PNA launched a nationwide agitation movement, demanding that the PPP government step down and a new election be held. Bhutto's PPP responded to the PNA's campaign with heavy-handed repression.

By this time, the politics of the period had affected the bar associations, where these political debates were playing out as well.[64] Leaders of several High Court bar associations, which belonged to sections of the urban middle class that opposed Bhutto's populist alliance of rural landholders and the working class, joined the PNA's protests. When Bhutto responded with arrests and detentions of these bar leaders, the Lahore High Court Bar Association hardened its stance against Bhutto.[65] By May 1977, Bhutto declared localized martial law in the areas that saw the greatest disturbances, namely the big cities of Lahore,

---

[62] *Sh. Karamat Ali* v. *The State*, PLD 1976 SC 476.
[63] These are different from the military court martials. Military court martials are courts composed of military officials that deal with internal military affairs. Military courts during martial law are courts composed of military officials that deal with civilian criminal cases unrelated to the military.
[64] 'Use of Bar Rooms as Political Platforms Condemned', *Dawn*, 21 March 1977; 'Lawyers Take out Procession in Lahore', *Dawn*, 25 March 1977.
[65] 'Lahore Lawyers Abstain from Courts', *Dawn*, 26 March 1977.

Karachi and Hyderabad. Bhutto called the military into these cities to enforce the law and curb the agitation movement. In doing so, he suspended all fundamental rights and authorized the establishment of specialized military courts ousting the jurisdiction of the civilian judiciary in these areas. Thus, by May 1977, Bhutto had brought the military back to the centre of the political arena, turning to it to help bring the PNA movement under control (Rizvi 2000).

The introduction of localized martial law and the suspension of the jurisdiction of the civilian courts raised important issues for the high courts. In two separate cases, the Lahore High Court and the Sindh High Court had to decide if the new localized martial law and the ouster of High Court jurisdiction in favour of military courts was constitutional.

In *Niaz Ahmed Khan* (1977) the Sindh High Court had to decide whether the declaration of martial law and the actions taken in the context of the establishment of martial law were legal.[66] The Sindh High Court tried to strike a difficult compromise in its decision. The court upheld the declaration of martial law as consistent with the emergency powers of the government, arguing that this declaration of martial law was meant to aid civil power, not replace it. But the court also held that the courts did not lose their jurisdiction, stating that if the military remained within its designated authority to act in aid of civil power, the courts had no jurisdiction to hold it accountable for its actions, but if it transgressed these boundaries, then the judiciary had the jurisdiction to challenge its actions. Under this ruling, the court's role was to determine when the military's actions exceeded the powers granted by the government's authority and hold it accountable for that. Thus, the Sindh High Court deferred to executive authority and upheld the expansion of military control, while still attempting to maintain its role and relevance.

In *Darwesh M. Arbey* (1977), the Lahore High Court went further than the Sindh High Court in challenging the government and the military.[67] The decision was made a month before the end of Bhutto's government, and the written judgment was issued after another military coup ousted Bhutto in July 1977. The court did not validate the supremacy the military was being given over civil power, and stated

[66] *Niaz Ahmed Khan v. The Province of Sind and others*, PLD 1977 Karachi 604.
[67] *Darwesh M. Arbey, Advocate v. Federation of Pakistan through the Law Secretary and 2 Others*, PLD 1980 Lahore 206.

that 'such sweeping arrangements, bringing the entire civil population of the province, within the ambit of the Pakistan Army Act . . . is totally against objects and reasons for which the Army Act is enacted'. The court both held the declaration of martial law to be invalid, and rejected the ouster of its jurisdiction, stating that the government could not divest the judiciary of all the judicial powers. The court stated 'the present Constitution neither envisaged the imposition of martial law nor the exercise by the Armed Forces of any judicial function'. *Darwesh Arbey* could be seen as a court assertively defending constitutional democracy, protecting its powers and opposing martial law, but the court also stated that 'if the Constitution is abrogated, set aside or placed in state of suspension . . . it might be possible to impose martial law outside the constitution. Such an action may or may not be justified by the doctrine of necessity.' The words of the court were consequential and ominous. The Lahore High Court had stated that martial law was not possible during a period of civilian rule under a constitution, but it left an opening for an extra-constitutional intervention outside the Constitution, justified by the doctrine of necessity. The court had therefore, in the same judgment, both invalidated the possibility of martial law under a civilian government and left open the possibility of martial law under an extra-constitutional military government.

The detailed written judgment was issued a month after the court had made its decision, by which time a military coup had taken place, in which General Zia-ul-Haq ousted Pakistan's first elected civilian government.

Thus, we see the beginning of a slow transition in the judiciary's role in the 1970s. The new constitutional arrangement had given the judiciary new autonomy from executive institutions and an expanded role it had not previously enjoyed, and when the elected executive branch attempted to restrict the judiciary's role, the courts opposed those attempts. However, at the same time, the decisions discussed here show that the judiciary continued to uphold executive discretion, safeguard the 'doctrine of necessity', preserve the autonomy of the military and uphold its prerogatives.

CONCLUSION

In sum, the reason that the Pakistani high courts upheld military dominance within the Pakistani political system in the 1950s and 1960s was that the military and affiliated elites were critical audiences influencing the internal workings of the judiciary, both through engagement with the process of judicial appointment and promotion processes, and through ties with the networks from which judges were being recruited. The judges who advanced their careers and built a reputation with their networks therefore, were those who supported military rule and cooperated in upholding it. Thus, the legal and policy preferences that were entrenched during this period in the judiciary helped ensure the judiciary collaborated with the military. This was not a judiciary hamstrung by limited authority or the reality of military dominance, but a judiciary that used its powers to legitimize and strengthen military rule. In the 1970s, during Pakistan's first period of civilian rule, we see how the new Constitution disrupted this arrangement, and began the separation of the judiciary from military. This started having an initial but limited effect on the jurisprudence of the courts during this period, but growing antipathy between the judiciary and the civilian government, and continuing ties between the judiciary and military, ensured the judiciary was more willing to use its new-found authority to challenge the civilian executive than the military.

CHAPTER THREE

THE CONTROLLED COURT (1977–1999, PART 1)
A Judiciary in Transition

In this chapter I describe changes in the Pakistani judiciary's behaviour towards the military between 1977 and 1999. The chapter is divided into two phases: (1) 1977 to 1988, Pakistan's longest uninterrupted period of direct military rule; and (2) 1988–1999, a decade of constitutional democratic rule. In each period, I discuss the prevailing political situation, the position and interests of the military and the judiciary's relationship with the military as demonstrated through its jurisprudence. Through this period, I show that the judiciary gradually shifted towards staking out a more independent position from the military, preserving and cautiously expanding its own role and jurisdiction.

1977–1988: A DECADE OF MILITARY RULE

Pakistan's brief interlude of constitutional civilian government came to a dramatic end in July 1977. The chief of army staff, General Zia-ul-Haq, ousted Bhutto's government and declared martial law. Federal and provincial governments were dismissed, and national and provincial assemblies were dissolved. The Constitution and fundamental rights were suspended under the new Laws (Continuance in Order) Order of 1977, the primary governing instrument of the new regime. The country was divided into martial law zones, each with a martial law administrator (MLA), directly responsible to the chief martial law administrator (CMLA), Zia-ul-Haq. Under this new political arrangement, the military was indisputably in control (Shah 2014a).

Initially, Zia described the coup as a temporary intervention to restore stability to the political system. Zia said he only wanted to restore law and order and hold free and fair elections and then transfer power to the elected representatives, ideally within ninety days. He banned political activity but pledged this was only a temporary action while the regime brought stability and created conditions conducive to free and fair elections (Rizvi 2000). But it soon became apparent that the new government was more interested in consolidating power than handing it over.

In October 1977, Bhutto was rearrested after being released on bail; he was tried for murder, and later executed in April 1979. Zia also carried out a countrywide crackdown against the PPP. Martial Law Order (MLO) 12 empowered law enforcement personnel to arrest persons who were working against security, law and order or the smooth running of martial law.[1] Under this order, the MLAs were granted wide discretion to arrest and detain civilians, and PPP officeholders, members and activists were arrested around the country. The regime used the pretext of the need for stability and accountability to repeatedly postpone elections, while issuing a host of MLOs that gave the regime widespread powers to control and repress political opposition, journalists and civil society.[2]

Zia's regime exceeded both the Ayub and Yahya regimes in the extent to which the military infiltrated the civil administration and the economy. Under Zia the military's intelligence apparatus greatly expanded, as the Inter-Services Intelligence's (ISI) S-directorate became deeply involved with the war against the Soviets in Afghanistan abroad, and its political cell disrupted and weakened the regime's political rivals at home. Zia appointed an unprecedented number of senior officers as ambassadors, secretaries and heads of autonomous public corporations (Shah 2014a). In 1980, the military reserved a statutory quota of 10 per cent in the three important civil services, thus replacing the military-bureaucratic collaboration of the Ayub era with the militarization of the bureaucracy (Shah 2014a).

---

[1] Shaikh Aziz, 'A Leaf from History: Furious Zia Gets Bhutto Re-arrested', *Dawn*, 15 June 2014.

[2] The regime was bolstered by the onset of the Soviet-Afghan War, as it became a critical ally of the Reagan government in dealing with Russia's invasion of Afghanistan in 1979, receiving American money and weapons to coordinate anti-Soviet resistance in Afghanistan.

Outside state institutions, the military's interventions into the economy assumed an unprecedented scope and scale. General Zia expanded and institutionalized Ayub Khan's practice of allotting agricultural and urban residential and commercial land to military officers, and the military's subsidiaries became monopolies (Siddiqa 2007). Military welfare foundations, such as the Fauji Foundation and the Army Welfare Trust, expanded into industrial conglomerates, investing in real estate, fertilizers, sugar mills, oil and gas and cement (Siddiqa 2007). Thus, within the first few years of Zia's regime a more expansive and repressive military-led political order was established.

By early 1981, Zia's regime abandoned all pretence of transience. In February 1981, Zia banned political parties. This included the PPP and the parties in the now disbanded PNA, which united with the PPP under the banner of the Movement for the Restoration of Democracy (MRD). In March 1981, the Supreme Court was conducting hearings challenging the legislative powers of the regime. At the same time, a Pakistani International Airlines flight was hijacked and taken to Kabul, allegedly by a terrorist group, Al-Zulfiqar, composed of former members of the PPP. Zia used the hijacking as an opportunity to claim that drastic measures were required to 'maintain the integrity and sovereignty of Pakistan' (Newberg 1995: 180). Accordingly, Zia introduced a new Provisional Constitutional Order (PCO) that was offered as a substitute constitution. It placed virtually all power in the hands of the military government, placed no limits on military rule and gave the president retrospective power to amend the constitution. Citizens were now subject to an ever-expanding list of martial law regulations and orders, resulting in the detention of thousands of civilians (Rizvi 2000). Political leaders could not travel between cities, and even indoor meetings were cause for arrest. Many political leaders, and civil society members left the country for fear of arrest (Rizvi 2000). Harsh punishments, including flogging and public hangings, were meted out by military courts.[3]

By 1985, Zia's regime began Pakistan's transition back to a civilianized system. Zia ensured his presidency was secured through a referendum that gave him a mandate to remain president for five more years. After securing his presidency, he organized parliamentary elections for February 1985. The elections were carefully managed by the military. They were held on

---

[3] 'MLC Convicts to Be Re-tried in Civil Court', *Star*, 28 November 1985; 'Lawyers to Set up Action Committee', *Star*, 1 April 1985.

a non-party basis, and members of the political parties of the MRD alliance, including the PPP, were detained around the country, and newspapers supporting the MRD were censored (Rizvi 2000).[4]

Zia's other step was to push through several constitutional amendments, which collectively came to be known as the 8th Amendment to the 1973 Constitution. The 8th Amendment made three significant changes to the constitutional order. First, executive power was decisively shifted from the directly elected parliament to the presidency. The president was given a range of discretionary powers with respect to the federal and provincial governments, including the power to dissolve the elected assembles under Article 58(2)(b). Second, Articles 62 and 63 of the Constitution gave the judiciary the power to disqualify elected representatives and electoral candidates from political office for not meeting a vague moral standard of morality and sagacity. Third, Article 270-A validated all martial law regulations, laws and orders and all actions taken under these law orders, including the decisions of military courts between 1977 and 1985. Once Zia had ensured that he wielded the most authority in the new system, that the elected legislatures were weakened by unelected presidential and judicial checks and that all prior actions of the military regime were given legal cover, he restored the 1973 Constitution, and in 1986 a new civilian government took power under the amended constitution, with Zia as president. The ruling coalition formed a party under the leadership of Prime Minister Mohammad Ali Khan Junejo, called the Pakistan Muslim League.

The Role of the Judiciary under Zia
During General Zia's regime, the shift of the judiciary from the military gradually became apparent. Initially, when Zia came to power, the judges of the Supreme Court had primarily been appointed to the judiciary during the 1950s and 1960s, when the institutional interlinkages between the military and judiciary were strongest and the norms of loyalty to, and collaboration with, the military were still entrenched.

When Zia seized power, he moved to ensure the judiciary's support, timed with his arrest of Bhutto on murder charges. He ended the state of emergency that had been kept in place by Bhutto since he

---

[4] In the absence of political parties, most of the candidates were powerful local notables in constituencies with the prior wealth and name recognition to win an election (Mohmand 2014).

came to power.[5] He also nullified all Bhutto's constitutional amendments 'to the extent that they affected the integrity and independence of the judiciary'.[6] Nullifying Bhutto's interventions in the judiciary not only served to alleviate any concerns of the judiciary and the legal community about the new dictatorship but also ensured that judges who had been held back by Bhutto received their expected promotions.[7] Zia nullified the controversial extension Bhutto had given to Chief Justice Yaqoob Ali, which served both to remove a judge who had ruled against the previous military takeover (see *Asma Jilani* (1972)), and promote judges whose elevation Bhutto had denied, and thus who harboured resentment towards the ousted prime minister. Zia also appointed the chief justices of the high courts of each province as the governors for their respective provinces, underlining the close collaborative relationship Zia sought to initially build with the judiciary. Finally, to consolidate the support of the judiciary, High Court judges were asked to take a new oath, a measure by which each judge signalled recognition of the new regime. Thus, in the early months, Zia established a collaborative relationship with the judiciary.

This collaborative approach soon yielded dividends. When Bhutto and ten other party leaders were reimprisoned in September 1977, and threatened with trial before military tribunals, Bhutto's wife Nusrat Bhutto filed a petition in the Supreme Court challenging the validity and legality of the martial law regime. In *Begum Nusrat Bhutto v. Chief of Army Staff and Federation of Pakistan* (1977), the Court under Chief Justice Anwar-ul-Haq ruled in favour of the new regime, validating military rule.[8] The Court held that 'the legal consequences of an abrupt political change should be judged, not by an abstract theory of law … but by a total consideration of the milieu in which the change is brought about'. In considering the 'milieu' in which Zia had seized power, the Court went through a list of failures of the Bhutto

---

[5] Lifting this state of emergency meant little, given that the Constitution and fundamental rights had been suspended.

[6] 'Freedom of Judiciary Ensured: CMLA Annuls Amendments to Constitution', *Dawn*, 23 September 1977.

[7] After Zia lifted the amendments, the president of the Lahore High Court Bar Association which had opposed Bhutto, 'expressed full support to the measures taken by the government to restore the dignity and jurisdiction of the superior court' (*Morning News* 1977).

[8] *Begum Nusrat Bhutto v. The Chief of Army Staff and Federation of Pakistan*, PLD 1977 Supreme Court 657.

government, and determined that Bhutto's electoral rigging had created a crisis that could not be resolved from within the constitutional framework, which made it *necessary* for the military to intervene. The Court took Zia's claim in its written statement at face value: that he merely intended to stay in power for a short duration 'to provide a bridge to enable the country to return to the path of constitutional rule' (Newberg 1995: 164). Thus, the Court resurrected the doctrine of necessity, validated the Zia regime's takeover as necessary to resolve the crisis Bhutto created and empowered the regime to take whatever actions were 'necessary' to return the country to constitutional democratic rule.

The judgment outlined the relationship that the judiciary envisioned for the military and the judiciary under the new regime. The Court was prepared to give the military wide discretion to carry out its aims, but it was not prepared to lose all the gains it had made under the 1973 Constitution. It granted the CMLA powers to 'perform all such acts and promulgate all legislative measures which have been consistently recognized by judicial authorities as falling within the realm of necessity'. The regime now had wide latitude to take executive and legislative actions, including even amending the constitution, as long as the actions could be demonstrated as being 'necessary' to accomplish the regime's stated goals.[9] However, the Court also ruled that the judiciary had to set the standard for what actions fell within the realm of 'necessity'. Further, the Court ruled that the 1973 Constitution was still the supreme law of the land, barring the parts of the Constitution that the regime had suspended, which meant the judiciary maintained its powers of judicial review of actions of the regime. Thus, the Court outlined a collaborative relationship, in which the military regime was provided wide discretion to take whatever actions were necessary to achieve its aims, and the judiciary had the power to determine the standard of necessity that these actions had to meet.

Perhaps the most important contribution the judiciary made to the new regime was in assisting the regime in eliminating the threat from Bhutto. The trial, conviction and execution of Bhutto for the murder of Mohammed Ahmed Khan Kasuri would go down as one of the darkest moments in the history of Pakistan's judiciary (Khan 2016). The trial of Bhutto was carried out in the Lahore High Court, where

---

[9] Judges who decided this case later came to regret granting the CMLA blanket powers to legislate and amend the Constitution (Haq 1993; Patel 2000).

the chief justice was Maulvi Mushtaq, a judge who had been denied his expected promotion by Bhutto but elevated to the position of chief justice by Zia, and was known for his acrimonious relationship with the ousted prime minister (Iqbal 2006).[10] The Lahore High Court ruled against Bhutto on all charges, including murder, and the case was appealed to the Supreme Court. The Supreme Court upheld the Lahore High Court verdict, as Chief Justice Anwar-ul-Haq held that any omissions, errors, irregularities or even illegalities (during the proceedings) were of such a nature as to not vitiate the trial (Schofield 1979).[11] During the proceedings, several judges who may have overturned the Lahore High Court decision were either retired or transferred from the bench, and new judges were promoted to the Supreme Court and to the bench on an ad hoc probationary basis (Khan 2016). The military also applied pressure to ensure a favourable verdict; as the son of one of the judges involved in the case narrated, 'my father was prodded and coerced by military officers. He received pressure from several groups opposed to Mr. Bhutto.'[12] In the end, four judges, all former members of the Lahore High Court, endorsed the decision of their junior comrades in the Lahore High Court, while the three judges from outside the Lahore High Court all acquitted Bhutto. With the help of the chief justice, Zia got the conviction he wanted through judicial manipulation, pressure, procedural irregularities and provincial and personal biases (Schofield 1979).[13] Thus, the senior judges of the Supreme Court, appointed during the 1950s and 1960s, continued to be loyal collaborators with the military.

By the time Bhutto was convicted, Zia, who had now appointed himself president, proceeded to dismiss the veneer of collaboration with civilian partners. By July 1978, Zia started complaining about the need for the 'speedy dispensation of justice', which was a pretext to set up a parallel judicial system of summary and special military courts of military officers and magistrates to deal with a wide range of

---

[10] Bhutto's defence team repeatedly appealed to the Supreme Court that Mushtaq's bias against him was apparent during the proceedings, including shouting and hurling abuses at the prime minister, but their appeals to change the bench were dismissed, 'Justice Mushtaq's Appointment Can't Be Assailed or Attacked', *Dawn*, 8 December 1977.

[11] *Zulfiqar Ali Bhutto and 3 others* v. *The State*, PLD 1979 SC 38.

[12] Interview No. L-10, 10 April 2017.

[13] Later, one of the judges who upheld the charges against Bhutto described the decision as the biggest regret of his career (Shah 2002).

criminal cases.[14] MLAs were given the power to transfer cases from civilian courts to military courts. Military court decisions could be appealed to the high courts, but in the absence of procedural requirements and a detailed evidentiary record, a successful appeal to the high courts would prove difficult. In August 1979, he promulgated Article 212-A to add to the constitutional framework, which expanded the jurisdiction of the military courts and stated that the jurisdiction of the high courts to issue writs, orders, injunctions against military courts or tribunals 'shall abate' although this did not apply to the Supreme Court (Jaffrelot 2015). The high courts were also divested of their jurisdiction to issue writs against the orders of MLAs. Thus, the very power the Supreme Court granted Zia to amend the constitutional arrangement was used to clip the judiciary's powers

If the judiciary was collaborating with the military, why did Zia curb the powers and jurisdiction of the judiciary? Unlike the 1960s, there was a growing divergence between the judiciary and the military on the role of the judiciary within Zia's regime, a divergence that was more apparent at the level of the high courts. In *Nusrat Bhutto*, the courts had preserved their right to determine whether actions taken by the regime were indeed necessary to achieve the regime's alleged aims. As the government grew more repressive, with MLAs increasing the number of detentions and transferring more cases from civilian courts to military courts, there was a flood of petitions to the superior judiciary challenging the actions of the MLAs and the jurisdiction of the military courts (Newberg 1995). The high courts took the responsibility placed upon them by the *Nusrat Bhutto* judgment seriously and sought to exercise their powers of judicial review over the orders of martial law authorities, to determine if these orders fulfilled the criteria of necessity.

Table 3.1 shows the clear difference between the Supreme Court and the high courts. Between July 1977 and March 1981, the Supreme Court only admitted twenty-two reported petitions challenging actions taken by the military regime, of which it ruled in favour of the military twenty-one times. On the other hand, the high courts admitted

---

[14] 'Zia Invites Suggestions: Speedy Dispensation of Justice', *Dawn*, 23 July 1978. The summary military court had only one judge, who did not have to have any legal training. Special military courts were made up of three people: a civilian magistrate and two ranking army officers. Full records were not made of the trials held in these courts, only summaries, and the accused were not entitled to be represented by a trained lawyer (Jaffrelot 2015).

TABLE 3.1   Proportion of reported High Court/Supreme Court decisions favouring the military regime (1977–1981)

	Supreme Court	High courts
Executive actions by MLAs	10/10	12/30
Legislative actions by MLAs	2/2	12/13
Judicial actions by military courts	9/10	35/79
Total favourable decisions	21/22	59/122

TABLE 3.2   Proportion of reported High Court decisions challenging military regime by year (1978–1980)

	1978	1979	1980
Executive actions by martial law authorities	9/18	7/9	2/2
Legislative actions by martial law authorities	0/5	0/6	1/1
Judicial actions by military courts	12/34	16/25	5/9

122 such petitions for hearing, of which they ruled in favour of the military only fifty-nine times. This highlights the close collaboration between the Supreme Court and the regime, and the clear divergence between the judiciary and the regime at the level of the high courts.

The high courts and the military regime increasingly diverged over what actions were 'necessary' to achieve the regime's goals as outlined in 1978. Initially, in 1978 the high courts upheld the jurisdiction of the military courts to deal with a wide range of questions, ranging from kidnapping and terrorism to hoarding and liquor possession.[15] However, by 1979, as the martial law authorities expanded the scope of their powers, detained more political prisoners and transferred more cases from the civilian to the military courts, the strain between the military and the high courts became more apparent, and the courts started issuing judgments more critical of military power (Newberg 1995). Table 3.2 shows how judicial contestation of the military increased steadily, with the high courts challenging the actions of martial law authorities in 37.5

---

[15] See *Nazeer Ahmed* v. *Abbas Ali Khan*, PLD 1978 Karachi 777; *Nyganad Askari* v. *State*, 1978 PLJ Lahore 519; *Manzoor Hussain* v. *State*, 1978 PLJ Lahore 229; *Mohammad Afraaq Ahmed* v. *Raunaq Ali*, 1978 PLJ Lahore 331.

per cent of reported judgments in 1978, and then in 57.5 per cent of judgments in 1979.

Individual judicial decisions further emphasize the growing divergence between the military and the high courts. In *Mumtaz Ali Bhutto and another* v. *Deputy Martial Law Administrator* (1979), the Sindh High Court objected to the detention of two former ministers in the PPP government, in a sweeping judgment that warned that the martial law authorities could not detain without any trial, insisted that the Constitution did entitle citizens to some rights and placed limits on state power to violate these fundamental rights beyond what was deemed 'necessary'.[16] The court placed limits on the necessity doctrine, saying that the courts have not conferred on the MLA 'the power to do anything that he may think best and render the power of judicial review nugatory'. The Sindh High Court went on to challenge several convictions under military courts, and other high courts followed suit, setting aside convictions where the High Court held that the military court did not have any jurisdiction.[17] In *Satar Gul* v. *MLA Zone B NWFP Peshawar* (1979), the Peshawar High Court voided the transfer of cases pertaining to possession and smuggling of drugs from civilian to military courts, questioning whether such actions met the standard of 'necessity'.[18] The regime was not prepared to accept these limitations placed on its authority and responded by tightening restrictions on the superior judiciary through new legislation, and expanding the powers and autonomy of the military courts.

Thus, as indicated in Table 3.2, by 1980, the courts issued far fewer judgments relating to the actions of MLAs and military courts. However, the response from certain judges was to start challenging the military regime's legislative powers, a question on which the courts had so far largely deferred to the regime. In *Yaqoob Ali* v. *Presiding Officer, Summary Military Court (1980)*, the Sindh High Court upheld Zia's constitutional amendments and his power to amend the Constitution and remove the judiciary's powers of judicial review, but Justice Mirza issued a famous dissenting opinion, in which he argued 'on no principle of necessity could the power of judicial review vested

---

[16] *Mumtaz Ali Bhutto and another* v. *The Deputy Martial Law Administrator, Section 1, Karachi and 2 others*, PLD 1971 Karachi 307.

[17] *Syed Essa Noori* v. *Deputy Commissioner, Turbat and 2 others*, PLD 1979 Quetta 189.

[18] *Satar Gul and another* v. *Martial Law Adminsitrator, Zone B N.W.F.P., Peshawar and 2 others*, PLD 1979 Peshawar 119.

in the Supreme Courts ... be taken away'.[19] The Balochistan High Court went further, ruling that Article 212-A, which took away the power of high courts to review the decisions of military courts, was void because it was inconsistent with the judgment in the *Nusrat Bhutto* case, and did not meet the test of necessity.[20] The courts were now openly debating the regime's legislative powers that were used to weaken the judiciary.

The period between 1977 and 1981 was a time of political transition. The military regime took power, ostensibly aiming to remain in power for a short period of time and collaborating with civilian partners to restore stability and constitutional democracy, a consensus that was outlined and upheld in the *Nusrat Bhutto* decision. However, over time this consensus unravelled, as the regime, backed by the Supreme Court, sought to use that consensus as a stepping stone towards greater executive discretion and consolidation of military authority, while the high courts worked to keep General Zia's actions within the limits of the consensus outlined in *Nusrat Bhutto*.

The Supreme Court was primarily composed of judges appointed during the 1950s and early 1960s when the institutional interlinkages between the judiciary and the military were at their highest, and the norm of collaboration between the two institutions was most entrenched. Thus, it was not surprising that the Supreme Court remained loyal to the military. At the High Court level, however, as I will explain in the next chapter, judges were mostly appointed from outside the civil service, from bar associations that were increasingly politically engaged. Thus, the younger generation of High Court judges diverged more from the military. The high courts subjected the actions of the regime to serious scrutiny, reminding the regime of its commitment to re-establishing constitutional democracy. The consensus between the two institutions finally fell apart in 1981, when Zia introduced a new PCO that consolidated all political authority with the military and slashed the jurisdiction of the judiciary.

---

[19] *Yaqoob Ali* v. *Presiding Officer, Summary Military Court, Karachi*, PLD 1985 Karachi 243.

[20] The regime was not happy with the decisions of the Balochistan High Court and had attempted to use coercive measures to prevent the High Court making this decision (Marri 1990).

The PCO's effect on the judiciary was devastating. It drastically weakened the judiciary and reshaped its composition to weed out all judges who would challenge the regime. All orders and actions taken by the regime were now considered to have been validly made and could not be called into question in any court on any grounds. Members of the armed forces, who occupied most leadership roles, were made fully immune to civil prosecution, and the courts would not hear cases pertaining to preventive detention or challenge any actions by the military courts (Newberg 1995). The judiciary was robbed of most of its jurisdiction, as military courts and MLAs now ran the country and were only answerable to the president.

Zia completed the subordination of the judiciary by ordering judges to take a new oath under the PCO. They were expected to pledge as follows: 'I will discharge my duties and perform my functions honestly, to the best of my ability and faithfully in accordance with Provisional Constitutional Order, 1981, and the law' (Jaffrelot 2015) By taking such a pledge, judges were forced to recognize the PCO and the reduction of the judiciary's authority, or risk being removed from the judiciary. Those judges who refused to take the oath, or who Zia refused to administer the oath to, were automatically removed. Most judges were willing to take the oath and keep their jobs. In total, fifteen judges of the Supreme Court and the high courts did not take the oath or refused to take the oath, which included four out of twelve judges in the Supreme Court, and eight out of twenty-five judges in the Lahore High Court (the largest High Court) (Khan 2016).[21] Zia justified the actions against the judiciary, saying he had only taken this action because, 'for the purpose for which the military took over, it was necessary that the country was administered in a particular form'.[22] He criticized the judiciary, saying 'it should be held accountable for its actions' and emphasized that the judiciary 'is held in high esteem but changes were required to make justice easily accessible'.[23]

From 1981 to 1985, the superior judiciary largely surrendered to military control. As one senior lawyer recounted, 'when Zia appointed the new Chief Justice, Justice Haleem, he asked Justice Haleem: "What is your view about the political situation in the country?" Haleem

---

[21] Hasan Akhtar, '12 SC, High Court Judges Did Not Take Oath under PCO', *Dawn*, 26 March 1981.

[22] 'SC and High Courts' Judges Sworn In', *Dawn*, 26 March 1981.

[23] 'Zia for Inexpensive, Speedy Justice to Masses', *Morning News*, 18 October 1981.

responded "I am not a politician. I do not want to be political" ... Zia was happy with his answer."[24] Thus, Zia chose a chief justice who he expected would stay away from politically salient issues.

Over the course of these five years, there were only thirty-eight reported judgments pertaining to military prerogatives, a far cry from the number of reported judgments between 1977 and 1981. Out of these thirty-eight judgments, only thirteen dealt with the actions of the MLAs and military courts. Further, very few of these cases dealt with salient constitutional questions. Khan (2016) writes that very few cases of constitutional importance were brought before the Lahore High Court during this period, and those raising important constitutional questions were returned by the office and were never fixed for hearing before the judges.[25]

This was the era of the *controlled court* in Pakistan, and the judiciary remained largely silent on the actions of the military regime.[26] The judiciary would seek out the advice of the government's lawyers on the powers of the judiciary, and whether there were any challenges to the actions of the martial law authorities that it could even accept for hearing.[27] In one particularly egregious case, a suspect was sentenced by a military court in absentia for a crime committed by someone else, in a case in which no evidence had been presented, and in which the convicted suspect had also been a victim .[28] A veteran lawyer highlighted the powerlessness of the judiciary during this period, stating:

> [I]f someone had been arrested or detained, as a young activist lawyer I would to go the judges seeking relief from the courts. Informally, they

---

[24] Interview No. L-10.

[25] There were some important exceptions such as *Fauji Foundation* v. *Shamim ur Rehman*, PLD 1983 SC 457. In this decision, the Court had to decide whether a legislative instrument issued during a martial law era that was designed to provide special privileges to an army-run sugar mill to prevent its dissolution was constitutional. In this landmark decision the Supreme Court outlined a very limited conception of judicial power, holding that it did not have the power to determine if a legislative instrument was passed in a *mala fide* way or not, and therefore could not overrule or reconsider a legislative instrument even if it was not passed through any parliamentary procedure. Thus, the Court during this period outlined a restrictive role for the judiciary.

[26] As outlined in Chapter 1, in the controlled court, the military shapes the judiciary's attitudes and actions by maintaining tight control over the careers of judges, that is, through close utilitarian interlinkages.

[27] 'Courts Powerless to Review ML Orders', *Star*, 11 May 1983.

[28] 'Transfer of Case to Military Court Criticized', *Dawn*, 20 March 1985.

would request the Advocate General or Assistant Advocate General for relief for the detainee, but they would refuse to hear these cases.[29]

Thus, Zia responded to the gradual divergence between the military and the judiciary by weakening the judiciary's authority and extending his control over the appointments and careers of judges. This controlled court was characterized by acquiescence to military authority. Judges cautiously avoided checking or challenging military supremacy, whether they supported the military or not.

Perhaps the only courts that saw limited but significant activity were the newly established Shariat (Islamic) courts, which were willing to review legislative statutes to determine if they comported with injunctions of Islam, and asserted that the independence of the judiciary was a fundamental Islamic principle (Cheema 2021). The Shariat courts did not take up petitions that would significantly challenge the military regime, and found ways to exercise their review powers within the contours of Zia's programme to bring the state's legal framework and institutions into conformity with orthodox Islamic injunctions. However, their willingness to review statutes *suo moto* (on their own accord), without waiting for a formal petition to be presented before the courts (Cheema 2021), highlighted the nascent willingness of judges to uphold principles and interests over a commitment to formal procedures.

Zia finally restored the Constitution at the end of 1985, ending Pakistan's longest spell of unchecked military rule. With the resumption of constitutional rule, the judiciary sought to regain its jurisdiction and relevance after years of silence. Shariat courts reasserted administrative law powers, particularly on questions of bureaucratic appointments, transfers and dismissals (Cheema 2021). Military courts were wound up, cases pending before military courts were transferred to civilian courts and the courts resumed their writ jurisdiction.[30] In this period of three years, the courts were flooded with petitions challenging actions that had been taken by the military courts and MLAs between 1977 and 1985, and habeas petitions against political detentions after the restoration of the constitution. The key challenge before the judiciary was whether the decisions made by the military courts and actions taken by MLAs could be challenged. The newly inserted Article 270-A created an effective ban on the re-evaluation of past actions by the military.

---

[29] L-11, 26 November 2016.
[30] 'MLC Convicts to Be Re-tried in Civil Court', *Star*, 28 November 1985.

TABLE 3.3   Reported judgments pertaining to MLAs and military courts (1986–1988)

	1986 (n=6)	1987 (n=5)	1988 (n=5)
Proportion of judgments against the military (%)	33	60	100

Senior lawyers and bar leaders called upon the judiciary to show more activism after years of silence and reopen decisions by military courts.[31] At this time, most of the judges had taken the oath under the PCO in 1981, acquiescing to Zia's direct control over their careers. Chief Justice Haleem had only recently been confirmed as chief justice, and many High Court and Supreme Court judges remained unconfirmed as additional and ad hoc judges (Iqbal 2006).

Table 3.3 shows that, initially, the judiciary avoided taking on the actions, privileges and immunities of the military leadership, martial law authorities and military courts. However, by 1987, the force of the numbers of petitions 'took its toll on the courts' (Newberg 1995: 193). By 1988, the high courts issued several important judgments chipping away at Article 270-A and paving the way for past actions and rulings of the martial law authorities to be challenged.

I discuss a few judgments pertaining to Article 270-A that provide a more complete picture of the judiciary's approach towards the military during this transitional period. The gradual increase in judicial contestation over these the years is illustrated by the shift in the judiciary's approach across these three decisions. In 1986, the Sindh High Court had to rule on the validity of an MLO that ousted the jurisdiction of the civilian Services Tribunal in cases where Airport Security Forces had forced employees into retirement.[32] The court dismissed the petition and held that Article 270-A provided a blanket immunity ousting its jurisdiction for reviewing any MLOs.

In 1987, in *Muhammad Bachal Memon v. Government of Sindh* (1987), the Sindh High Court again revisited the scope of Article 270-A, to decide whether the court's jurisdiction under Article 199 was superseded

---

[31] 'Call to Reopen Decisions by Military Courts', *Frontier Post*, 29 March 1985; Makhdoom Ali Khan, 'Review Procedure: A Long Way Short of Justice', *Dawn*, 15 May 1988.
[32] *Nazar Muhammad Khan v. Pakistan*, PLD 1986 Lahore 428.

by the immunity provided under Article 270-A.[33] The court held that Article 270-A provided MLOs with immunity, but the judiciary retained its jurisdiction in certain cases, if it was shown that the judgments of military courts were completely out of jurisdiction or clearly *mala fide*. This set a very high bar for successfully challenging the orders and actions of martial law authorities but created the possibility for the courts to hear some petitions challenging these orders and actions. The court said: 'In view of the score of challenges made by aggrieved persons on innumerable grounds against convictions by Martial Law Courts, it may have been more conducive to public confidence ... if some sort of opportunity of hearing had been provided to the aggrieved parties to vent their grievances.' Thus, the Sindh High Court made the first dent in Article 270-A by asserting its jurisdiction over a small set of cases, justified by the volume of people affected by the actions of martial law authorities.

Soon after, the Lahore High Court accepted seven petitions challenging the judgments and sentences of special military courts and made a more far-reaching judgment in *Ghulam Mustafa Khar v. Pakistan* (1987).[34] The prosecution in this case made the argument that the judiciary had given Zia's regime a mandate to take what actions were necessary to achieve the short-term aims set out in the *Nusrat Bhutto* case, but the PCO of 1981 and subsequent actions violated the requirements of necessity, and thus their immunity could not be upheld.[35] The court was not willing to go as far as upholding challenges to all actions taken by the regime since 1981, but the court did expand the scope of the judiciary's power to entertain challenges to past decisions of military courts. The court held that it had jurisdiction to hear cases that betrayed malice by the military courts, were outside the jurisdiction of the military courts or were *coram non judice* (held in the wrong venue for such a case). The decision allowed the high courts to hear many petitions since many convicts had not been given fair trials by the military courts, and *Khar* was hailed as a major legal breakthrough.[36]

---

[33] *Muhammad Bachal Memon* v. *Government of Sindh*, PLD 1987 Karachi 296.

[34] *Ghulam Mustafa Khar* v. *Pakistan*, PLD 1988 Lahore 49.

[35] Badarul Islam Butt, 'LHC Puts of Hearing of Petition: Ia Has Violated Mandate of Supreme Court', *Muslim*, 8 February 1987.

[36] 'A Historic Decision', *Nation*, 20 November 1987; 'A Historic Judgment', *Daily News*, 19 November 1987; 'H.C. Competent to Review Decisions of M.L. Authorities', *Frontier Post*, 19 November 1987.

Thus, the courts chipped away further at Article 270-A to expand their own jurisdiction, while still maintaining the broader immunity provided by the article. The Supreme Court upheld the Lahore High Court's decision in an appeal in 1988 stating that interpreting Article 270-A to take away the High Court's jurisdiction to review acts that suffered from defects of jurisdiction, or were *coram non judice* or were *malafide*, would be an interpretation that would allow 'absurd results to follow'.[37] By this time, Zia was already dead, and the country was preparing for elections. This did not mean the judiciary upheld many challenges against the actions of martial law courts, but the courts expanded the jurisdiction of the high courts to hear such challenges.

Perhaps the most significant case challenging Article 270-A was *Benazir Bhutto* v. *Federation of Pakistan* (1988). During the martial law era, Zia had banned political parties from organizing and only permitted elections on a non-party basis. Once Zia dissolved Junejo's government and called for new elections, Benazir Bhutto, the leader of the PPP, petitioned the Supreme Court to revoke the MLO banning political parties from running for elections. The regime claimed that Article 270-A protected this MLO. The Supreme Court overturned Zia's restriction on political parties contesting elections, cleared the path for party-based elections and narrowed the scope of MLOs protected by Article 270-A.[38] In supporting political parties against the regime, the judiciary attempted to create a 'symbolic break with the past' of complicity with the military (Khan 2015).

Beyond this, the Court reasserted its fundamental rights jurisdiction after years of silence, expanded its original jurisdiction to loosen the requirement of an aggrieved party in a case of public interest and moved beyond the focus on procedural rights, in the interest of substantive 'socio-economic justice'.[39] Adopting the concept of public interest litigation as developed in Indian jurisprudence, the Court expounded a new theory of legal interpretation, stating that the 'law has to serve as a vehicle of social and economic justice which this court is free to interpret', and 'it is needless to insist on a rigid formula of proceedings for the enforcement of fundamental rights'. Thus, the Court outlined a broad social vision of an 'egalitarian society', and

---

[37] *Ghulam Mustafa Khar* v. *Pakistan*, PLD 1989 SC 26.
[38] *Benazir Bhutto* v. *Federation of Pakistan*, PLD 1988 Supreme Court 416.
[39] Jurisconsult, 'SC Judgement – I – Law, a Vehicle of Social, Economic Justice', *Daily News*, 30 June 1988.

described the role of the Court as interpreting the law, Constitution and legal procedures in service of realizing this vision. In a sweeping judgment, the Court had asserted its original jurisdiction over fundamental rights, overturned a significant MLO and articulated a broader role as a protector of political and socio-economic rights.[40] Thus, during this brief period, the judiciary sought to reassert its role, quickly but carefully opening up spaces to challenge the actions of the military regime through the judiciary.

The trends in jurisprudence during Zia's regime made the gradual divergence and changing priorities of the judiciary apparent. The judges appointed during the heyday of judicial–military collaboration dominated the courts at the beginning of this period but became a minority over time. Gradually, the judiciary sought to carve out a more independent role, and judges sought legitimacy with the network of professional lawyers that increasingly opposed unfettered military rule. The evolving preferences of the judiciary became more apparent once Zia died and democracy was restored in 1988.

1988–1999: UNSTABLE MULTI-PARTY DEMOCRACY

After General Zia died in a plane crash in 1988, democratic rule returned to Pakistan. The period from 1988 to 1999 was the longest stretch of democratic rule in Pakistan's history. But the civilian political parties did not win democracy from the army or force the army to retreat to the barracks. Instead, the military permitted the resumption of democratic rule, and never entirely returned to the barracks. The army exerted an effective veto on all matters of foreign and defence policy.[41] The ISI maintained a political cell that continued to interfere in the political affairs of the state, manipulating political coalitions and institutional arrangements to its advantage (Talbot 1998). Zia's constitutional arrangement was also maintained, ensuring that the unelected branches, particularly the presidency, continued to exercise power over the elected branches. The president was Ghulam Ishaq Khan, a member of Zia's cabinet and a close bureaucratic ally of the military.

---

[40] According to one interviewee, '[t]he Chief Justice got a call from Zia who was very unhappy with the judgment', Interview No. L-10.

[41] Benazir retained Zia's foreign minister as her own, indicating the military's continued dominance of foreign policy (Talbot 1998).

Thus, the military, even while out of power, maintained considerable control and influence over the new political dispensation.

When Benazir Bhutto's PPP took power in 1988, and she became prime minister, she faced a powerful army allied with a bureaucracy, and the opposition of several political parties that depended upon military support and patronage.[42] The country was essentially ruled by a 'troika' of the president, prime minister and the chief of army staff. Bhutto sought to bring the military's intelligence agencies under some sort of civilian control, replacing its leadership and trying to carry out an internal investigation, which created resentment in the ISI (Rizvi 2000). She clashed with the president over who had power to appoint officers to senior positions in the armed forces. The army jealously guarded its professional domain and was not willing to tolerate any civilian interference. By 1990, Bhutto had alienated the military, and the Corps Commanders of the military conveyed their dissatisfaction with Bhutto to President Ishaq (Talbot 1998). Within a month the president used his powers under Article 58(2)(b) to dismiss Bhutto's government and dissolve the National Assembly, on charges of corruption, political horse-trading and failure to enforce law and order and discharge legislative functions.

The presidential dissolution of elected governments became a recurring occurrence during the 1990s. Once elected governments sought to exercise power independently and also play a role in shaping foreign and defence policy, they fell out of favour with the military and the presidency and faced presidential dissolution. Whether it was Bhutto's PPP or the right-wing Pakistan Muslim League led by Nawaz Sharif (PML-N), they both met the same fate. Finally, by 1999, with the growing economic crisis, international isolation and military opposition to government policies and interference within the military, the military under General Musharraf carried out a coup, bringing an end to eleven years of democratic rule.

During this tumultuous period there were four themes that ran through the politics of the time, which ensured the military's continued supremacy. First, political parties adopted an approach of perpetual confrontation, always seeking to undermine and delegitimize each other, and turning to the military and judiciary to assist or validate

---

[42] She was the daughter of the former Prime Minister Zulfiqar Bhutto, who had been executed by Zia.

efforts to bring down the opposing parties. This turned the judiciary and military into unelected arbiters of partisan political conflicts.

Second, there was a growing problem of political and administrative corruption in government institutions, exacerbated by the weakness of the leading political parties and their continuing conflicts that helped entrench negative impressions of the political class, and also led to growing reliance on the military for routine administrative tasks. Particularly after 1997, the army was deployed to carry out the census, root out ghost schools, deliver educational services, build roads and take over key policing roles (Talbot 1998) Thus, just as the public grew increasingly disillusioned with elected civilian governments, given the persistent maladministration, corruption and regular dissolutions and elections, the military's presence and visibility in administrative affairs increased.

Third, as the governments pushed an agenda of economic liberalization to revive a flagging economy and dysfunctional public sector, the governments encouraged the military's assumption of the work of the public sector and the expansion of its commercial interests. The government provided special benefits, exemptions and privileges for the military's expanding commercial and landed ventures (Siddiqa 2007). By 1999, Nawaz Sharif recognized just how vast the military's economic empire had grown and sought to bring an end to the tax breaks provided to its welfare organizations, a move that furthered the military's antagonism towards Sharif's government (Siddiqa 2007).

Fourth, the civilian governments had to confront a steadily worsening law and order situation, with increasing sectarian and ethnic violence around the country, particularly in the commercial capital, Karachi. By the mid-1990s, Karachi entered a state of virtual civil war, which led to mounting criticism of the government's handling of the law and order situation. The government came to increasingly rely on the military to handle internal policing responsibilities as well. In 1997, the Anti-terrorism Act was introduced to provide a basic legal framework for counterterrorism, which established a new system of anti-terrorism courts and gave law enforcement agencies, including military and paramilitary forces, special discretionary powers at the expense of certain fundamental rights. In 1998, Nawaz Sharif went even further, declaring a state of emergency and ordering the military to establish military courts to tackle the problem of terrorism in an expedited manner.

Hence, with the military arbitrating political affairs, managing administrative tasks and internal policing, and expanding into the primary economic actor in the state, there was little doubt that the military remained the most powerful institution in the state, and this ultimately set the stage for the military's return to direct power in 1999.

Judicial–Military Relations during the Democratic 1990s

With the resumption of constitutional democracy, the polity was characterized by a deep dissonance both between the elected and unelected branches of government, and between the leading political parties, a dissonance that was exacerbated by the amended constitution, not overcome by it. This placed the judiciary in a position of unprecedented relevance to navigate the dissonance, interpreting the new constitutional framework to resolve the regular conflicts that plagued the state during this period. As Chapter 4 details, during this democratic period, the role of the military and other executive institutions, as audiences for the judiciary, continued to decrease. The judiciary remained cautious in challenging the military, particularly initially, but over time, judges increasingly affirmed their independence from executive institutions, and asserted their jurisdiction over a wider range of military prerogatives.

In the aftermath of Zia's dictatorship, the judiciary had to deal with the legacy of the regime, particularly the actions of the late dictator, and the large number of petitions that came before the courts challenging the actions of military courts.

After Zia's death, before Bhutto won the 1988 elections, the judiciary was first called upon to determine the constitutionality of Zia's exercise of power under Article 58(2)(b) to dissolve the assemblies. In *Haji Saifullah* (1988), the Court found President Zia's dissolution order to be illegal.[43] The majority opinion stated that the power of dissolution can only be used by the president in a narrowly circumscribed set of objectively extraordinary situations. However, surprisingly, the Court did not grant the relief of the restoration of the Assemblies, saying that 'interrupting the election process was politically infeasible' (Newberg 1995: 221). Given the strong stance the Court took against Zia's dissolution of the assemblies, the Court's decision not to resurrect the assemblies was unexpected. One lawyer familiar with the proceedings stated that '12 judges were to announce the judgment and PM Junejo was invited by the Court by the CJ [chief justice]

---

[43] *Government of Pakistan* v. *Muhammad Saifullah Khan (Haji Saifulllah)*, PLD 1988 Supreme Court 43.

himself to be in the courtroom for the final announcement. We all took this as an indication that Junejo would be reinstated.'[44]

Some years later, the former chief of army staff, Aslam Beg, publicly claimed at the Lahore Press Club that he had pressured the Court not to reinstate the assemblies.[45] Beg said that he had sent a message to the chief justice that if the Court wanted democracy to return, then the Court should not restore the assemblies. Beg's admission highlighted that even after Zia's death the military continued to be able to wield pressure and influence over the Court. The Court's response to Beg's statement also emphasized how concerned the judiciary was about appearing susceptible to military pressure. The Court issued a contempt of court notice to Beg and summoned the former chief of army staff to appear before the Court. During the Supreme Court proceedings judges criticized him for his statements and defended the judiciary.[46] However, after defending the Court's image against Beg's statements, the Court chose not to punish him.[47] The saga of the *Haji Saifullah* case demonstrated both the continued leverage of the military over the judiciary, but also the judiciary's deep concern with its own reputation as an independent institution.

The judiciary accepted several petitions challenging military court decisions during the martial law era. There were eighteen reported judgments during this period dealing with military court judgments from Zia's martial law era, out of which the high courts overturned the judgments in ten cases. Initially, the courts were more cautious in overturning such judgments. In *Nazir Ahmed Saleemi* v. *Province of Punjab* (1991) the Lahore High Court deemed military courts sentences to be constitutionally protected, and in *Khadim Hussain* v. *Government of Pakistan* (1992), the Lahore High Court avoided reconsidering the military court decision, due to the misplacement of part of the record of the case.[48] But as the era of martial rule grew more distant the courts were more willing to open these past cases to greater scrutiny. In *Sabur ur Rehman* v. *Government of Sindh* (1996), a plurality of Supreme Court judges ruled that civilian courts could assess the factual proceedings of a

---

[44] Interview No. L-1, 15 May 2017.

[45] 'Supreme Court Summons Gen Beg', *Dawn*, 14 February 1993.

[46] 'CJ Feels Everything Was Done According to a Horrible Plan', *The News*, 21 February 1993.

[47] *Contempt of Court Proceedings against General Mirza Aslam Baig*, PLD 1993 SC 310 (e).

[48] *Nazir Ahmed Saleemi* v. *Province of Punjab*, 1992 ALD 141; *Khadim Hussain* v. *Government of Pakistan*, 1992 PCrLJ 1623.

TABLE 3.4   Reported judgments pertaining to the military's economic prerogatives (1990–1999)

	1990–1994 (n=54)	1995–1999 (n=73)
Proportion of judgments against the military (%)	37	38

past military court case, if the concern was that the military court had made the decision in the absence of evidence.[49] Justice Mian held that the Court could not go into the question of the sufficiency of evidence, whereas Justice Siddiqui held that the Court could assess evidence, to the extent of determining whether there was no legal evidence in support of the decision of the military court. Ultimately, the third judge on the bench sided with Justice Siddiqui's position regarding jurisdiction to assess evidence, but held that there was adequate evidence to prevent any interference in this particular decision. Thus, as Zia's era faded into history, judges grew emboldened to scrutinize the decisions made by his military courts.

As the military's economic interests expanded, decisions pertaining to the military's economic prerogatives generated the largest proportion of military-related jurisprudence. As Table 3.4 illustrates, the judiciary remained largely deferential to the military on questions of economic prerogatives through most of this period, with little change across the decade

The judiciary in general upheld the special exemptions and privileges granted to the military's land and commercial ventures. For instance, in 1993 and again in 1998, the judiciary upheld the special status of military-owned companies and military-affiliated institutions, deciding that their special status of being connected to the armed forces exempted these companies from respecting workers' rights. In Wah Cantonment, a military-owned housing scheme that formerly only housed members of the military but now included substantial civilian populations and private businesses, a union of sanitation workers of the Cantonment Board applied to be registered as a trade union, but were refused by the Registrar of Trade Unions.[50] While the right to form a union is a fundamental right under the Constitution, the exercise of

---

[49] *Sabur ur Rehman* v. *Government of Sindh*, PLD 1996 SC 801.
[50] *Aman* v. *Federation of Pakistan*, 1993 SCMR 1837.

this right can be restricted on reasonable grounds, when it pertains to the members of the armed forces for the 'maintenance of public order'. The Supreme Court chose to read this exception broadly, arguing that since the Cantonment is 'connected with the Armed Forces' and their upkeep is a 'service which is directly concerned with the Armed Forces', therefore this 'public order' exception applied to Cantonment employees. The Court argued that, if Cantonment workers unionized, they would be able to call for strikes and disrupt services required by the Armed Forces of Pakistan and thus compromise public order. Therefore, it was reasonable for the Cantonment authorities to reject the unionization of these sanitation workers.

This was further reaffirmed in 1998, when workers at the Army Welfare Trust Cement Plant in Nizampur sought to form a trade union. The management of the plant held that, since the company was directly connected with and incidental to the Pakistan army, it could deny the workers the right to unionize. The appellate court held in favour of the management, stating that the Industrial Relations Ordinance, which entitled employees to form unions, did not apply to employees of the defence services, and since the Army Welfare Trust was established to serve the interests of members of the defence services, the Industrial Relations Ordinance did not apply to its holdings either. Thus, the judiciary held that the hundreds of thousands of people employed in factories and mills around the country that were connected to the military were not permitted to enjoy the same workers' rights that were enjoyed by employees in the rest of the economy.

This is not to say that the judiciary always decided in favour of the military on economic matters during this period. However, a majority of the decisions where the courts decided against the military were procedural matters, such as where the courts intervened in the administration of the property of landholders and tenants in military cantonments, to ensure the administrators fulfilled notification and hearing requirements.[51] But for the most part the military's economic prerogatives were upheld by the judiciary.

However, over time the judiciary grew more willing to take assertive decisions contesting the military in salient cases. As we see from Table 3.5, the Supreme Court challenged the military more often after 1995 than before.

---

[51] See *National Bank* v. *Islamic Republic of Pakistan*, 1992 SCMR 1705. 'Allotment of Plot: Meraj Khalid's Petition Accepted', *Dawn*, 19 April 1988.

TABLE 3.5   Supreme Court's reported judgments pertaining to
military prerogatives (1990–1999)

	Supreme Court	
	1990–1994 (n=18)	1995–1999 (n=20)
Proportion of judgments against the military (%)	39	60

This increase in judicial contestation was especially apparent in the
judiciary's increased efforts to protect judicial power. The courts expanded
their jurisdiction during this period and resisted any efforts to fragment
their authority. With the growing law and order crisis, the executive
established new court systems to provide speedy convictions in cases of
violence, kidnapping and terrorism, but the judiciary pushed back.

In *Mehram Ali* (1998), the Supreme Court weighed in on the validity
of the new Anti-terrorism Act promulgated in 1997.[52] The Act gave
civil and military forces discretion in carrying out security operations,
including relaxing rules about use of force during operations. The Act
also established a parallel judicial system of anti-terrorism courts that
operated outside the judiciary, where rules of procedure including rules
of evidence were relaxed in order to provide speedy convictions in
terrorism cases. The Court upheld the Act but made a series of amendments. In particular, the Court imposed restrictions on the armed
forces' discretion in detentions and the use of force, placed the anti-
terrorism courts under the purview of the high courts, vested appellate
power in the high courts and staffed the new courts with judges from
the lower courts rather than executive officers.

Subsequently, in *Liaquat Hussain* (1999), the Court went further to
affirm its judicial power resisting any fragmentation of its authority from
allied civil and military institutions.[53] After Prime Minister Sharif
declared a state of emergency in 1998, the government put out an
ordinance amending the Pakistan Army Act to expand the purview of
military field martial courts to try civilians charged with several offences
including kidnapping and terrorism, and also give the military the

---

[52] *Mehram Ali v. Federation of Pakistan*, PLD 1998 SC 1445.
[53] *Liaquat Hussain and others v. Federation of Pakistan through Ministry of Law Justice and Parliament*, PLD 1999 SC 504.

power to assist anti-terrorism courts in the processing of cases. These statutory amendments would ensure that the entire anti-terrorism infrastructure, from the security operations to the detention and conviction of suspects, would be managed and supervised by the military. The Court ruled decisively against this measure, deeming it unconstitutional, and held that the creation of any parallel judicial system that fragmented the authority of the judiciary would be deemed unconstitutional. The Court also held that an unconstitutional act could not be deemed legal because it was deemed 'necessary' to restore law and order, thus also rejecting the legality of the 'doctrine of necessity' that had been used to uphold previous military coups.

The *Mehram Ali* and *Liaquat Hussain* judgments articulated the judiciary's position that judicial power is vested exclusively in the judiciary, and the executive branch can neither share this power with the judiciary nor influence how the judiciary exercises this power. In *Mehram Ali*, the Court describes judicial power as the power to 'interpret, construe and apply the law' and the role of the judiciary as ensuring that 'none of the organs of the state or the government functionaries act in violation of any provision of the constitution, or of any other law'. The Court read the Constitution as stating that 'supervision of the judiciary vests in the high courts which is exclusive in nature, comprehensive in extent and effective in operation'. Thus, it was only willing to allow the creation of anti-terrorism courts if they fell under the supervision of the high courts, and refused to allow the creation of military courts, since they would fall outside the supervision of the high courts. The Court also stated that the 'right to have access to justice through independent courts is a fundamental right', emphasizing both the exclusive power of the high courts over judicial institutions, and the separation of the judiciary from the executive. *Liaquat Hussain* and *Mehram Ali* affirmed the judiciary's separation from executive institutions, including the military, emphasizing that executive and judicial institutions could not share judicial powers, nor could civilian and military executive institutions maintain interlinkages with the judiciary.

Through its jurisprudence, the judiciary separated itself from executive institutions, including the military, and expanded its jurisdiction over certain prerogatives of the military, even as it remained cautious about making decisions against the actions and interests of the military. On the one hand, the courts made very few decisions holding military officers accountable for their actions. Major Amir of the ISI, who was accused of using his office and government money to help over throw Benazir Bhutto's first government, was exonerated by the courts, even though he went on to state that 'if he had to overthrow a PPP government he would do it again'; Brigadier Imtiaz, who had also participated in attempting to sabotage the PPP's first government, was also exonerated .[54] In 1994, the judiciary accepted a petition alleging that the ISI's political cell had financed an alliance of right-wing parties opposed to the PPP called the Islamic Jamhoori Itthead to help the alliance win the election against the PPP in 1990. General Aslam Beg himself acknowledged that the ISI had interfered in the election.[55] After conducting a series of hearings between 1994 and 1996, the Supreme Court effectively dropped the case without any decision

On the other hand, the courts admitted an increasing number of petitions for the redressal of grievances from those affected by security operations. The Sindh High Court relaxed its procedure for accepting petitions in the mid-1990s, accepting applications against detentions, enforced disappearances and torture by security forces that were not formal petitions but were moved through telegrams and hand-written letters addressed to the chief justice, who then converted these into constitutional petitions.[56] The court also called in government officials to explain why people had been detained by the military during operations.[57] Even though the judiciary rarely took formal actions overturning the actions of the military or holding military and para-military soldiers accountable, the courts opened themselves up as forums for people to bring grievances against the military and ask difficult questions of security officials.

Thus, when it came to protecting and expanding the power and jurisdiction of the courts the judiciary grew more assertive, especially in the second half of the 1990s, even if that entailed asserting itself against the military. The jurisprudence of the period indicated how the judiciary continued to gradually diverge from the military and assert its independent role. The judiciary expanded its jurisdiction, and relaxed its procedural rules, to hear cases pertaining to the military courts of the

---

[54] A. Rehman, 'Revival of Judicial Activism', News, 24 July 1997.
[55] Interview No. L-62, 26 May 2017; 'Beg Acknowledges Presence of Angels in 1990 Elections', The News, 10 February 1993.
[56] Nusrat Amin, 'Approach the High Court', The News, 1 January 1993.
[57] 'SHC Asks for Report on Solitary Confinement of Political Leaders', The News, 4 March 1993.

Zia era, and petitions from victims of security operations, and also protected itself from any fragmentation of its authority in favour of the military and law enforcement agencies. Courts were cautious about using their powers to make decisions that *overruled* actions of the military, but they worked to expand their jurisdiction over the actions of other institutions, including the military.

CONCLUSION

This chapter provided a history of the different phases the judiciary moved through from the imposition of martial law in 1977 to the imposition of martial law in 1999. The judiciary began by collaborating with the military regime and then sought to expand its own role within the structure of the military regime, finding itself at odds with the military. After a period of imposed deference, control and fragmentation by the military, the judiciary sought to claim its legitimacy and independence, expand its role and preserve its judicial functions. As I detail in Chapter 4, the judiciary's legal and policy preferences gradually diverged from the military, as the institutional interlinkages between the military and judiciary diminished.

CHAPTER FOUR

BETWEEN THE BARRACKS AND THE BAR (1977–1999, PART 2)

A Judiciary in Transition

In this chapter, I seek to explain the trajectory outlined in Chapter 3. I first show that regime-related factors, namely the prevailing political configuration and the authority and influence of the military, did play a role in shaping the judiciary's military-related jurisprudence, but they cannot alone explain the incremental shift in the approach of the judiciary over the course of this period, and the transformation of the role the judiciary sought to play in the political system. I then argue that the incremental shift in the judiciary towards increased independence from the military and expansion and promotion of its own jurisdiction was linked to a change in the audiences that shaped legal and policy preferences within the judiciary during this period. The military's institutional interlinkages with the judiciary diminished, and the judiciary's interlinkages with the politically active bar of professional lawyers grew, which reshaped the norms and preferences of the judiciary. It is important to point out that this shift took place gradually, and thus there was an institutional lag before the effects of this shift were fully realized, which will become apparent in Chapter 5. However, without understanding these shifts it would be difficult to explain the changing approach of the judiciary towards the military over the course of this twenty-year period. I use a combination of sociological data on judges, archival information on judicial appointments and bar association politics, and interviews with judges and lawyers to trace this gradual but impactful shift.

VARIATION IN REGIME STRUCTURE

Regime-related factors refer to the nature of the state's political power structure and the space available to the judiciary to assert itself within this power structure. Courts act more assertively against other state institutions when the political system is more fragmented, raising the cost of repealing judicial decisions or reducing judicial authority for the other political actors (Chavez 2004; Ferejohn et al. 2007; Rios-Figueroa 2007). Conversely, when political power is more concentrated and political authority is unconstrained, such as during a military regime, the courts accordingly act deferentially. Judges will act assertively based on their understanding of the political environment and how other political actors can and will exercise their authority. Therefore, if judges believe that a regime's authority is declining and the regime is likely to be replaced, then their strategy might be to act assertively against the outgoing regime to gain the favour of the incoming regime (Helmke 2005). Similarly, when the judiciary is initially granted authority, judges will tend to act with restraint, in the expectation that the newly gained powers might also be lost to more entrenched political actors, and judgments will only grow more assertive over time (Ginsburg 2003). These regime-related factors all played a role in shaping the patterns of assertiveness during this period.

The initial rupture between the judiciary and the military could be explained by the centralized nature of General Zia's military regime. When Zia came to power, judges expected the new regime to operate with the same power structure used by previous dictators. Under Ayub Khan, the military leadership stood at the apex of the political system, but the military did not try to rule alone, as the bureaucracy and the judiciary were integrated into the same power structure. Thus, judges simply assumed they would play the same role they had played in the previous military regime, upholding the broad structure of the praetorian state, but carving out a space within this system as a venue to protect procedural rights, monitor the lower echelons of the administrative bureaucracies and check the dangers of arbitrary rule. Chief Justice Anwar-ul-Haq and Maulvi Mushtaq, for example, two judges who had played a key role in collaborating to uphold Zia's political agenda in the early years, expected that Zia would share power with them, in exchange for their collaboration. As one lawyer explained, 'Anwar ul-Haq was ambitious and was even interested in being Zia's president'.[1] However, Zia was more interested in centralizing control within the military and did not seek alliances with civilian institutions; rather, he sought to capture or control civilian institutions, and eliminate any political threats. This power structure could not accommodate civilian institutions like a judiciary with an independent jurisdiction, and therefore even collaborative judges like Anwar-ul-Haq and Maulvi Mushtaq were removed, and the consensus between the two institutions unravelled.

The changing nature of the regime was also a factor in explaining the silence of the judiciary between 1981 and 1985 during Zia's most repressive era, and its expanding role after 1985 with the resumption of constitutional rule. Between 1985 and 1988, the political opening created by the restoration of the Constitution and a new civilian government provided an opportunity for the judiciary to expand its jurisdiction, opening up the past orders and actions of the military regime to legal challenges. The historic *Benazir Bhutto* decision, issued in the last year of Zia's regime, which upheld the right of political parties to participate in elections, overturning the orders passed by Zia's regime, indicated that the judiciary was flexing its muscles in response to a changing political environment. A lawyer involved with the *Benazir Bhutto* decision explained that 'in 1988 Benazir Bhutto had been back for two years, Junejo (Zia's prime minister) had allowed her back and allowed her to set up her party. For the first time you could think of a future without Zia. That must have emboldened the judges.'[2]

Finally, the cautious pace of the judiciary's increasing assertiveness after the resumption of democracy in the 1990s can be explained by the duration of the democratic regime. In a newly restored constitutional democracy, a judiciary seeking to gradually entrench its power and avoid retaliation from other political actors would act deferentially towards the most powerful incumbent political actors, which, in this case was the military (Ginsburg 2003). Accordingly, the judiciary would only act more assertively over time as the constitutional framework grew more entrenched, creating more space for the judiciary to act more assertively. Therefore, after the resumption of democracy, the initial judicial caution, and gradually increasing judicial contestation

---

[1] Interview No. L-10.
[2] Interview No. L-62.

of the military, can be explained by the judiciary's response to the increasing entrenchment of the constitutional democratic system.

Hence, from the initial divergence between the two institutions, to the complete deference during the PCO era, and then the gradual increase in assertiveness after the resumption of constitutional democratic rule, we see variation in the judiciary's assertiveness towards the military that can be explained by variation in the nature of the regime and the judiciary's expectations about how the military would operate in that political environment.

However, these regime-related factors do not provide a complete explanation for the judiciary's actions during this period, as the jurisprudence of this period shows that the judiciary was not only responding to regime-related factors in deciding whether to act assertively. The content of the decisions shows that over time the judiciary was steadily seeking to play a different and more expansive role in the political system. The judiciary that emerged during Zia's regime appeared to differ from the judiciary of the 1960s, in terms of the role it sought to play. These changing legal preferences became apparent by the late 1980s, particularly in the *Benazir Bhutto* decision. In *Benazir Bhutto*, the Court made a judgment favouring political parties, but also used the judgment to open up the possibility of public interest litigation. In public interest litigation, the courts could relax key procedural rules and restrictions to uphold public interests in cases of fundamental rights.[3] The Court articulated the judiciary's new role of enforcing socio-economic rights and improving access to justice, all of which had little to do with the key question of the ban on political parties in the case. Thus, the judiciary was not simply responding to an opening up of political space to make more assertive decisions; it was also defining a new role for itself in the political system – an evolving role that cannot be explained purely through regime-related factors.

During the democratic era, the judiciary was not simply growing gradually assertive over time with the entrenchment of the democratic system, it was also recalibrating its role in the political system, by expanding its jurisdiction and relaxing procedural rules, and staking its legitimacy on asserting independence from the military and other executive authorities. Therefore, this changing articulation of the role

---

[3] Public interest litigation in Pakistan was adapted from across the border in India, where it served to ease direct access to the courts in India, and increase the profile and power of the judiciary (Khan 2015).

of the judiciary emphasizes that the judiciary was not simply responding to changes in the regime but also to changes within the judiciary itself. Regime-related factors certainly played an important role in explaining variation in the judiciary's assertiveness towards the military, but this explanation is incomplete without also considering changes in the judiciary that could explain its changing role in the political system and assertion of independence from the military.

JUDICIAL QUEST FOR LEGITIMACY

After 1977, there was a growing divergence between the Supreme Court and the high courts on the question of the power of the courts to check the actions of Zia's military regime. The judges of the Supreme Court differed from some of the younger, High Court judges. In 1977, the Supreme Court was mostly composed of more senior judges appointed to the high courts during the 1950s and early 1960s during the heyday of judicial–military collaboration. On the other hand, new judges were joining the High Court after the fall of Ayub Khan, and these judges were more assertive towards the military. Any explanation for the change in judicial behaviour must explain what made the attitudes of these High Court judges different from their senior counterparts.

Judicial decision-making is also shaped by the need to acquire and maintain legitimacy. Legitimacy is conceptualized as diffuse support (Caldeira and Gibson 1995), which means that there is a public commitment to defending the institutional structure and authority of the judiciary, regardless of the outcomes of individual decisions (Staton 2010). Scholars hold that when a judiciary carries legitimacy then other branches of government cannot pressure or induce decisions or avoid compliance with decisions (Milner 1971; Caldeira 1986; Mondak 1993; Caldeira and Gibson 1995; Gibson et al. 1998). Legitimacy is ultimately seen as deriving from perceptions that the judiciary is fair and impartial (Tyler 2009; Staton 2010). Judiciaries that are perceived as susceptible to political influence suffer from a lack of legitimacy (Kapiszewski 2012). Therefore, judges seeking to build legitimacy as a bulwark against attempts to defy or undermine judicial authority would be keen to appear fair and impartial.

Khan (2015) argues that, in expanding its jurisdiction and altering its role in the political system after the restoration of the constitutional democracy in 1988, the judiciary was guided by a need to reclaim legitimacy that had been lost during the years of being subordinated under the Zia regime. One former judge, who had been a lawyer representing the government in the *Mustafa Khar* (1989) decision, described an interaction in the court during the case. He said the judge asked the attorney general 'if tomorrow the government passed a law saying all bald people will be put to death, then you are saying the law is protected, Mr. Attorney General, how can you sleep at night?? To this the attorney general said, "if you people (the judges) have been sleeping for eleven years, how can you sleep now?"'[4] This exchange explains the reputation the judiciary was seeking to move away from: as first a collaborator and then a silent spectator during the repression of the Zia era. Thus, the judiciary's changing approach to the military was also motivated by a need to gain legitimacy.

But legitimacy from whom? Judges would seek legitimacy, first and foremost, from those groups who paid the most attention to judicial decisions: those with whom judges interacted the most and who informed the public about the content of judicial decisions, shaping public understanding and approval of the courts. The groups that paid closest attention to judges and provided them with the most feedback on their actions and their authority are the fellow members of the legal complex, especially the lawyers populating their courts. As I show in the next section, the network of professional lawyers became the primary audience for judicial decision-making, and it is in seeking legitimacy from this audience that the judiciary articulated norms of independence from the military, and socio-political judicial activism.

A CHANGE IN JUDICIAL AUDIENCES

I argue that an audience-based explanation is crucial for explaining the shift of the Pakistani judiciary over this period, from collaborating with the military to carefully establishing its independence from the military. From 1973 to 1999, three processes unfolded concomitantly that incrementally reshaped the legal and policy preferences of the judiciary – the indigenization of Pakistan's judiciary, the politicization of the bar from which judges were recruited and the separation of the judiciary from the executive. These processes altered the judiciary's relationship with the military, reducing institutional interlinkages between the two institutions and the military's ability to shape the institutional

---

[4] Interview No. J-44, 28 November 2017.

preferences of the judiciary. In short, the military's role as a critical audience for the judiciary gradually diminished.

Instead, the judiciary drew closer to the bar of professional lawyers, which developed both utilitarian and normative interlinkages with the judiciary, thus altering the judiciary's legal and policy preferences. These gradual changes had incremental effects on the jurisprudence of the judiciary and its relationship with the military. Prior to this period the judiciary was loyal to the military and integrated into the collaborative power structure of the military, bureaucracy and judiciary. Over the course of this period, the judiciary shifted out of the orbit of the military and drew closer to a politically mobilized bar of professional lawyers that emphasized political activism, an expanded role for the judiciary and opposition to military rule and political party elites. Here I discuss these three processes and explain the impact they had on the institutional interlinkages of the judiciary with other institutions and on the preferences within the judiciary. To conclude, I discuss how the changes in the judiciary help explain the evolution of the judiciary's military-related jurisprudence during this period.

Indigenization of the Judiciary
During the 1950s and early 1960s, the majority of Pakistan's judiciary emerged from the bureaucratic elite and the lawyers who were either trained as barristers in the United Kingdom or worked as lawyers for the British Empire in the Indian subcontinent. However, over time this changed. First, after 1973, no judges came from the bureaucratic elite of the civil service, although this practice had already reduced during the late 1960s. This removed one significant network of elites from the ranks of the judiciary.

Second, as Pakistan's economy evolved so the professional incentives for Pakistan's elite barristers to become judges declined. Under Ayub Khan, Pakistan's private economic sector advanced and commercial law and litigation developed in response (Asian Development Bank 2008). As private commercial law and litigation started blossoming, the compensation available to lawyers working in private litigation firms quickly outpaced the salaries available for judges, and money became a growing incentive for joining the private legal profession. A gap emerged between younger lawyers who joined the profession for monetary reasons, and older judges who were drawn by the privileges and perks of being a judge. A senior judge in the early 1970s, Justice Sajjad Ali Jan, admonished the new generation of lawyers, warning them that 'money should not be the only consideration for advocates as they had to fulfill their . . . duties towards the nation'.[5]

Judges' salaries did not keep up with the monetary advantages of being hired by a leading law firm, affecting the attractiveness of becoming a judge. Chief Justice Ajmal Mian writes in his memoirs that when approached to become a judge of the Sindh High Court in 1977, he found it 'a very difficult decision as at that time all my children were of school-going age . . . and providing education in good institutions for five children was not an easy task' (Mian 2004: 43). He described how his clientele as a lawyer included major banks who paid very well, which he left to become a judge. Thus, professional lawyers were concerned about the monetary sacrifice that they had to make if they chose to become judges.

This disparity in compensation increased during the 1980s since the judiciary lagged behind other state intuitions in terms of institutional reform, and private law continued to become more profitable, particularly as the drive towards privatizing and liberalizing the economy accelerated in the late 1980s and early 1990s (Asian Development Bank 2008).

A young lawyer, after passing the bar exam at the age of twenty-one or twenty-two, worked with a senior partner for several years. A lawyer with about only four or five years' experience and qualifications could be offered remuneration on the basis of sharing legal fees in addition to a salary. After several years he or she could choose to branch out and start their own firm, or become a partner in that firm. It took typically about eight to ten years to reach the level of partner. Major multinational companies also typically hired lawyers with five to ten years' experience.[6] Lawyers with multinational companies and senior partners in leading commercial law firms earned very well. There was no limit on remuneration for senior partners.[7]

On the other hand, a lawyer could only be appointed a High Court judge after the age of forty-five, once he or she had at least ten years' of work experience as a High Court lawyer. By this point in his or her career, a successful elite lawyer was likely to be a senior partner in a law firm, or working with a major multinational organization, making a

---

[5] 'Lawyers Urged to Revive Ideals of Legal Profession', Muslim, 12 March 1976.
[6] 'All You Wanted to Know about Law . . . and Were Too Afraid to Ask', News, 17 March 1995.
[7] Ibid.

significant income. As a judge, he or she would be a government employee and not entitled to a private practice, with all its associated compensation. There were perks associated with becoming a High Court judge, but these did not compare to the wealth and privilege afforded to a successful senior partner at a law firm. Further, the judiciary's financial resources were dependent upon the budget provided by the federal government, which, particularly during Zia's era, were kept limited. Ali writes that 'the Chief Justice could not incur even a small expenditure without the beggings of the Finance and Interior Ministry'.[8] Newspaper reports from the early 1990s described the state of neglect in the high courts, with limited money, resources and staff. Thus, there were opportunity costs associated with choosing a career as a High Court judge.

This difference was exacerbated for lawyers who went to study abroad. An education in the UK was steadily moving out of reach for most potential judicial appointees. There were no more judges from the federal civil service with a government-funded foreign education. By the 1980s, Justice Patel said that 'becoming a barrister had become so expensive because the cost of living in England was now very high ... As a result, few Pakistanis living in Pakistan could afford to become barristers', and those who could would look for careers that compensated them for the investment made in their education.[9] Another leading lawyer of the era, Khalid Ishaque, also said that going abroad would give lawyers 'training specially for the commercial world'.[10] These elite lawyers would then be offered jobs at the most lucrative commercial law firms on their return, either through their personal family networks or by virtue of their increasingly rare and sought-after credentials. Thus, lawyers who gained an expensive foreign education belonged to an elite with easy access to the rewards of commercial law and litigation and were more interested in pursuing careers in commercial law than pursuing judicial careers.

This disparity has been further exacerbated since the 1980s and 1990s. In my interviews, I learned that by the time foreign-educated lawyers, engaged in commercial law and litigation, reach the age of forty-five, if they were approached to become judges, they had to choose between the limited steady income of a judge or the high

---

[8] Sarmad Ali, 'The Judiciary and Social Change', *Muslim*, 21 July 1991.
[9] 'All You Wanted to Know about Law ... and Were Too Afraid to Ask'.
[10] Ibid.

compensation they were already used to in commercial law and litigation. A retired judge explained that:

> The problem is salary in private practice is very good. I had a successful practice as a tax lawyer. When I became a judge I had to take out of my savings. A judge would make maybe Rs. 1–1.2 million per year. However, a lawyer at a good firm can make Rs. 4–5 million per case. And successful lawyers were unwilling to sacrifice this. As a judge I offered the judgeship to several senior partners of leading law firms in Karachi multiple times but they all refused.[11]

Who replaced them in this vacuum? As the number of law schools in Pakistan grew, the bar rooms filled up with more middle-class, locally educated lawyers. Between the 1970s and 1990s, bar associations rapidly grew in size. A former president of the Karachi Bar Association said it 'had 100 members in 1947, and by the 1980s it had 1,700 members and today [2017] it has over 10,000 members'.[12] There was a large influx of lawyers during this period, most of whom could not get jobs in elite commercial law firms. These locally educated lawyers were primarily from middle-class backgrounds for whom the salary and perks of a High Court judgeship still promised considerable social mobility and economic stability. Thus, as the elite lawyers increasingly gravitated towards the promise of commercial wealth, middle-class lawyers were drawn to the mobility provided by the judgeship. This is not to say that elite lawyers with a foreign education never became judges, but a decreasing proportion of such lawyers were drawn to the judgeship, while there was a growing pool of locally educated lawyers available for recruitment (see Figure 4.1). The changing sociology of the bench was encapsulated by one former High Court judge from the 1990s who said:

> I did not like the lifestyle … Those who stay on the bench now are those who have a different lifestyle from me. In the earlier years you had a Westernised elite. It was a colonial leftover. As times changed and the political situation changed, the atmosphere of courts has changed. Thus, a different order of people emerged in the bench. And the majority were not Westernized now.[13]

[11] Interview No. J-65, 14 March 2017.
[12] Interview No. L-42, 1 April 2017.
[13] Interview No. J-60, 18 April 2017.

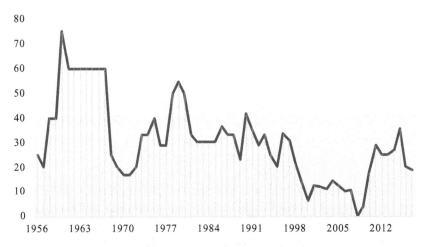

Figure 4.1 Proportion of Supreme Court judges educated abroad (1956–2017)
The study is missing educational information for nine judges who also served during this period.

There were two consequences of this change. First, the close network of Western-educated military, bureaucratic and judicial elites fragmented, as judges now came from a wider pool of middle-class, locally educated lawyers. The legal and judicial elites of the 1950s and 1960s were beneficiaries of the late colonial order, and subsequently of bureaucratic and military rule, and thus were willing supporters of the established autocratic political order of the period. However, this younger pool of lawyers did not have the same elite ties with the military and bureaucratic elite, nor had they enjoyed the same benefits from military rule. Hence, they were not natural collaborators with the military.

The second consequence is more counterintuitive but equally significant. As the number of law schools and law colleges churning out lawyers increased, the standard of the legal education changed. A former Supreme Court judge who taught in law schools for twenty-five years said that 'in the 1960s the education was good enough and if you had that education you could be a competent lawyer, but since the 1960s, the quality of legal education has changed'.[14] Siddique (2014) explained that lawyers and legal practitioners dominate the law schools. The Pakistan Bar Council, the national elected organization of Pakistan's lawyers that regulates the profession, also primarily regulates

[14] Interview No. J-15, 1 April 2017.

legal education. The result of the control of practising lawyers over legal education is that there is no dedicated legal academia, as professional lawyers largely determine academic curricula, set standards and teach. Given that these lawyers are already quite busy, they tend to teach in their spare time, giving limited time and attention to teaching responsibilities. The approach to teaching law is very vocational, teaching law students about the laws pertaining to claims of the litigants, with little to no training in broader themes of formal judicial procedure, constitutional law and legal doctrine that inform the work of a High Court judge. Ghuman (1992) points out that the university education was usually spread over a period of only two years and taught in short classes by legal practitioners, which meant that the actual class time did not exceed three hours a day, spread over a total of ten months.[15] After qualifying, lawyers had to complete a six-month compulsory apprenticeship, but found that they could manoeuvre to have a certificate of training without undergoing it.[16] There were also no credible bar examinations governing entry into the legal profession, leading to an overpopulation of lawyers lacking procedural training (Siddique 2014). This meant that locally educated judges did not have the same extensive training in positive law and doctrines of interpretation that their counterparts attained from the earlier generation of British-trained lawyers.

Judges, less familiar with legal positivism, also feel less bound by formal law and legal procedures. Therefore, there has been an increasing emphasis on outcomes as opposed to procedure in the jurisprudence of the court. Judges care about the development of their reputation in the courtroom, and without the same procedural focus of judges of the previous era, the judges focused on outcomes as a way to develop a reputation and gain the esteem of the lawyers. As one former judge explained, in the absence of adequate training in legal formalism, these judges compensated by attempting to appear 'effective and bold among the lawyers in their courtrooms'.[17] He said:

> Judges who do not consider themselves bound by procedure promise to do substantive justice. The concept comes from the judges' own ... training ... You put on a show. You have to be seen to know. Judges were playing to an audience, creating an impression, building a reputation.[18]

---

[15] Ghuman, 'The Legal Profession in Pakistan'.
[16] Ibid.
[17] Interview No. J-33, 21 March 2017.
[18] Interview No. J-33.

Thus, the indigenization of the judiciary meant that judges, locally educated as lawyers within an educational system run by the local bar, were increasingly concerned about building esteem within the bar through outcomes that were popular with the lawyers populating their courts. This process increased the normative interlinkages between the bar and the bench, as lawyers were able to impose reputational costs and benefits on judges. As a former Supreme Court judge pointed out: 'To get a better education. Some go abroad. these people represent the elite class, they are not the common people. They may be considered to be competent as judges, but they do not have that kind of compassion for the masses.'[19] The locally educated judge was more attuned, if not to the concerns of the masses, then at least to the middle-class networks of lawyers from which he or she came, and with which he or she sought to build a reputation and, thus gain esteem.[20]

Thus, as judges were increasingly recruited from the non-elite segments of the bar, the distance between bar and bench decreased, and the normative interlinkages between the judges and the bar increased. Judges increasingly sought to build esteem with lawyers by loosening procedural restrictions and making decisions they deemed would be well received and popular among the lawyers of the bar.

Politicization of the Bar

As more judges were recruited from networks of locally educated lawyers, and the normative interlinkages between bar and bench increased, the next question is: what legal and political preferences developed within the bar?

Pakistan's legal profession was organized with two leadership structures: bar councils and bar associations. The bar councils are the regulatory bodies of the legal profession, established under the Legal Practitioners and Bar Councils Act, 1973. Each province has a provincial Bar Council elected by advocates across the province, and the Pakistan Bar Council, the primary regulatory body, is elected by

---

[19] Interview No. J-15.

[20] It is also noteworthy that nearly all High Court judges have been men, and there has been, at the time of writing, only one woman Supreme Court judge. This dominance of men across the judiciary, and across the legal community more broadly, has important implications for the esteem-building strategies of judges and the internal culture of the judiciary, which are beyond the scope of this book to adequately discuss.

members of the provincial bar councils. The leading government lawyer of each province, the advocate general, functions as the official chairman of the Bar Council, and the attorney general functions as the official chairman of the Pakistan Bar Council. However, they are merely figureheads, and the real authority lies with the Executive Committee of elected lawyers. Thus, the Bar Council is largely independent, ensuring that the profession is largely self-regulated.

The bar associations are the professional associations of lawyers. In Pakistan, these bar associations are elected bodies that are autonomous and controlled and managed by lawyers. Hundreds of bar associations exist at each administrative level – tehsil, district and provincial – and bar associations representing particular professional interests within the law also developed, such as the tax bar association. These bar associations represent the professional interests of lawyers. The major provincial capitals had especially large bar associations, including the Karachi Bar Association, the Lahore Bar Association and the Lahore High Court Bar Association, which represents the High Court lawyers of Punjab. The Karachi Bar Association and the Lahore High Court Bar Association form the primary focus of this discussion of the bar.

As explained in Chapter 2, in the early years Pakistan's bar associations were small, and the major urban bar associations were still led by elite lawyers with close ties to the government, who aimed to become judges or executive officers. Thus, even though there were certainly politically active lawyers throughout Pakistan's history, the bar associations initially did not take organized political stands or lead the way on political issues.

This began to change, first with the wave of popular mobilization against Ayub Khan, and then with the democratic dispensation after 1972. The political activity of the period also swept up the bar associations. 'With the new political dispensation, the bar got divided along more political lines. Few issues transcended political and partisan divisions. The Bar got involved in politics individually but not institutionally.'[21]

The political opposition to Bhutto made concerted efforts to win over the urban bar associations. By 1977, this yielded dividends, as leading bar associations in urban capitals took organized stands against Bhutto's allegedly rigged re-election in March 1977, and even

---

[21] Interview No. L-9, 4 December 2016.

mobilized in opposition.[22] In Lahore, when Bhutto's government arrested and detained agitating lawyers, the Lahore High Court Bar Association demanded the government and the Election Commission resign and new elections be held .[23] Between March and May 1977, the Lahore High Court Bar Association issued resolutions against the actions of Bhutto's government, and removed members of the bar association who had been elected to political office as members of the PPP (Sidhwa 1989). When Zia finally ousted Bhutto, several major bar associations supported military intervention, especially after Zia initially removed some of the curbs Bhutto placed on the judiciary. The Lahore High Court Bar Association 'expressed full support to the measures taken by the interim (Zia) government'.[24] Thus, during the 1970s, the bar associations grew more engaged with political issues, and were more willing to agitate for political causes.

A critical juncture in the evolution and politicization of the bar associations was in the early years of Zia's military regime. When Zia came to power, he initially banned all political activity. He made repeated pledges that he was merely paving the way for free and fair elections, but he spent his first eight years focusing on minimizing political activity as he depoliticized the state. In March 1978, Zia made a limited concession to political activity, as he lifted the ban on elections to professional bodies, which included bar associations. It is unclear what his motives for lifting the ban were.[25] Perhaps at this time Zia was interested in maintaining a collaborative relationship with civilian allies, and leading bar associations had opposed Bhutto's government, so he probably did not foresee any threat from the bar.

The resumption of political activity in the bar associations had two unexpected effects. First, bar associations became one of the few venues available for political activity, and bar association elections provided an opportunity for political lawyers to take on leadership roles. Bar associations increasingly attracted the interest and attention of political lawyers. In 1979, the Lahore High Court Bar Association resolved to

[22] 'Lawyers Role during Movement Unforgettable, Says Wali', *Muslim*, 9 February 1978.

[23] 'Lawyers Take out Procession in Lahore', *Dawn*, 25 March 1977; 'Lahore Lawyers Abstain from Courts', *Dawn*, 26 March 1977.

[24] 'LHC Bar President Hails Removal of Curb on Judiciary', *Morning News*, 26 September 1977.

[25] 'H.C. Bar Body Elections', *Dawn*, 20 March 1978; 'Lawyers Urged to Educate People Whom to Elect', *Dawn*, 20 January 1978.

restore the membership of lawyers who also had membership in the PPP after their membership was cancelled in 1977. Thus, politically active lawyers, including those belonging to the PPP and opposed to Zia, grew more engaged with the bar associations.

Second, bar association elections received increased attention, being one of the few elected political positions in the country. By the early 1980s, bar association elections in the major urban centres became widely publicized and hotly contested.[26] Newspapers reporting on the elections to the Karachi Bar Association described the electoral activity at the time:

> The Karachi Bar Association is gripped with election fever. The air is thick with passionate claims, pledges and declarations of the grand variety. These elections take place under the scenario of the country's political problems, all this unrest and frustration has surfaced and hit the KBA [Karachi Bar Association] like a whirlwind.[27]

In another report, the same newspaper reported: 'In all fairness one should say that it is commendable living as we are in an age of apathy and indifference that organizations such as the KBA should continue to rekindle the electoral flame'.[28] Thus, the bar association elections drew considerable attention and interest, during a time of otherwise limited open political activity.

By this time bar associations were much larger than they were in the 1950s and 1960s. One former judge pointed out that 'when Pakistan came into being, the legal profession was a gentleman's profession. Now it was not a profession of choice for the majority of lawyers, it was a profession by default.'[29] The elite character of the urban bar associations had clearly faded, and this affected the way bar elections were fought, and the issues upon which they were fought. One veteran bar leader explained that most lawyers in the bar 'were now more concerned with what was happening in their neighbourhoods or with the masses, as they did not have much of a stake in the legal system'.[30] Thus, political issues became more important for organizing campaigns, mobilizing support and winning bar elections than purely professional issues.

---

[26] 'Bar President Hopes for Joint Political Declaration', *Muslim*, 8 July 1983; 'LHCBA Presidential Candidates', *Pakistan Times*, 23 February 1984.
[27] Suhail Nigar, 'All the Karachi Bar-Men', *Star*, 1 April 1982.
[28] Suhail Nigar, 'The Quest for Power', *Star*, 24 May 1984.
[29] Interview No. J-19, 23 April 2017.
[30] Interview No. L-42.

By 1980, there was growing opposition to Zia's rule within the legal fraternity, given the regime's growing reliance on military courts. 'Military courts were seen as a direct threat to the legal profession itself' as it reduced litigation in the civilian courts where they practised.[31] Lawyers in Karachi, Lahore and other urban centres started protesting against Zia's military regime in a series of demonstrations.[32] By 1981, with the PCO consolidating Zia's control over the judiciary, opposition within the bar grew stronger.

However, a veteran bar leader explained that:

> Bar members were not united. In the bar there were activists and there were opportunists and careerists who were more interested in gaining government approval to move forward in their careers. Therefore, to get people united on issues, we had to form a group that kept fighting and winning elections, as the different groups in the bar would follow the bar's leadership.[33]

Groups of lawyers allied against Zia around the country held a National Lawyers' Conference in 1981. One of the organizers of the conference said, 'we spoke against martial law and then we took a procession out against military rule'.[34] The Lawyers' Conference also provided politicians banned by Zia with a platform to speak out against military rule. After the Lawyers' Conference, lawyers opposing the military regime formed political groupings in their respective bar associations and campaigned to win bar elections.

Thanks to the changing size and demographics of the bar, the increased political interest in bar elections and the need for a platform for challenging the regime, bar elections now became centred around support for, and opposition, to the military regime. In the Lahore High Court Bar Association, Karachi Bar Association and other bar associations, groups of politically active lawyers opposed to Zia's regime secured victories.[35] With anti-Zia activists winning bar elections, the bar became a platform for opposing the regime.

Presidents of the bar associations, including Abid Hussain Minto and Hafeez Lakho, held meetings with defunct political parties and student

---

[31] Ibid.
[32] 'Pakistani Lawyers Stage March to Protest Zia Rule', *Dawn*, 22 August 1980; 'Lawyers Ignore Strike Call', *Business Recorder*, 3 March 1980.
[33] Interview No. L-9.
[34] Ibid.
[35] 'Minto LHC Bar Chief', *Dawn*, 26 February 1982.

and trade union leaders, and asked them to back their opposition movement against Zia and 'join its struggle for the restoration of democracy' and the 1973 Constitution.[36] The MRD, an alliance of banned political parties opposing Zia, allied with bar associations, rallied in their support and used the bar as a venue to speak out against the regime.[37] Efforts against the regime were coordinated across bar associations around the country by the Pakistan Lawyers' Coordination Committee.[38]

Zia responded by cracking down on the autonomy of the legal profession. The 1973 Legal Practitioners and Bar Councils Act was amended to remove peer review from the licensing of lawyers, thus reducing the Bar Council's power to regulate the entrance of lawyers into the profession (Newberg 1995). The regime also cracked down on bar associations, arresting and detaining bar leaders who protested the amendments to the Legal Practitioners' Act.[39] Lawyers protested by walking out of courtrooms, carrying out processions wearing black arm bands, courting arrest and organizing hunger strikes.[40] Judges who refused to sign Zia's PCO became heroes and were invited to speak before the bar, while lawyers who joined Zia's rubberstamp parliament were expelled from bar associations.[41]

There was a clear generation gap within the bar. Some senior lawyers and former leaders of the bar associations supported the government's reduction in the autonomy of the legal profession, stating '[t]here is no precedent or practice ... permitting political activity in a Bar Association' and condemning the fact that 'Bar Associations had been

---

[36] 'KBA Members Meet Politicians', *Dawn*, 2 November 1982; 'Political Parties to Join Lawyers' Struggle', *Star*, 31 October 1982; 'Aitzaz to Confer with Politicians', *Dawn*, 20 July 1983; 'Bar President Hopes for Joint Political Declaration', *Muslim*, 8 July 1983.

[37] Interview No. L-42.

[38] 'Bar President Hopes for Joint Political Declaration', *Muslim*, 8 July 1983; 'Lahore Bar Body Endorses Hunger Strike Decision', *Dawn*, 31 May 1983.

[39] 'Bar Body Amendments: Faisalabad Lawyers Boycott Courts', *Dawn*, 20 July 1982; 'City Lawyers Protest', *Star*, 10 October 1982; 'Lawyers Arrest "Dastardly Act"', *Star*, 11 October 1982.

[40] Murtaza Malik, 'Lawyers Condemn Amendment', *Muslim*, 19 July 1982; 'Lawyers' Release Sought', *Dawn*, 22 February 1984; 'Lawyers to Set up Action Committee', *Star*, 1 April 1985; 'Lawyers' Convention on November 28', *Dawn*, 18 November 1985; 'Country-Wide Protest Meetings by Bar Councils', *Star*, 29 March 1985.

[41] 'City Bar Asked to Reverse Decision: Expulsion of 4 Members', *Muslim*, 6 April 1982.

providing platforms to politicians'.[42] But the younger generation of bar lawyers were engaged in politics and mobilized against the military dictatorship.[43] Opposition to the military establishment continued to be the platform upon which lawyers ran for bar elections and won.[44] Over time, the same groups winning bar association elections went on to organize and win elections in the bar councils as well, thus placing the regulation of the legal profession in the hands of politically active lawyers who opposed the military regime. The 1984 elections to the presidency of the Lahore High Court Bar Association clearly high-lighted the shift within the bar, as outlined in these newspaper reports:

> All the three Presidential candidates have announced their support for the 1973 Constitution and the immediate restoration of democracy in the country. However, lawyers who call themselves 'progressives' have announced their support for Chaudhry Khalid Mahmud.[45]
>
> Khalid Mahmud was appointed a judge of the High Court in 1977 but he resigned within six months of his appointment. He stands for the restoration of the 1973 Constitution and an undiluted democracy.[46]

Khalid Mahmud, a former judge who refused to serve under Zia and had proven his pro-democracy credentials, won the High Court bar election, an election that demonstrated the consensus across the bar electorate in opposition to military rule. This new consensus was not just evident in Lahore. As one newspaper report stated about the Karachi Bar Association, '[t]he Karachi Bar no longer carries on the traditions of the Bar and has become a melting point for all kinds of anti-establishment groups and views'.[47]

Thus, in the early 1980s, a combination of (1) changing size and demographics within the bar, (2) increased public and political interest in bar elections and (3) regime actions against the judiciary, all helped to create opportunities for politically active lawyers opposed to the military regime to take leadership roles within the bar associations. This led to the mobilization of the bar associations against the regime, and the entrenchment of norms of political activism and opposition to

---

[42] 'Dialogue between Bar, Government Suggested', *Business Recorder*, 22 July 1982; 'Lawyer without Politics?', *Dawn*, 27 July 1982.
[43] 'Lawyers Convention on November 28', *Dawn*, 18 November 1985.
[44] 'Khalid Mahmud Elected LHC Bar President', *Dawn*, 24 February 1984.
[45] 'Hectic Activity for LHCBA Election', *Pakistan Times*, 22 February 1984.
[46] 'LHCBA Presidential Candidates', *Pakistan Times*, 23 February 1984.
[47] Nigar, 'The Quest for Power'.

military rule within the major bar associations. At a time when the judiciary and the bar were developing closer normative interlinkages, the bar was developing a new normative consensus opposing collaboration with the military.

By the end of Zia's regime in 1988, and the resumption of democratic rule, bar associations had embraced political engagement and activism, but this did not mean the legal community was necessarily supportive of rule by Pakistan's political parties. Pakistan's political parties were decimated by Zia's regime. After years spent in the wilderness, when democratic rule resumed, these political parties were weak with few direct connections to voters, and dependent upon autonomous local actors ranging from landlords and tribal leaders, to clientelist exchanges through brokers, kin groups and local party leaders (Mohmand 2014). In this system, elite corruption, in-fighting and governance failures plagued the political governments during the 1990s.

After the resumption of democracy, political parties recognized the importance of gaining the support of bar associations. Just as pro-democracy lawyers had used the bar as a platform to oppose military rule, political parties supported groups within bar association elections in order to ensure those groups used their platform to speak in support of that political party and in opposition of their political rivals.[48]

However, while political parties got increasingly engaged with the activities of bar associations and solicited the support of groups of lawyers, the bar associations still prioritized maintaining distance and autonomy from political parties.[49] There was a clear distinction between those members of the legal profession who opted for politics as their careers and those who were still lawyers by profession.[50] Even groupings within the bar that were affiliated with political parties maintained a distance from party direction, and would make alliances

---

[48] In 1995, for example, when the Lahore High Court Bar Association election was won by a lawyer with the support of the Pakistan Muslim League, soon after the High Court bar association put out resolutions criticizing the government of the Pakistani People's Party and calling for its dissolution and fresh elections in the province of Sindh. Latif Sheikh, 'PML(N) Candidates Sweep LHCBA Election', *Frontier Post*, 25 February 1995; 'LHCBA Calls for Sindh Government's Dismissal', *Dawn*, 2 March 1995.

[49] 'LHCBA Is Now Politically Non-aligned', *Dawn*, 7 March 1996;.

[50] 'The President Speaks', *News*, 25 March 1992.

and arrangements that ran counter to the interests of the party leadership.[51] As a senior political office-holder who was also a practising lawyer, explained, 'lawyers are a community unto itself, and party affiliations were always secondary'.[52] In the 1992 elections for the Lahore High Court Bar Association, the candidates emphasized how they maintained distance and detachment from political parties, as close ties to political parties were seen as detrimental within professional associations that strongly guarded their autonomy. Thus, even as bar associations grew more politically active and engaged, they maintained a degree of autonomy from the political parties.

The urban middle-class lawyers of the bar associations were disdainful of what they saw as the corruption and incompetence of elite-driven political parties. Bar leaders during the 1990s regularly spoke out against the perceived corruption of political parties. In 1992, Hamid Khan, the president of the Lahore High Court Bar Association, said in a speech:

> Corruption in the ranks of the government has exceeded all imaginable proportions. The country has been rendered into a cauldron of hate and prejudice. The stories about bribery, graft, commissions and other methods of corruption can put to shame the worst during the Byzantine Empire. The main concern of legislative members is the transfers and postings of their favourites with the evident motive of making money and to use such favourites for oppressing and tyrannizing their opponents.[53]

In 1995, the vice chairman of the Pakistan Bar Council attempted to throw himself into a cage of lions protesting unemployment, corruption and lawlessness, and chided the judiciary for not intervening in this state of affairs.[54]

Thus, in the late 1980s and 1990s, the bar associations expanded their political priorities beyond democratic rights to speak out and mobilize on all matters of state, including foreign policy, economic policy and welfare, and they distrusted the intent and capability of

---

[51] Frequently, the bar wings of rival political parties would join each other to back the same candidate in bar elections.

[52] Interview No. P-5, 2 January 2021.

[53] 'The President Speaks'.

[54] Birjees Nagy, 'Saving Judiciary and the Legal Profession for the Public', *Frontier Post*, 25 August 1995.

elected state institutions.[55] The bar represented the ambitions and frustrations of Pakistan's urban middle class, and this included frustration with entrenched elites and their reputation for corruption. Aziz (2015) explains that there has been an ascendant aspiration in the middle class that seeks to assert 'its control over the political process through an anti-corruption movement' and 'deliver clean politics'. As a senior lawyer reminded his bar association, 'the purpose of the bar association should not be to promote the interests of the lawyers but to advance the public interest'.[56] For the section of the middle class represented in the institution with which they had the strongest linkages, the judiciary represented the vehicle for pursuing an anti-corruption agenda.

During the 1990s, courts were seen as routes for resolving the problems of 'weak parties in an uncertain polity'(Newberg 1995: 230). As the high courts were called on to intervene in disputes between presidents and parliaments, governors and chief ministers, ruling parties and opposition, and federal and provincial governments, the judiciary's visibility and significance as an arbiter of Pakistan's dissonant politics became increasingly evident, and leading voices within the bar wanted to see the judiciary move beyond just arbitrating institutional disputes to actually intervening in the functioning and policymaking of these governing institutions. Justice Khosa, chief justice of Pakistan in 2019, who was a lawyer in the 1990s, wrote as a lawyer at the time that 'legislators passed their time passing motions about breaches of privileges, and the judiciary had to arrest this repugnancy' (Azeem 2017: 224). The National Lawyers' Conference of 1993 resolved that 'the judiciary, particularly the superior courts, at this critical juncture should serve as a symbol of liberty, equality and social justice ... if the judiciary of Pakistan remains a silent spectator, its death as a lifeline of society could be inevitable'.[57] Dr Khalid Ranjha, a prominent lawyer and bar association leader from Lahore, said:

> The courts can take *suo moto* (self-moved judicial actions without a petitioner moving the courts) action in the affairs pertaining to political

---

[55] 'Genocide of Iraqis Condemned', *Dawn*, 1 February 1991; Farooq Lodhi, 'Independent Judiciary Is an Integral Part of Democracy', *Daily News*, 21 March 1993.

[56] 'Bar Association Should Promote Public Interest', *Frontier Post*, 18 January 1991.

[57] Lodhi, 'Independent Judiciary Is an Integral Part of Democracy'.

corruption to save the system . . . Courts should take *suo moto* of all the corruption of the political culture and take those to task who conduct themselves in breach of political ethics.[58]

Thus, many bar associations wished to see the judiciary assert its independence from other state institutions, elected or unelected, and play a broadly expansive role in the political system, intervening in the affairs and actions of other state institutions and ruling on a broad range of political and socio-economic issues, in order to remove corruption and ensure the state acted in the public interest. The president of the Sindh High Court Bar Association articulated this consensus most clearly when he stated in 1999:

> The edifice of our democratic system is built upon the foundations of illiteracy and ignorance . . . promises of just governance have become fairy tales . . . We need to structure a judiciary to even strike down laws which in its considered opinion are harsh, unjust . . . or counterproductive.[59]

Thus, the bar associations had evolved considerably to become large associations teeming with lawyers from less privileged backgrounds, with less of a stake in the established political order and more attuned to the political and socio-economic concerns of the middle-class communities to which they belonged. In the absence of alternate political venues, politically active lawyers turned the bar associations into vehicles for challenging military rule and helped entrench a norm of anti-militarism and political activism within the bar. With the end of military rule, this political activism was translated into a broader agenda of socio-economic and political reform that was to be realized through an active judiciary with an expansive role in the political system. An anti-elite consensus established itself within the bar. The focus of this anti-elitism was often a moving target, shifting between generals, politicians and bureaucrats, depending on the political and institutional context of the time, but either way, the sentiment in the bar was that the judiciary's role was to confront, rather than collaborate with, these elites. By the 1990s, this consensus of political and judicial activism was entrenched through the bar associations in the major urban centres. As judges were increasingly recruited from and socialized in the bar, and developed closer normative interlinkages with the bar,

---

[58] 'Suo Moto Action Is a Must', *Nation*, 15 September 1995.
[59] 'System of Good Governance Has Collapsed', *Business Recorder*, 13 May 1999.

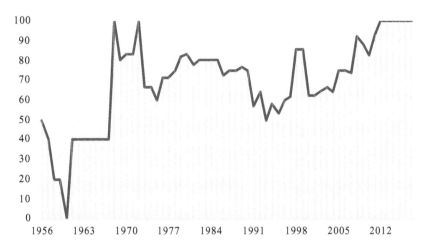

Figure 4.2 Proportion of Supreme Court judges recruited from the bar of professional lawyers (1956–2017)
This graph does not include the information on the professional background of four judges.

they became more attentive to the preference for independence and political and judicial activism that developed in the bar.

Separation of Judiciary from the Executive
By the 1990s, the military's normative interlinkages with the judiciary had gradually diminished. The 1973 Constitution began the process of separating the judiciary from the bureaucracy and ended the recruitment of judges from the executive branch. Most judges were now recruited laterally from the bar of practising lawyers, and only a minority were promoted from the judicial bureaucracy of the lower courts (see Figure 4.2). Further, with the indigenization of the judiciary, the judiciary was now recruited from the network of middle-class lawyers that was more distant from the military and bureaucratic elite.

However, even as the normative interlinkages changed, the military continued to maintain utilitarian interlinkages with the judiciary, that is, the military and affiliated elites remained in a position to impose material costs and benefits on judges. Between 1973 and 1994, no government facilitated the constitutionally mandated separation of the judiciary from the executive, as the executive branch still had significant control over judicial appointments and transfers and the judicial budget. Under the ideal system of judicial appointments, as explained in Chapter 2, a list of nominations for judgeships was prepared by the relevant High Court's chief justice, and the nominations went through a series of tiers of executive and judicial consultation before the president made the final decision on the nomination after completing consultation. In practice, however, the executive branch had the discretion to abuse this process and appoint judges without going through meaningful consultation.

This was clearly highlighted during Zia's regime. Under Zia, politicians lost all influence in the matter of appointments of judges, and most judges appointed under Bhutto had either resigned or been removed.[60] The recruitment of judges was primarily in the hands of Zia and a handful of judges, serving or retired, and a few other influential men such as Zia's attorney general, Sharifuddin Pirzada, and Chief Secretary Ghulam Ishaq Khan, who had close relationships with General Zia and his junta.[61] Lawyers had to stay in the 'good books of the generals in power' in order to become judges.[62] Chief justices of the High Court and Supreme Court did nominate candidates for the judiciary, but ultimately only those candidates would be confirmed who were deemed acceptable by the military regime. Therefore, they were unlikely to nominate candidates who were likely to be rejected. The safest pathway to become a judge was being appointed as a government lawyer for the regime. The offices of the attorney general, advocate general or additional advocate general became nurseries for appointment to the superior courts.[63] Given Sharifuddin Pirzada's position as both attorney general and law minister, he exercised considerable sway in both the appointment of government lawyers and selection of judges from the pool of government lawyers. As a veteran politician explained:

> Judicial appointments at the time were controlled and strongly manipulated by the attorney general. He managed appointments in order to have a judiciary that would be pliable to the military regime. Sharifuddin Pirzada had the primary say, and the chief justice had a more limited say.[64]

---

[60] Khalid Javed Khan, 'Judiciary in the Whirlwind', *Dawn*, 7 October 1994.
[61] Interview No. L-3, 22 May 2017.
[62] Hamid Khan, 'Judiciary – Institution in Decay – I', *Dawn*, 14 October 1994.
[63] Ibid.
[64] Interview No P-5.

Thus, even as judges were increasingly appointed from the bar of practising lawyers, the military regime selected lawyers who were politically conservative and unwilling to 'rock the boat' and had proven this through their time as government lawyers.[65]

Zia's regime enforced control over the judiciary during this period through his powers to confirm and transfer judges. Justice Ilyas was elevated as a judge of the Lahore High Court in 1977, but after Zia seized power he transferred him back down to the subordinate judiciary.[66] Only once a judge is confirmed is his or her tenure secured. The intended practice was that a judge was appointed as an additional judge to the High Court or the Supreme Court before being confirmed after a year or two with an ad hoc status. However, Zia's regime routinely violated this expectation, maintaining the ad hoc status of judges. Chief Justice Haleem was appointed as the acting chief justice of the Supreme Court in 1981 but was not confirmed until late 1984, over three years later. Zia used the same tactic with the chief justices of the high courts, appointing a senior judge as the acting chief justice, but 'only confirming him as Chief Justice in the last month or so of his appointment'.[67] This was done with the expectation that an acting chief justice would be more obedient than a confirmed chief justice, given that his tenure remained insecure. Ali described this practice as follows: 'What can a judge do when the sword of confirmation hangs over his head? An Adhoc judge needs a lot of courage, sense of duty and high degree of idealism ... to risk his job by annoying the powers that be, who can send him home.'[68] Thus, the military-led executive maintained utilitarian interlinkages with the judiciary, and those who moved forward in their judicial careers were lawyers and judges who were willing to acquiesce to military dominance. Lawyers who favoured boldness or assertiveness were unlikely to be selected as judges, and those who were selected knew they had to remain deferential in order to be promoted or confirmed. The extent to which regime control over judicial careers impacted judicial decision-making even came up before

---

[65] Interview No. L-3.

[66] Similarly, in 1985, Zia transferred and demoted the acting chief justice of the Balochistan High Court for allegedly passing an order that displeased the military authorities. 'Transfer of Acting Chief Justice: Balochistan High Court Bar Protests', *Dawn*, 30 March 1985; 'Saga of a Judge', *Nation*, 26 October 1996.

[67] Abdullah Jan, 'More than Half of PHC Judges Serving on an Adhoc Basis', *News*, 10 March 1995.

[68] Ali, 'The Judiciary and Social Change'.

the courts, when a petitioner asked the Supreme Court to change the composition of the bench hearing a case against the government, because those judges had been appointed by Sharifuddin Pirzada, who, as attorney general and law minister, was both arguing the case before them and could initiate disciplinary proceedings against them. The petitioner held that judges 'would feel too beholden to Sharifuddin Pirzada for their appointment, or they would feel too intimidated in his presence because of his power to initiate disciplinary proceedings'.[69] Justice Javed Iqbal, the acting chief justice of the Lahore High Court, typified this norm of avoiding any confrontation in the controlled judiciary, stating in 1982 that 'the judiciary in Pakistan currently enjoyed as much power as was necessary in a civilized ... Islamic society'.[70] A senior lawyer explained: 'During Zia's time judges would always be concerned about the military's reaction. The judges were concerned: what does the military want? We do not want to offend the military.'[71] This was the era of the *controlled court* in Pakistan, where a norm of submission to the will of the military dominated the internal culture of the military. Under Ayub's regime, the judiciary used its power to support the military, while the judiciary under Zia accepted that it was powerless to challenge the military. Justice Iqbal described the judiciary during his tenure under Zia as 'helpless' (Iqbal 2006).

After Zia's regime ended, the civilian governments sought to build the same utilitarian interlinkages with the judiciary, seeking to control the judiciary in the same way that Zia had. Bhutto did not have the opportunity to appoint any new judges in her first term. Nawaz Sharif, in his first government, made no improvement in the appointment process. Khan explains that appointments under Sharif remained arbitrary, 'as the politicians and the Chief Justice appointed their favourites'.[72] One senior lawyer explained that 'during the 1980s and early 1990s, you had to be close to the [military] establishment or to a political party and you became a judge'.[73] Further, Nawaz also maintained Zia's practice of maintaining the ad hoc status of senior judges,

---

[69] *Malik Hamid Sarfaraz v. Federation of Pakistan*, PLD 1979 SC 991.
[70] 'Freedom within Limits: Judiciary Cannot Ask for More Powers: Javed Iqbal', *Muslim*, 9 November 1982.
[71] Interview No. L-5, 15 May 2017.
[72] Hamid Khan, 'Judiciary – Institution in Decay – II, *Dawn*, 14 October 1994.
[73] Interview No. L-42.

and in 1993, the high courts of three provinces had ad hoc chief justices and over a third of judges for the Supreme Court were ad hoc appointees.[74]

However, after the restoration of democracy, leading lawyers and the bar associations started criticizing the judicial appointment system, advocating for the separation of the judiciary from the executive and a new judicial appointment system.[75] In 1992, the president of the Lahore High Court Bar Association, Hamid Khan, openly criticized the judges that had been appointed in recent years, stating that 'some of the judges appointed were not even known as advocates and the majority of lawyers practising in the High Court learnt about them when they were already judges'.[76] In 1992, the bars of the Lahore High Court and district courts unanimously resolved that 'the method of appointment of judges be restructured so that persons of doubtful and suspect character and conduct should not be appointed', and in an unprecedented move boycotted the oath-taking of newly appointed judges whom they did not deem qualified.[77] A new consensus had also emerged within the bar that if judges did not enjoy security of tenure and were not protected against arbitrary executive action in matters relating to their appointment, then the judiciary could not function independently.[78] Instead, the presidents of the bar associations recommended that the practice of appointing ad hoc judges be ended, the executive be given minimal say in judicial appointments and the chief justice of each High Court consult with the bar about the competence and reputation of a candidate.[79]

---

[74] 'Six New SHC Judges Take Oath of Office', *Dawn*, 25 March 1992; Farooq Lodhi, 'Independent Judiciary Is an Integral Part of Democracy', *Daily News*, 21 March 1993. It is noteworthy that by 1994, the judiciary had gained financial autonomy. In *Government of Sindh* v. *Sharaf Faridi* (1994), the Supreme Court ordered the 'immediate separation of the judiciary from the executive branch', including guaranteeing financial autonomy. See *Government of Pakistan* v. *Sharaf Faridi*, PLD 1994 SC 105.

[75] 'What Is Delaying Separation of Judicial from Executive Powers?', *The News*, 27 October 1987; 'Need Stressed to Purge Judiciary of Corruption', *Morning News*, 11 December 1989.

[76] 'Appointing Judges', *The News*, 25 March 1992.

[77] 'LHCBA Boycotts Oath-Taking Ceremony', *Muslim*, 30 May 1992; 'Lawyers Go on Indefinite Boycott', *Frontier Post*, 14 October 1992; 'Bar, Bench Develop Differences', *Dawn*, 10 January 1992.

[78] Ash'ar, 'Erosion of the Judiciary's Independence', *Dawn*, 8 May 1998; Lodhi, 'Independent Judiciary Is an Integral Part of Democracy'.

[79] 'City Bars for Restructuring Judges' Appointment Procedure', *Frontier Post*, 20 July 1992.

When Benazir Bhutto took office a second time, the PPP was convinced it had to appoint judges to the high courts that would favour them. Given that the judiciary upheld Zia's coup, the execution of Bhutto and the dissolution of Benazir Bhutto's government in 1990, many members of the PPP believed that a strong institutional bias against the PPP was locked into the judiciary. A lawyer affiliated with the PPP explained the party's belief that 'between 1988 and 1999 there was a compact between the judiciary and the army against the PPP. The Court was anti-Benazir and the PPP. Judges who had convicted and hanged Bhutto [Benazir Bhutto's father] were serving judges on the [Supreme Court] bench.'[80]

Bhutto's government sought to reshape the bench by appointing judges from networks of lawyers and legal practitioners who belonged to the PPP. In 1994, 'Benazir wanted to appoint twenty judges all chosen by her for the Lahore High Court and nine judges were chosen for the Sindh High Court, without any input from the judges', which judges feared would 'change the entire face of the court'.[81] Questions were raised about the credentials and capability of these judicial appointees as some were allegedly 'people who had not even seen the High Courts ever'.[82] One of these appointees was simply a PPP party member who had run for a seat in the previous election and lost, before Bhutto granted him an appointment as a High Court judge.[83] Bhutto also promoted judges who she believed would favour the PPP and demoted judges who she felt would undermine the party's interests, and the Supreme Court was packed with as many as seven ad hoc judges, almost half the total strength of the Supreme Court bench (Khan 2016).[84] Bhutto's attempts to pack the courts with loyalists generated widespread condemnation from the bar associations and opposition parties.

The Supreme Court granted leave to an appeal against Bhutto's appointment of twenty judges to the Lahore High Court to consider

---

[80] Interview No. L-1, 15 May 2017.
[81] Interview No. L-88, 5 June 2017.
[82] Ibid.
[83] Interview No. J-19.
[84] Not only did she appoint Chief Justice Sajjad Ali Shah, who had been one of the dissenters in the Court's decision to uphold the presidential dissolution of the PPP government in 1990, over a more senior judge, she also demoted the highly respected chief justice of the Sindh High Court, Justice Nasir Aslam Zahid. See Hamid Khan, 'Judiciary – Institution in Decay – I', Dawn, 10 October 1994.

the constitutionality of such appointments in *Al-Jehad Trust* v. *Federation of Pakistan* (1996).[85] The oral arguments over the next several months in the Court dealt with fundamental questions about the role and independence of Pakistan's judiciary. The government lawyers argued that executive involvement in the process of judicial appointments did not undermine judicial independence, and that judicial independence commenced with a judge's oath-taking, after which the executive could not interfere in their judgments.[86] However, the opposing counsel, a prominent lawyer and bar leader, Akram Sheikh, vehemently opposed this contention, stating that even if judges suddenly became impartial after taking the oath, '[h]ow will that change the public perception of the judge firmed up over the years?'[87] Thus, the opposing counsel outlined a position held by many within the legal community: that judges appointed through executive interference lacked credibility and legitimacy.

In a landmark decision, which came to be known as the *Judges'* judgment, the Court declared the government's appointments to the Lahore High Court unconstitutional and significantly reduced the control of the executive in judicial appointments.[88] On the question of ad hoc judges, the Court held that the appointment of ad hoc judges in the Supreme Court was unconstitutional, High Court chief justices could only have an acting position for a period of fifty days and additional judges must be confirmed within a short period of time. On the question of judicial backgrounds, when recruiting judges from among advocates of the High Court, a record of actual experience as an advocate was necessary during the mandatory period of ten years of practice to qualify for judicial appointments, thus preventing the government from simply appointing loyalists as opposed to experienced lawyers. Finally, on the question of judicial appointments the Court altered the consultation process that had been in place by reinterpreting the 'consultation' between the executive and the chief justices on judicial appointments to be binding on the executive.[89] Under this

---

[85] *Al-Jehad Trust* v. *Federation of Pakistan*, PLD 1996 SC 324.

[86] 'Consultation of CJ Becomes Consent after President's Acceptance', *The News*, 9 February 1996.

[87] 'Independence of Judiciary: Aitzaz Contention Opposed', *The News*, 5 March 1996.

[88] *Al-Jihad Trust* v. *Federation of Pakistan*, PLD 1996 SC 324.

[89] The Court adopted a similar formulation of the 'consultation' process to that adopted in India, just two years earlier.

new framework, the president still appointed the judges, but the opinion of the chief justice of Pakistan and the chief justice of the relevant High Court as to the fitness and suitability of a candidate for judgeship was entitled to be accepted, unless there were very strong reasons for the president to disagree, and these reasons must pertain to the candidates' judicial capabilities. Thus, the chief justices of the high courts and Supreme Court now had the primary say in judicial appointments, and the executive was expected to accept their choices unless they had compelling reasons to oppose the choices made by the chief justices.

The judgment reflected the consensus that had developed within the legal community regarding the crucial role of the process of judicial appointments in ensuring judicial independence from other executive institutions, whether civilian or military. The Court's judgment echoed Akram Sheikh's argument regarding an independent appointment process and public confidence, holding that the 'people at large should have faith in the independence of the judiciary'. The Court also acknowledged that utilitarian interlinkages between the judiciary and executive institutions affected judicial decision-making, stating that 'the junior judges may feel that by having good terms with the government in power, he can become the chief justice ... this will destroy ... public confidence in it [the judiciary]'. Thus, the arguments put forward from the bar regarding a lack of confidence in judges appointed through an executive-dominated appointment process provided the rationale for the judiciary's decision to alter the appointment process. Now judicial appointments, promotions, transfers and confirmations were primarily in the hands of the chief justices.[90]

Bar associations around the country celebrated the verdict of the judiciary, and pushed for its rapid implementation, opposing any delay or compromise by the executive, and even refusing to appear in the courts of judges whose appointment had been deemed unconstitutional.[91] Initially the PPP government opposed the decision and refused to implement it. However, combined pressure from the bar associations, political opposition and even the president finally forced the PPP

---

[90] 'Appointments without CJ's Consultation Invalid', *Nation*, 3 April 1996; Asma Jahangir, 'SC Ruling: A Judicial 'Coup', *News*, 21 March 1996;.

[91] 'SC Judgement: Lawyers to Observe Token Hunger Strike', *The News*, 9 April 1996; 'Lawyers' Reaction', *The News*, 25 March 1996; 'SHCBA Forms Eight-Man Implementation Committee', *Dawn*, 27 March 1996; 'SC Verdict in Judges Case: PBC Committee Rejects Compromise', *Dawn*, 30 March 1996.

government to comply.[92] In September 1996, Bhutto denotified the judges who had been laid off by the *Al-Jehad* decision.[93]

The *Al-Jehad* decision would probably not have been possible without the fragmented politics of the time, with a hostile opposition, assertive presidency and politically engaged military all willing to back the judiciary's assertion of independence from the executive institutions, as long as the executive branch was controlled by the political party they opposed. During the proceedings, Sharifuddin Pirzada, in his capacity as *amicus curia*, argued against the ills of the very form of judicial dependence that he had helped ensure under General Zia. However, the decision's impact would resonate beyond the context of the PPP government.

The decision placed the chief justices in control of the judicial appointment process. The judicial appointment process was always a negotiation between officers of the executive branch and the judiciary, but, prior to the *Al- Jihad* decision, the formal appointment powers ensured the executive branch had more leverage in the negotiations, as the president had the discretion to reject candidates nominated by the judiciary. This meant that judges and executive law officers would consult over nominated candidates, but they were unlikely to propose or shortlist candidates that the president was likely to reject. The *Al-Jihad* decision significantly altered the negotiating powers of the chief justice during the process of judicial appointments. Now the chief justice's advice was binding on the president, making it harder for the president to reject the chief justice's choices. Judges and executive officers still negotiated over appointments, but they were now unlikely to propose or shortlist candidates that the *chief justice* was likely to reject, and once the chief justice had selected a candidate, this selection was binding on the president. Government discretion in appointing and confirming ad hoc judges and selecting the chief justices of the courts was reduced, further limiting executive control over judicial careers. Thus, primacy in judicial careers shifted from the government to the chief justice.

---

[92] 'PML Demands Implementation of SC Judgment', *Dawn*, 13 April 1996; 'The Judiciary vs Illegal Appointments', *Frontier Post*, 8 October 1996.

[93] On the question of seniority in appointments, in *Malik Asad v. Pakistan*, the judiciary held that the senior-most judge of each High Court and the Supreme Court should be appointed as the chief justice of each court, ending executive discretion in selecting chief justices. See *Malik Asad Ali v. Federation of Pakistan*, PLD 1998 SC 161.

Before, when the executive institutions, such as the military, military governments or elected governments, wanted to impact the selection of judges, they could do so directly, through the powers allotted to them in the appointment process. Now generals and political parties would seek to cultivate and co-opt chief justices of the high courts in order to influence the appointment and promotion process. A retired chief justice from this period explained that the decision expanded the powers of the chief justice, and it was now up to the chief justice to decide whether he wanted to consult with the government about appointments, and 'confirm their choices' in the judiciary or not.[94]

The bar sought a formal role in the consultation process, but even though this formal role was not granted, the *Al-Jihad* decision opened an informal role for the bar in judicial appointments.[95] The Pakistan Bar Council announced that it would keep a vigilant eye on the process of review and regularization of newly appointed judges in high courts.[96] One former judge explained the change produced by the *Al-Jihad* decision. He said that before the judgment, there were three important considerations for becoming a judge: 'where [which law firm] did you start as a junior? Did you make a name [with judges] in the courtroom? What kind of contacts in uniform, and in executive office did you have?'[97] He added: 'Uniformed and bureaucratic contacts were useful through the mid-90s, but the Al-Jihad decision changed this.' After this, the development of a 'professional reputation as a lawyer' gained importance, which meant building a reputation with High Court judges, especially the chief justice, and with senior bar lawyers and bar leaders became crucial. The judge explained further:

> Reputation in the bar room is very important. You cannot hide your conduct from the bar room. Problems can be created for unwanted judicial appointments ... disruptions in the court, whispering campaigns against him. I have seen this happen as a judge.[98]

Another senior lawyer explained to me why the bar associations advocated for the implementation of the decision, stating that 'through

---

[94] Interview No. J-2, 19 February 2021.
[95] 'PBC Wants a Say in Judges' Appointment', *Dawn*, 1 December 1996.
[96] 'Bar Council to Watch Judges Performance', *Muslim*, 19 April 1996.
[97] Interview No. J-19.
[98] Ibid.

this decision the bar was becoming a stakeholder in the appointment process. Before *Al-Jehad* they were not stakeholders'.[99]

Now that judges were the primary appointing authorities, they could not pass blame for poorly made appointments on to the executive, and faced considerable pressure from the legal community to which they belonged if they made controversial choices that were unpopular among leaders within the legal community. Being former lawyers them-selves, judges were also more willing to take the advice of senior lawyers in appointing judges. After *Al-Jihad*, one experienced lawyer opined:

> If you go only by quality of appointments made, it would not be inaccurate to say quality of appointments improved. 1997–1999 appointments of judges were those who should have been judges. They were all successful lawyers, with a reputation in the bar. The CJ was in a position where he had to take full responsibility for judicial appointments before the bar.[100]

This did not mean that the judicial appointment process inevitably became more meritocratic. It remained an opaque process, without clear rules and criteria for appointment, providing considerable discretion to the primary appointing authorities in making selections. The opinions of those who had personal or professional proximity to the chief justices of the High Court and Supreme Court carried considerable weight, and this included judges' family members in the legal profession, colleagues from their law firms and chambers they previously belonged to, or senior lawyers and bar leaders who had direct access to the judges. Stakeholders in the legal community had always influenced the choices made by the chief justices, but historically, given the primacy of the executive institutions in the appointment process, and the military's control over the executive branch for most of that history, the support of those close to the military-led executive was often more critical to actually being shortlisted and selected for appointment. As the importance of executive institutions decreased, and bar leaders became vocal about judicial appointments, the role of reputation among senior lawyers and bar leaders became increasingly important in judicial appointments.

Thus, by 1996, the transition of the judiciary away from executive authorities, including the military, was largely complete. Not only had

---

[99] Interview No. L-10.
[100] Interview No. L-50, 18 May 2017.

the normative interlinkages between the judiciary and the military been broken, but with the *Al-Jihad* decision, the utilitarian interlinkages between the judiciary and executive authorities, including the military, had greatly diminished. On the other hand, the bar had not only developed normative interlinkages with the judiciary, it had also developed utilitarian interlinkages with the judiciary, making it a critical audience for judges.

AUDIENCES SHAPING THE JUDICIAL TRANSITION

The three processes described so far in this chapter reshaped the legal and policy preferences of the judiciary. This institutional transition provides the best explanation for the gradual changes in the jurisprudence of the courts outlined in Chapter 3.

Beginning in the late 1970s, we witness the difference between the senior judges on the Supreme Court who had been appointed during the 1950s and 1960s and the junior judges in the high courts who had been mostly appointed in the late 1960s and 1970s. As the judiciary was separated from the executive, more High Court judges were being recruited from outside the executive. These judges came from a bar that was less distant and detached from mass politics compared to its predecessors. Further, for these judges, the initial years of experience on the bench occurred under the empowering 1973 Constitution and was spent resisting Bhutto's efforts to undermine their constitutionally granted powers. These judges differed from their seniors on the question of the political role and independence of the judiciary.

The biographies of the senior-most judge of the Supreme Court and the junior-most judge of the Supreme Court at the time of the introduction of the PCO in 1981 help highlight the change in the judiciary. Justice Anwar-ul-Haq, the chief justice, was a former civil servant educated at Oxford University, who had been a member of the civil service under British rule and continued to serve in the bureaucracy until he was appointed a High Court judge in the Lahore High Court during Ayub Khan's regime. Justice Fakhruddin Ebrahim, who had just been promoted to the Supreme Court in 1981, a few months prior to the introduction of the PCO, had studied at Sindh Muslim (SM) Government Law College in Karachi and went on to become a successful lawyer, before briefly becoming attorney general in Bhutto's government for a year, after which he was elevated to the Sindh High Court in 1973. Thus, Justice Ebrahim served as a young lawyer when Ayub Khan fell, and became a judge under the 1973 Constitution, appointed by an elected civilian government.

Justice Anwar-ul-Haq, as chief justice, most actively sought a collaborative relationship with the Zia regime. As the author of the *Nusrat Bhutto* decision, he gave Zia wide discretion, and then in subsequent judgments authored by him, he further augmented that discretion. He also devised the oath that all judges were expected to take in 1977, carefully removing any mention of the 1973 Constitution from the oath, to ensure that judges, by taking the oath, recognized Zia's constitutional order (Patel 2000). Under Anwar-ul-Haq, the Supreme Court rarely challenged the military regime. He did not conceal his bias against the populism of Bhutto and the PPP, asking senior lawyers in 1978 to 'educate the people' so they do not repeat the mistake of electing the wrong representatives in the general election.[101] Anwar-ul-Haq sought to establish the close collaborative relationship with Zia that Cornelius and Munir had enjoyed with Ayub Khan.

On the other hand, Justice Ebrahim, as a Sindh High Court judge, was one of the judges who authored the *Mumtaz Bhutto* decision that restricted the detention powers of the military regime, placing the judiciary in a position to check the military regime's actions. He had been appointed by Bhutto, and thus, given both his professional background and his appointing authority, Ebrahim had fewer linkages with the military. By 1981, Justice Ebrahim and several other judges who had been involved in jurisprudence at the High Court level that sought to place some checks on the MLAs were in line to be elevated to the Supreme Court, indicating the movement of the Court away from a collaborative approach to the military. Ebrahim refused to take an oath under Zia's PCO in 1981 and became an outspoken critic of the military regime in subsequent years.

The two biographies show how judges who were primarily recruited from the bar of locally educated lawyers that had grown more politically active sought to play a more active and less collaborative role as judges than their predecessors. Thus, the internal culture of the judiciary was beginning to shift, and this shift started in the high courts, slowly percolating up to the Supreme Court, as judges moved from the High Court to the Supreme Court, which explains the contrasting approaches taken by the Supreme Court and high courts during this period.

---

[101] 'Lawyers Urged to Educate People Whom to Elect', *Dawn*, 20 January 1978.

It is important to state here, though, that the changes in the judiciary were still only limited. Most judges were still unwilling to actually challenge the laws promulgated by the regime, and the majority of judges still took the oath under the restrictive PCO of 1981 to preserve their careers.

During the period from 1981 to 1985, we see no increase in contestation of the military from the judiciary, but this was a period where the judiciary was under the tight control of the military, with its jurisdiction narrowed, making it very difficult for the judiciary to challenge the military. However, when this period ended, the judiciary faced a crisis of legitimacy. With a politically active bar now opposing the military, judges recruited from the bar grew increasingly concerned about their reputations with the bar. This became apparent from the retirement speech of Justice Iqbal, who had served as Zia's chief justice in the Lahore High Court:

> During General Zia's dictatorial rule the superior judiciary was irreparably damaged ... Judges were required to take repeatedly the oath of allegiance, which made each judge a controversial functionary. Those judges who continued to serve in the courts were accused of being collaborators of dictatorship. Those judges who were ejected from the judiciary claimed to be Shaheed [martyrs], and those who resigned called themselves Ghazi [warriors]. (Iqbal 2006: 224)

Justice Iqbal's speech highlights the reputation crisis faced by judges who had chosen to serve under Zia's PCO, while judges who did not serve under Zia became heroes in the bar. This legitimacy crisis faced by judges helps explain the judiciary's approach after the resumption of constitutional democracy. The decisions in the late 1980s – opening up military courts to legal challenges, striking down the martial law ordinance banning political parties and articulating a new socio-economic role – were all significant breakthroughs after the dormancy of the previous few years. Khan (2015) argued that these decisions of the court were spurred by a need to reclaim legitimacy for the courts. This legitimacy was sought from the community of lawyers from which judges emerged, which judges went back to after retirement, and which populated the courtrooms in which these judges worked. The landmark decisions the judiciary took were in line with the growing consensus within the bar that favoured opposition to the military courts during Zia's martial law regime and a broader political and socio-economic role for the judiciary after the regime ended.

Over the course of the 1980s and 1990s, most judges in the high courts and Supreme Court were recruited from the bar populated by urban middle-class lawyers. The upheavals of the late 1960s and 1970s, the authoritarian suppression of the 1980s and the political dissonance and dysfunction of the 1990s all impacted the legal culture within the legal community, and a populist consensus emerged within the bar around independence from, and opposition to, both military and political party elites, who were seen as either repressive or corrupt, and, in either case, unwilling to act in the public interest. Increasingly, lawyers pushed for judges to demonstrate their independence from other state elites, and to intervene in the political and policymaking processes of other state institutions. As the judiciary grew more visible in resolving disputes between state institutions, and the growth of public interest litigation reduced the procedural and jurisdictional restrictions on judicial interventions into political and socio-economic questions, lawyers urged courts to expand their role in governance. In *Khan Attaullah Khan Tareen v. District Magistrate DC Multan*, an advocate petitioned the Lahore High Court to intervene in the issue of the deteriorating condition of the roads. While the court declined to intervene, it stated that 'the technical approach for the case is not the answer, as the problems of citizens are assuming serious proportions'.[102] A prominent activist petitioned the Balochistan High Court to intervene in a deal being struck regarding the selling of gas fields, which the petitioner said went against the 'national interest'.[103] Thus, bar association resolutions, and the growing number of petitions inviting judicial intervention into matters of executive and legislative institutions, signalled the rising enthusiasm in the lawyers' community for a more independent and interventionist judiciary and increasing criticism of judges who were unwilling to confront executive power.

In the late 1990s, the growing role the bar was playing in the affairs of the bench was evident. When a conflict emerged between two groups of judges on the Supreme Court, leaders of the bar associations intervened to mediate the dispute between the two factions and help resolve the issues (Khan 2016). After the *Al-Jehad* decision, the bar began closely monitoring judicial appointments and the

---

[102] *Khan Attaullah Khan Tareen v. District Magistrate, Multan*, 1997 MLD 229 Lahore.
[103] *Abdul Hayee v. Govt of Balochistan*, 1997 PLD 37 Quetta.

conduct of judges.[104] As a Supreme Court judge from the late 1990s explained, 'who is a judge's audience? It is basically first the lawyers, second the media. And then it is the political groupings.'[105]

As the bar grew more mobilized and organized, and the gradual changes within the judiciary drew the judiciary closer to the bar, judges' reputations within the lawyers' community grew increasingly important. As one senior lawyer explained:

> Keeping the lawyer's community happy is very important to a junior judge, it is everything to them. Judges are very vulnerable in that way, they cannot speak for themselves, they have no public outlet, and they need a collegium within the body of lawyers. Yes, the primary control over the judge's career lies with the senior judges but you need to keep your reputation with senior lawyers, because other judges then shun you if the body of lawyers, especially senior lawyers and leading figures in the bar, shun you.[106]

In this environment, judges needed to demonstrate their independence from executive institutions in order to maintain their reputations. Judges would emphasize at least a rhetorical commitment to independence from the executive branch and safeguarding of the public interest. For some, it was sincere, as these were the ideas they were socialized with, as former lawyers influenced by the emerging legal culture in the 1980s and 1990s; for others, it was strategic, in order to enhance their reputation with the lawyers' community for material and non-material reasons.

Once the judiciary reduced the utilitarian interlinkages with the executive institutions, the importance of this new role conception became more evident in the jurisprudence of the judiciary. Judicial pronouncements of independence from civil and military institutions were evident in the *Al-Jihad*, *Mehram Ali* and *Liaquat Hussain* decisions discussed earlier, and these decisions were cheered on by vocal and influential sections of the bar. The courts also initiated *suo moto* proceedings to look into the deteriorating law and order situation in the state, working conditions for school teachers and political

---

[104] 'SC Moved over Non-confirmation of Three LHC Judges', *Dawn*, 16 June 1999; 'A Judge Should Avoid Exposure in Private Functions: Kalanauri', *Nation*, 14 October 1999.
[105] Interview No. J-15, 1 April 2017.
[106] Interview No. L-60, 5 June 2021.

appointments to government bureaucracies, among other issues.[107] Through this public interest litigation, the high courts and Supreme Court were directly intervening in the administration and policymaking of executive institutions, ostensibly to ensure these institutions acted in the interest of the public. This expansion and preservation of jurisdiction was also directed towards the military. Whether it was addressing detentions and torture during security operations or opposing the establishment of parallel military-run judicial systems, the courts were more assertively expanding their jurisdiction towards the latter half of the 1990s.

This is not to say that other audiences did not matter to the judiciary, and that the internal culture of the judiciary can be reduced to a tussle between the military and the bar. Political parties tried to establish interlinkages with the judiciary and influence judicial behaviour as well.[108] However, given the history of longstanding military dominance within the executive branch, and the alignment of many political and bureaucratic elites with the military, including Nawaz Sharif's PML-N, until the late 1990s, the judiciary's utilitarian and normative interlinkages with the military and pro-military elites, and the gradual waning of these interlinkages over time in favour of the bar, have shaped the internal judicial culture more than other political stakeholders.

Justice Wajihuddin, the most junior judge on the Supreme Court in 1999, exemplified the change that had taken place in the judiciary. Justice Wajihuddin had graduated from SM Law College in Karachi, and was a practising lawyer during the 1980s. He was the president of the Karachi Bar Association in 1981, when the Karachi Bar Association was mobilizing in protest against Zia's regime. He became a High Court judge in 1988, and became chief justice of the Sindh High Court, before being elevated to the Supreme Court in 1998. Justice Wajihuddin was a bar leader and practising lawyer during a time when an agenda of political activism was being promoted in the bar. When he became chief justice of the Sindh High Court, this

---

[107] Masood Haider, 'Sajjad Ali Shah Talks to Newsmen: SC to Take Suo Motu Action on Karachi', *Dawn*, 6 July 1997; 'The Judiciary vs Illegal Appointments', *Frontier Post*, 8 October 1996; 'LHC Takes Suo Moto Action on Letter', *Dawn*, 15 February 1999.

[108] As mentioned, the PPP's attempts to appoint loyal judges triggered the Supreme Court's decision to reduce executive discretion in judicial appointments.

150

activism travelled with him, as he conducted the largest number of *suo moto* actions during the 1990s. Justice Wajihuddin's understanding of the judiciary was best exemplified in a speech he gave in 1997, when he said '*suo moto* and public interest litigation initiated by the superior courts are the hall mark of our judicial activism ... And it is the legal community, the lawyers, which ultimately must come to man the judiciary and judicial offices.'[109] For Justice Wajihuddin, a close relationship between the bar and the bench, and an expansive role for the judiciary, were cornerstones of the judicial philosophy he expounded.[110]

The changing approach of the judiciary towards the military can therefore be best explained by a change in legal and policy preferences within the judiciary. Importantly, this transition was only complete by the end of the 1990s, and thus the full impact of this evolution would only be seen in subsequent years after 2000, which is discussed in Chapter 5. However, this evolution of the judiciary is the best explanation for the variation in the judicial behaviour towards the military during this period. As a senior lawyer I spoke to explained:

> Reputation with the bar matters because (1) if you are accepted well with the bar, then your appointment is likely to be less to be controversial. (2) The judges want legitimacy from the bar as well ... for their legacy ... In short, lawyers are the constituency of the judge.[111]

CONCLUSION

To summarize, the judiciary shifted from active collaboration with the military to growing more independent from the military and seeking a more expansive role and wider jurisdiction over the period 1977 to 1999. The military continued to wield considerable influence over the judiciary through much of this period, and sought to control the courts, and the waxing and waning of military power played an important role in explaining the variation in judicial behaviour towards the military. However, my argument is that the changes in the longstanding

---

[109] 'Suo Moto, Public Interest Litigation Hallmark of Judiciary's Activism', *Frontier Post*, 2 September 1997.
[110] Justice Wajihuddin also refused to take oath under the next military dictatorship in 2000.
[111] Interview No. L-42.

institutional interlinkages between the judiciary and other institutions best explain the changes in the legal and policy preferences of the judiciary. As the military's interlinkages with the judiciary diminished, it ceased being a critical audience for the judiciary, while the politically active bar of professional lawyers became an increasingly effective audience impacting both the esteem and, later, the careers of judges. This change in audiences best explains the change in legal and policy preferences within the judiciary, and, as I show in Chapter 5, its impact was fully realized in the judiciary's behaviour towards the military after the turn of the century.

CHAPTER FIVE

THE CONFRONTATIONAL COURT (1999–2017)

The Judiciary Challenges Military and Civilian Power

INTRODUCTION

In this chapter I describe and explain the judiciary's increasing assertiveness towards military and civilian branches of government between 1999 and 2017. The chapter is divided into two sections. The first section discusses the trajectory of judicial–military relations during this period. It is divided into three phases: (1) 1999 to 2005, the early years of General Musharraf's rule when the judiciary remained cautious; (2) 2005 to 2008, when the judiciary and military clashed, leading to the fall of the military regime; and (3) 2008 to 2017, the period of constitutional democratic rule. In each period, I discuss the prevailing political situation, and the judiciary's relationship with the military as demonstrated through its jurisprudence. Through this period, I show that the judiciary adopted a more assertive approach towards the military, beginning with contesting the military's economic prerogatives, and gradually shifting to challenging the military's political agenda and undermining the foundations of the regime, before seeking to take its place alongside the military as the overseer of Pakistan's democratic political order.

In the second section, I explain the judiciary's confrontational approach to the military and civilian centers of power. I argue that, notwithstanding the importance of other factors, the incremental shift in the judiciary towards increased independence from the military and growing institutional interlinkages with the politically active bar of professional lawyers, as described in Chapter 4, reshaped the legal and policy preferences of the judiciary. This change in audience manifested itself in the activist and populist norms and preferences of the judiciary during this period. I use information on judicial appointments and bar association politics, judicial rhetoric on and off the bench, and interviews with judges, lawyers, politicians and journalists to demonstrate how the judiciary developed the legal and policy preferences underlying the judiciary's confrontational approach to both the military and civilian governments.

THE EMERGENCE OF THE ASSERTIVE JUDICIARY

Consolidation of Musharraf's Regime (1999–2005)

On 12 October 1999, the military seized power once more, ending the tumultuous democratic decade. In the year prior to the coup, the military had fallen out with the elected government of Nawaz Sharif. Sharif, in a bid to forestall the coup, forced the chief of army staff, General Pervez Musharraf, into retirement, while he was on a visit to Sri Lanka, and then, in a final act of desperation, sought to divert the plane carrying Musharraf back to Pakistan from landing as scheduled. However, by then it was too late, as the military took over the airport and other key state facilities, and, after his plane landed, Musharraf announced the military takeover. Musharraf followed the template of previous coup d'états, declaring a state of emergency, holding the Constitution in abeyance, sacking the government and suspending the national and provincial assemblies (Shah 2014a). He also issued a new PCO, No. 1 of 1999, as the primary governing instrument of the new regime.

However, Musharraf, perhaps concerned about his international legitimacy in a post-Cold War era where democracy had become a global norm, sought to give his regime a 'softer' and less militaristic image (Levitsky and Way 2010; Shah 2014a; Grewal and Kureshi 2019). Musharraf declared a state of emergency but refused to formally impose martial law and chose the nebulous and corporate title of 'chief executive' as opposed to the more authoritarian title of 'chief martial law administrator' used by previous dictators, stating: 'This is not martial law, only another path towards democracy' (Shah 2014a: 187). Musharraf also kept fundamental rights officially intact and did not ban political parties. There was no blanket press censorship, and he promised to liberalize private television and radio channels.

Musharraf established two key institutions to consolidate his rule. He created a military-dominated National Security Council, which was to advise him on all matters of governance and foreign policy.

The National Security Council was served by a cabinet comprising businessmen and technocrats without connections to political parties. Musharraf also created the National Accountability Bureau (NAB) to reorganize the political order. He made the drive against corruption 'the centerpiece of his rhetoric' and blamed Pakistan's problems over the previous few decades on the corruption of the political class (Shah 2014a). NAB was headed by a military officer and was given a broad mandate to investigate complaints of corruption. Dozens of politicians were fined or put out of action, particularly from the two leading political parties, Bhutto's PPP and Sharif's PML-N (Jaffrelot 2015). However, members of two institutions, the military and the superior judiciary, were exempt from the jurisdiction of NAB, highlighting the selective accountability being practised by the regime.[1] Nawaz Sharif was tried on charges of hijacking and terrorism for his fateful decision to divert the plane bringing Musharraf back to Pakistan, and after an eventful trial, which will be discussed in more detail, he was sent into exile.

After the attacks of 11 September 2001, the Pakistani military became a critical front-line ally in the US-led fight against Al-Qaeda (Shah 2014a). In return for Pakistan's cooperation, coup-related sanctions were lifted and large sums of Western military and economic aid helped bolster the regime. With his political rivals out of the country, an improving economy and good relations with the west, Musharraf's rule was consolidated, and the military planned out a long-term political arrangement with the military at the helm.

In anticipation of the resumption of constitutional rule, Musharraf followed the strategies used by his predecessors. He first ousted the figurehead president and appointed himself president. In April 2002, he held, and predictably won, a controversial referendum that was intended to legitimize his rule for five more years. In August 2002, he introduced a new package of constitutional reforms known as the Legal Framework Order (LFO) to restructure the parliamentary system. Executive power was shifted once more from the elected parliament to the presidency, the role of the National Security Council was formalized and Article 270-AA validated all the actions taken by the regime since it seized power. Having ensured his presidency for five more years and institutionalized the role of the military at the helm of Pakistan's

---

[1] Kamran Khan, 'Military, Judiciary Declared "out of Bound" for NAB,' *News*, 12 December 1999.

constitutional order, Musharraf organized parliamentary elections in October 2002. Since he allowed political parties to run, Musharraf had to ensure that a party aligned with the regime's interests won the election. Musharraf founded the Pakistan Muslim League – Quaid (PML-Q) just before the election: an amalgamation of local notables and politicians who defected from other political parties, primarily the PML-N. The new parliament was sworn in, and the PML-Q, with a comfortable majority, amended the Constitution in line with Musharraf's LFO, thus institutionalizing Musharraf's civilianized military regime.

During Musharraf's regime, the military's imprint on the Pakistani economy grew further. By 2007 the army controlled about 12 per cent of the arable land owned by the state, with this rural land valued at over $11 billion (Siddiqa 2007). The army also acquired highly valued urban real estate, as defence housing societies proliferated and expanded around the country (Siddiqa 2007). Military-run and affiliated companies were given vast funding to expand their activities, and some companies expanded their commercial ventures abroad. Retired military officers took up other roles in private ventures, on the boards of major private companies and in administrative positions in universities (Shah 2014a). Under Zia the country saw the militarization of the bureaucracy, and under Musharraf the country saw the militarization of the private sector economy.

By 2005, Musharraf's military regime was firmly established, as its political opponents had been exiled and Musharraf held both the offices of the president and the chief of army staff, while the military's role at the helm of the state was formalized, and its role in the economy and society expanded.

Judicial–Military Relations under Musharraf's Regime
Initially, when Musharraf took power, the judiciary proceeded cautiously. Supreme Court judges held a meeting two days after the coup and decided to preside the courts and continue business as usual.[2] Article 2 of the PCO maintained that the country would be governed as nearly as possible in accordance with the 1973 Constitution, and allowed the conditional functioning of the courts, as long as the enforcement of the Constitution did not conflict with the PCO.

---

[2] Nasir Iqbal, 'SC Continues Hearing of Cases despite Government's Ouster', *The News*, 14 October 1999.

Chief Justice Saeeduzzaman Siddiqui had met with Musharraf who he claimed had given him an assurance that the judiciary would continue their role under the Constitution and judges would not be expected to swear a new oath under the PCO.[3] Musharraf even ordered judges to take an oath under the original Constitution and before a person nominated under that Constitution.[4] Thus, the regime assured the judiciary that its takeover was only intended to be temporary before a return to constitutional rule.

However, the judiciary could not postpone dealing with questions about the legality of the regime for too long, as two important petitions came before the Court: the arrest and trial of Sharif, and a petition by his party challenging the coup. In a replay of Zia's takeover, the judiciary had to rule on the validity of the military coup, and the criminal guilt of an ousted prime minister. The Court admitted the petition challenging the coup and the PCO in December 1999 and scheduled regular hearings of the case.[5] The Court also issued notices to all the bar associations of the country, and the leading government lawyers in each province, to appear before the courts and give their legal advice in the case.[6] Mere days before the Court began its hearings, Musharraf reneged on his assurance to allow judges to continue in office without taking a new oath. The government announced a new Oath Act, according to which judges were expected to swear an oath to the very PCO that was being challenged in this petition. The text of the Oath of Office order stated:

> Whereas in pursuance of the emergency, and the Provisional Constitutional Order No. 1 of 1999, as amended, the constitution of the Islamic Republic of Pakistan, has been held in abeyance. Whereas Pakistan is to be governed as nearly as may be in accordance with the Constitution and the Chief Executive has and shall be deemed to always have had the power to amend the constitution. ... And whereas to enable the judges of the Superior Courts to discharge their functions, it is necessary that they take oath of their office.[7]

---

[3] Interview L-14, 15 March 2017.
[4] Sajid Zia, '1999 and the Judiciary', Nation, 20 December 1999.
[5] 'PML Urges SC to Undo Military Action', Dawn, 23 November 1999; 'SC Has to Decide against Validity of Army Take-Over', Frontier Post, 17 November 1999.
[6] 'SC Bench to Hear Petitions against Coup', Dawn, 2 December 1999; 'SC Admits Writs against Army Takeover', Dawn, 7 December 1999.
[7] 'Text of Oath of Office (Judges) Order 2000' Dawn, 27 January 2000.

Why did the regime now require an oath from the judges?

Musharraf was concerned that the judiciary would not provide him the broad mandate for altering the constitution and entrenching military rule, as he desired. Therefore, he used the oath to force these judges to accept his new PCO and purge judges who were expected to challenge the regime, as it would be difficult for judges to rule against a constitutional order to which they had sworn an oath.[8] A majority of judges took the oath in order to preserve their careers.[9] Significantly, however, six justices of the Supreme Court, including the chief justice, refused to take the oath and chose to step down. At the High Court level, several judges who the military saw as potential threats were refused the oath, and thus were automatically removed from the judiciary.[10] Several prominent High Court judges were initially reluctant to take the oath, including Justice Jawwad Khawaja of the Lahore High Court and Justice Sardar Raza and Nasir ul Mulk of the Peshawar High Court, but their colleagues convinced them to take the oath so they could stay on the bench.[11] Thus, a majority of judges took the oath to preserve their careers, but the en bloc refusal by Supreme Court judges undermined the credibility and legitimacy the military sought to gain from a favourable verdict from the Court. Musharraf had purged the judiciary of potential challengers and ensured the judiciary would uphold his coup, but the show of defiance by a large group of Supreme Court judges was unprecedented and demonstrated the growing independence of the judiciary from the military.

---

[8] Interview No. J-4, 18 June 2017. A retired judge claimed that the government had been in discussions with Chief Justice Siddiqui about the petition challenging the legality of the regime, and Siddiqui had said: 'Elections should be in 90 days. If you do this we will dismiss all petitions [challenging the coup]. There will be no PCOs. And no amendments to the Constitution which will be restored. But Musharraf said no.'

[9] Ashraf Mumtaz, '89 Superior Court Judges Take Oath under PCO: Two Judges of LHC Stand Retired', *Dawn*, 27 January 2000.

[10] Ashraf Mumtaz, '2 Judges of LHC Stand Retired', *Dawn*, 27 January 2000; Intikhab Amir, 'PHC: 11 Take Oath, 2 Lose Jobs', *Dawn*, 27 January 2000. Justice Rashid Rizvi of the Sindh High Court, for example, was not called for the oath because, among other reasons, 'he was known to go after the Rangers [the military's paramilitary outfit] a lot in court'. Interview No. J-65, 14 March 2017.

[11] 'Judges' Oath-Taking under PCO Eclipses All Events at PHC', *Frontier Post*, 31 January 2000; 'Why the Judges Quit', *Dawn*, 22 January 2000.

In *Zafar Ali Shah* v. *Pervez Musharraf* (2000), the Court granted Musharraf the judicial validation he sought.[12] During the proceedings, the new chief justice, Irshad Hasan Khan, stated that politicians acted as dictators when in power and 'they spoke of rule of law but scandalized the judiciary'.[13] When the counsels challenging the coup argued that the Court had unambiguously buried the doctrine of necessity that had been used to validate previous military coups in *Liaquat Hussain* (1999), Justice Irshad responded that 'science had progressed to an extent that even the dead can be brought to life'.[14] There was hardly any uncertainty that the judiciary would uphold the coup. In April 2000, the Court upheld Musharraf's coup on similar grounds as had been used in the *Nusrat Bhutto* case to uphold Zia's coup. The Court resurrected the doctrine of necessity once more, listing all the transgressions of the previous government and holding that the situation that had arisen did not have a constitutional solution, and necessitated an extra-constitutional intervention. The Court's decision gave Musharraf's regime far-reaching powers, approving Musharraf's seven-point plan for Pakistan, providing him with a generous period of three years before holding elections and even granting him the powers to take whatever legislative actions he deemed necessary to accomplish his aims.

But the Court held that the 1973 Constitution remained the primary legal instrument for the state, and the judiciary maintained its powers of judicial review and enforcement of fundamental rights. The Court went a lot further than the *Nusrat Bhutto* decision in articulating the role for the judiciary in the new regime. It held that the 'judiciary is called upon to enforce the Constitution and safeguard the Fundamental Rights and freedom of individuals' and 'foster appropriate legal and judicial environment where there is peace and security in the society of life, protection of property, and guarantee of essential rights'. Justice Irshad stated that judicial independence is 'conducive to economic growth and social development' and even claimed the Court would overturn any validly passed constitutional amendment which 'could undermine the independence of the judiciary'. Thus,

---

[12] *Syed Zafar Ali Shah* v. *Pervez Musharraf*, 2000 PLD SC 869.
[13] Zabe Azkar Hussain, 'A Comment on CJ's Comment on Doctrine of Necessity', *News*, 13 March 2000.
[14] Zabe Azkar Hussain, 'A Comment on CJ's Comment on Doctrine of Necessity', *The News*, 13 March 2000; 'The Verdict', *Dawn*, 7 April 2000.

even as the Court granted Musharraf the discretion he asked for, it granted itself a far broader role than previous coup-validating judgments had done. The judiciary had moved from an implementer of positive law in *Dosso* (1958), to an enforcer of executive accountability in *Nusrat Bhutto* (1977), to a policymaking institution safeguarding fundamental rights, peace, economic growth and social development in *Zafar Ali Shah* (2000).

The second critical verdict was the trial of Nawaz Sharif. Just as in Bhutto's trial twenty years ago, in the plane-hijacking case the government sought the death penalty from the courts.[15] Sharif's trial was carried out before the same anti-terrorism courts he had created during his regime. Military intelligence officials and members of the Rangers were in regular attendance at the court to monitor the proceedings. Justice Shabbir found their presence disruptive and ordered the officials to leave the courtroom; when they refused to vacate the courtroom, he referred the case to the court of the more senior Justice Jafri.[16] Later, during the proceedings, the court considered imposing a reporting ban when Sharif's defence team gave evidence that led to two of Sharif's leading lawyers stepping down from the case.[17] Most disturbingly, one of Sharif's defence lawyers was assassinated, and his murder caused immense fear in his panel of lawyers.[18] A lawyer involved with the case said, 'during the trial, with Iqbal Raad's assassination, who got the message? This was a pressure tactic, a message to the lawyers and the presiding judges.'[19] After deliberations the court convicted Sharif on all counts, except attempted murder and kidnapping, but, unlike Bhutto, the court spared him the death penalty, sentencing him to life imprisonment instead. The government appealed the decision to the Sindh High Court, asking for the death penalty to be given. The High Court upheld the decision of the lower courts, including the life sentence, and Justice Osmany opined that the sentence should have been reduced to three years.[20]

[15] 'Nawaz's Indictment Again Delayed till 20th', *Frontier Post*, 14 December 1999; 'Nawaz' Speedy Trial Court Comes Back to Haunt Him', *Nation*, 16 November 1999.

[16] Nusrat Amin, 'Intruders in the Court?', *The News*, 23 January 2000;.

[17] Rory McCarthy, 'Sharif Defence Lawyers Quit over Threat of Reporting Ban', *Guardian*, 28 February 2000.

[18] 'Murder of Forgotten PML-N Lawyer Recalled in Supreme Court', *News*, 9 September 2011.

[19] Interview No. L-84, 26 November 2016.

[20] *Muhammad Nawaz Sharif v. State*, PLD 2002 Karachi 152.

These judgments highlight both the similarities and differences between the judicial–military relations during the early years of General Zia and the early years of General Musharraf. After the institutional changes in the judiciary over the past three decades, the institutional interlinkages between the judiciary and military had greatly diminished, and the judiciary was not as loyal or subordinate to the military. The Court provided the military with the mandate to rule and legislate that it demanded, just as it did before, but only after the Court was purged of several of its senior judges, and the Court upheld its power to overturn any legislation that undermined the judiciary. The judiciary also convicted the ousted prime minister, thus eliminating the regime's primary political opponent, but it did not acquiesce to the regime's demand for an execution. One lawyer highlighted the change that had emerged in the court. 'Even after taking the oath, this was not a kangaroo court, they did not give the death sentence. In Nawaz Sharif's appeal, Justice Osmany actually dissents and reduces the sentence. You will not get a judgment between 1981 and 1988 like that.'[21]

Between 1999 and 2002, the judiciary, operating under Musharraf's PCO, remained cautious about challenging the military regime. Just as in the four years under Zia's PCO, the judiciary only reported a limited number of cases (forty-nine) pertaining to military prerogatives during this period and upheld the military's prerogatives in a majority of these cases. A High Court judge from this period explained the predicament of the judiciary: 'During the Musharraf period, you had the burden of the PCO, powers had been drastically curtailed. The high courts were particularly circumscribed.'[22]

The Court's decision-making on Musharraf's controversial referendum and constitutional amendments highlighted the judiciary's caution. The constitutionality of the referendum was challenged before the Supreme Court. Three days before the referendum was held, in short order, the Court rejected the petitions in *Hussain Ahmed v. Pervez Musharraf* (2001) on the grounds that the petitions were premature and dealt with mere hypotheticals since the referendum had not happened and allowed the referendum to proceed.[23] Months later, after the referendum had taken place granting Musharraf an overwhelmingly

---

[21] Interview No. L-94, 18 March 2017.
[22] Interview No. J-2, 25 November 2017.
[23] *Hussain Ahmed v. Pervez Musharraf*, 2002 PLD SC 853.

favourable result, the Court ruled that an appeal to the popular sovereign of Pakistan was a democratic exercise, and upheld its constitutionality. The Court under Chief Justice Shaikh Riaz Ahmed was going out of its way to avoid challenging the regime, waiting to see how the referendum played out and what its political consequences and fallout were, and only deciding once its outcome and impact were clear (Khan 2016). Similarly, in *Watan Party* v. *Chief Executive, President of Pakistan* (2002), where Musharraf's constitutional amendments were challenged, the Court simply sidestepped dealing with the petition by declaring that the petition was non-maintainable as the petitioner was not affected by the amendments and therefore did not have legal standing to file the petition.[24] This Court, like its predecessor in the mid-1980s, chose caution and deference when confronted with Musharraf's political agenda.

Yet the judiciary was more assertive when it came to protecting its own authority and independence. When Musharraf made complaints committees with serving members of the Pakistan army, to hear cases against public officials in the early days of the regime, the Lahore High Court struck them down, declaring these complaints committees to be unconstitutional.[25] Then, 'even at the height of Musharraf's martial law, he could not put any MLAs, and he could not establish military courts, as this was unacceptable to the judges'.[26] Chief Justice Irshad also negotiated with Musharraf to ensure he did not install military courts, as had been done under previous regimes.[27]

Thus, the judiciary was not willing to broker any intrusion into its powers as the key venue for arbitration and dispute resolution or any fragmentation of its authority, and was focused on preserving its institutional interests during this period.[28] The courts conceded to the military's broader political agenda but checked attempts to circumvent the judiciary's authority and independence. Even during the early years of the military regime, when the regime's strength and repression was at its highest, the judiciary was charting a more independent course

---

[24] *Watan Party* v. *Chief Executive, President of Pakistan*, 2003 PLD SC 74.
[25] Interview No. J-50, 16 November 2016.
[26] Interview No. L-94.
[27] Interview No. J-16, 6 June 2017.
[28] We also see a similar resistance to the fragmentation of its authority in *Khan Asfandyar Wali* v. *Federation of Pakistan*, 2001 PLD SC 607.

In November 2002, Musharraf restored the 1973 Constitution, subject to several amendments that shifted the balance of power towards the presidency. The restoration of constitutional rule was partly prompted by the Court's decision in *Zafar Ali Shah*, which had ordered elections in three years, and international pressure for some movement towards democratic rule. But most importantly, the regime was confident that, in the absence of political opposition, this was a promising opportunity to establish a long-term constitutional regime with the military at the helm.

With the return of the judiciary's jurisdiction, the high courts heard more petitions regarding the military's prerogatives. The judiciary remained cautious about challenging the military's primary political prerogatives. In *Pakistan Lawyers Forum* v. *Federation of Pakistan* (2004), the Court heard petitions challenging Musharraf's legislation and constitutional amendments that his loyal parliament had passed, including the 17th Amendment that formalized the transfer of power to the presidency and immunized the regime's past actions from legal challenges, and the 'President to hold another office Act 2004', which allowed Musharraf to hold both the offices of president and chief of army staff.[29] The Court rejected all the petitions and upheld the constitutional amendments and Musharraf's authority to hold two offices. The Court accepted the government's word that the parliamentary elections had been democratic, and, based on this, determined that any constitutional amendments passed by a democratically elected parliament were procedurally valid and therefore could not be subject to judicial scrutiny. The Court stated that '[t]he 17th Amendment is not merely a *proforma* rubber-stamping by parliament of the various constitutional amendments made by General Pervez Musharraf through the LFO. Instead, it can be seen ... that Parliament has independently applied its mind ... and has then reached an independent conclusion.' On the question of whether the president's power to hold two offices violated the parliamentary system and balance of power between the president and the elected parliament, the Court stated that Pakistan was no longer a purely parliamentary system, and therefore there was no reason to consider this concentration of power in the presidency a violation of the parliamentary system. Thus, this case highlighted the judiciary's restrained and deferential approach in cases pertaining to the regime's political authority and legislative actions.

---

[29] *Pakistan Lawyers Forum* v. *Federation of Pakistan*, 2005 PLD SC 719.

TABLE 5.1   Comparison of reported judgments pertaining to the military's economic prerogatives (1988–1999 and 2002–2005)

	1990–1999 (n=127)	2002–2005 (n=44)
Proportion of judgments against the military (%)	38	63

However, with the growth of the military's landed and commercial interests and deeper penetration into the economy, the judiciary issued an increasing number of judgments pertaining to the military's economic prerogatives. As Table 5.1 shows, the judiciary was now more willing to challenge the military's economic prerogatives than during the previous decade, even though the military was directly in control of the political system, making such contestation riskier.

Individual decisions further showcase the judiciary's more assertive approach towards the military's economic prerogatives. The expansion of the military-run Cantonment housing schemes and Defence Housing Authority (DHA) generated petitions challenging the administration and procedures used by military authorities to run these vast housing schemes. During this period, the courts increasingly exercised jurisdiction over the procedures used by the military authorities to manage their vast landed interests and housing schemes. In *Pakistan Defence Officers' Housing Authority Karachi v. Shamim Khan* (2005), the Court determined that it had the jurisdiction to interfere in the DHA's granting and rescinding of plot allotments, to determine if the authorities had followed procedures or acted discriminately.[30] In *Clifton and Defence Traders Welfare Association v. President, Clifton Cantonment Board, Karachi* (2003), the Sindh High Court held that, before authorizing the construction of billboards, the military authorities had to gain the consent of people affected by the billboard construction, as billboards were a public nuisance and authorizing their construction without consent was a violation of fundamental rights.[31] Justice Mushir Alam dismissed the Cantonment's objection that there was a technical bar on the judiciary interfering in the decision of the Cantonment,

---

[30] *Pakistan Defence Officers' Housing Authority v. Shamim Khan*, 2005 PLD SC 792.
[31] *Clifton and Defence Traders' Welfare Association v. President, Clifton Cantonment Board, Karachi*, 2003 PLD Karachi 495.

stating that 'courts as sanctuaries of justice are not to be persuaded by technicalities', and must 'act in the aid of justice and adopt such interpretations that may serve the cause of justice'. Justice Alam then discussed the challenges of urban governance, and criticized government agencies for not formulating a policy on advertisements, stating that it is 'anomalous that various civic agencies operate in this city, and all are oblivious of their responsibiliti(es)'. He then proceeded to provide guidelines for affixing advertisement hoardings. In this judgment we see the contours of the 'public interest' approach the high courts would increasingly take in the coming years: a prioritization of 'just' outcomes over adherence to technical constraints, a critique of governance by executive institutions that morally merits judicial intervention and guidelines for executive institutions for formulating policy in the interest of the public.

The increased scrutiny of the military's commercial interests by the high courts was in line with an increased focus on socio-economic litigation and human rights issues, and an expansion of its jurisdiction to deal with such issues.[32] Public interest litigation referred to the idea that if a matter of significant public importance arose, and it related to the enforcement of fundamental rights, procedural restrictions should not impede the hearing of these cases.

Under Article 184(3) of the Constitution, the Supreme Court could also directly exercise jurisdiction to tackle cases of 'public interest' pertaining to fundamental rights. Siddiqi (2015) writes that before 2002, the Court accepted only a few constitutional petitions under Article 184(3), but this number went up from eleven in 2001 to forty-two in 2002, and then fifty-eight in 2003. Ghias (2010) explains that there was a rapid pace of neoliberal economic growth under Musharraf, particularly after the surge in foreign direct investment since 2001, and aggressive liberalization policies were pursued by Musharraf's prime minister, Shaukat Aziz. In this period of rapid growth, new governance challenges emerged, and the focus of public interest litigation was to protect populations negatively affected by the economic changes. The judiciary expanded its role by managing the socio-economic fallout of

---

[32] Other cases checking the prerogatives and autonomy of Cantonment and DHA authorities during this period included *Shahid Aleem* v. *Pakistan Defence Officers' Housing Authority*, 2005 CLC 1624, *Yasmeen* v. *Beach Developers* 2003 YLR 1109 and *Rabia City, Residents Welfare Association* v. *Cantonment Board, Faisal Cantt.*, 2003 MLD 627.

the liberalization process, which brought the military's economic interests and the rights of those affected by the military's economic operations and activities under increasing judicial scrutiny.

Thus, two trends were clearly apparent. On the one hand, the judiciary did not contest the military regime's political agenda, authority and governance structure, showing cautious deference and instead blaming the political class for the failures that brought about the need for the military regime and its legislative overhaul of the parliamentary system (Khan 2015). On the other hand, the judiciary emphatically protected its own jurisdiction and authority, and then asserted and expanded its role in intervening on questions of socio-economic justice, expanding its jurisdiction over the military's economic prerogatives. Even in the face of a powerful military regime, the courts continued to act cautiously upon the legal and policy preferences that had started to take root in the judiciary during the 1990s: protecting the independence and authority of courts from military intervention, and expanding the judiciary's role in socio-economic issues, increasingly contesting the military's prerogatives on these questions.

The Military and the Judiciary Clash (2005–2008)

On 29 June 2005, Chief Justice Siddiqui retired and the next seniormost judge, Justice Iftikhar Chaudhry, was appointed chief justice.[33] Justice Chaudhry was promoted to the Supreme Court when he took the oath in 2000, and he was a member of the bench for several important judgments that upheld the regime's authority and political agenda. Thus, the military did not anticipate any difficulties with a chief justice who was considered to be a Musharraf loyalist (Khan 2015). It was hard to imagine that within two years he would play a pivotal role in bringing about the downfall of the military regime.

Between 2005 and 2006, some ruptures started appearing in the steadiness of Musharraf's regime, with a rise in Islamist terrorism spreading from Pakistan's troubled tribal areas, a growing separatist insurgency in Balochistan and increased political opposition from the religious right. However, Musharraf retained a comfortable majority in parliament, managed to keep the alliance of religious parties under control and maintained close relations with the United States, all while

---

[33] Since the key political events during this period involve the judiciary, I do not separate the discussion of the general political environment from the discussion of the role of the judiciary during the period 2005–2008.

his political opponents remained in exile. Therefore, the regime did not foresee any real political threat (Jaffrelot 2015).

Thus, there was no clear political opening or fragmenting of political authority that enabled the judiciary to assert itself and confront the military. Instead, during this period the institutional preferences that had developed over the previous two decades manifested themselves in a jurisprudential approach that strongly favoured independence from the military and an expanded, visible role for the judiciary, which claimed to represent the public interest against other power centres, including the military. Given the reduced interlinkages between the judiciary and the military, the judiciary was unlikely to accept a subordinate role to the military regime.

Under Chief Justice Chaudhry, the most significant change taking place was the explosive growth in public interest litigation. One of the first steps that the Supreme Court took up was to reactivate the Human Rights Cell of the Court to reduce the backlog of human rights cases and other public interest litigation cases (Khan 2015; Siddiqi 2015). The Human Rights Cell received numerous complaints about human rights violations and converted these into formal human rights petitions. The Court also took up an increasing number of cases *suo moto*, if it determined that an issue was one of significant public importance and raised the question of the enforcement of fundamental rights. Between 2002 and 2004, the Court only took *suo moto* action in fourteen cases, but this went up to fifteen *suo moto* cases in 2005 alone (Siddiqi 2015). Similarly, the number of human rights cases before the Court went up from zero in 2005 to eighty in 2006.

The initial focus of the public interest litigation under Chaudhry involved regulating the process of economic liberalization by intervening in issues such as unsafe high-rise construction, questionable land acquisitions and zoning of prime real estate, regulation of price controls that effected the prices of basic commodities and transparency in the privatization of state enterprises (Ghias 2010). The literature on this period tends to focus exclusively on Chief Justice Chaudhry's public interest jurisprudence and describes this as his carefully crafted and path-breaking strategy to judicialize governance and build legitimacy for the Supreme Court (Ghias 2010; Khan 2015). Undoubtedly, Chaudhry was responsible for the rapid surge in public interest litigation and a new phase of judicial activism by the Supreme Court, but, as the discussion of the period from 2002 to 2005 shows, the high courts were already engaging with the regulatory challenges posed by the new liberalizing economy. This expansive role for the judiciary was not pioneered by Justice Chaudhry but was percolating upwards from the high courts before being adopted by the Chaudhry court.

However, under Chaudhry, what was unprecedented was his interference in the security prerogatives of the military regime. During the war on terror that the military and intelligence agencies had been fighting since 2001, a growing number of people had been reported missing who had allegedly been detained in undisclosed locations as a part of counter-terrorism activities. These enforced disappearances were reported by newspapers and human rights groups. In December 2005, after noting a newspaper article about the enforced disappearances, the Court took *suo moto* action and directed the government to either produce the detainees or provide information about their whereabouts.[34] The *suo moto* intervention invited a flood of petitions, and the Court was now intervening in the fallout from military operations. The Supreme Court was not the only court intervening in military court cases. The Sindh High Court followed the Court's lead, and in *Abdullah Baloch* v. *Federation of Pakistan* and *Naz Bibi* v. *SHO*, the court exercised jurisdiction over enforced disappearances, and asked for the production of disappeared detainees.[35]

The missing persons cases also highlighted a new aspect of jurisprudence under Chaudhry. The Court started taking *suo moto* notice of issues based on newspaper articles. If a news item struck a chord with an individual judge, the chief justice could directly convert it into a petition. Khan (2015) explains that this created a feedback loop between the Supreme Court and the media: as the newspapers and electronic media reported on an important policy failure or human rights issue, the court took notice of it, and the media outlets publicized the court's actions. With the passage of time, as the number of *suo moto* cases increased rapidly, the courts became media favourites, picking up issues that had been the focus of media coverage. The Court developed an unprecedented level of visibility. The *suo moto* power was a potent tool in the hands of the chief justice, as there were no prescribed standards or criteria for determining if an issue was worthy of *suo moto* action, and it was entirely at the discretion of the chief justice if he wanted to intervene, making it easy for him to respond to popular sentiments and issues that would maximize the visibility, popularity and

---

[34] Reema Omer, 'Justice for the 'Disappeared'', The News, 29 July 2013.
[35] *Abdullah Baloch* v. *Federation of Pakistan*, 2006 PLD Karachi 584; *Naz Bibi* v. *SHO*, 2006 PCrLJ 1447.

impact of the courts.[36] Bar associations lauded and celebrated the judiciary's increased interventions in a wide range of governance issues, and scrutiny of policies and actions undertaken by the military regime.

While initially the judiciary's renewed activism was focused on low-level governance problems that did not directly challenge the military's core interests, this began to change as the judiciary grew more ambitious in challenging the military, starting with the missing persons cases. The turning point came when the Court stalled the privatization of Pakistan's largest state-owned steel mill through its public interest litigation in *Watan Party v. Federation of Pakistan* (2006).[37] While this case did not deal directly with the military's prerogatives, this privatization was a cornerstone of Musharraf's economic agenda. The petition before the Court claimed that the steel mill's assets were sold for a price lower than their value, and asked the Court to review the privatization process. A nine-member bench of the Court asserted it had jurisdiction to intervene in the privatization process, claiming '[n]ormally, this Court will not scrutinize the policy decisions or to substitute its own opinion in such matters ... However, in this case, we are seized not with a policy centric issue as such but with the legality, reasonableness and transparency of the process of privatization of the project.' This became the method through which the Court turned policy issues into justiciable questions, by framing bad policy as a problem created by unreasonable or non-transparent processes, thus constituting a violation of fundamental rights. The proceedings of the case shed light on the concerns and priorities of the judges. Justice Chaudhry observed that although the court does not formulate policies, it had a mandate to 'adjudicate as to whether the privatization policies were in the national interest ... or not'.[38] As Justice Chaudhry articulated the court's policymaking priorities, Justice Buttar voiced the Court's policy preferences, stating that 'entities having strategic importance cannot be sold to foreign investors, and privatization of state-owned strategic entities is against the universal law'.[39] The remarks of the judges during the proceedings showed that they had little concern for legal requirements, procedure or precedent, and the restraints these placed upon the

---

[36] 'SC Stresses Need to Check Abuse of Power', *News*, 4 December 2006; 'Iftikhar Known for Taking Suo Moto Notice', *The News*, 10 March 2007.
[37] *Watan Party v. Federation of Pakistan*, 2006 PLD SC 697.
[38] 'SC Questions Privatisation of Strategic Entities', *News*, 1 June 2006.
[39] Ibid.

judiciary's ability to intervene in policymaking, as the Court articulated a broader mandate to determine whether policies were being made in the national interest and referred to universal principles rather than statutory law.

As one senior lawyer, who was highly critical of the judgment, opined: 'Any objectivity and established legal principles were sacrificed because of Chaudhry's sense of "justice".'[40] In its judgment, the Court determined that the procedure through which the government had determined the sale value of steel mill assets was 'unreasonable', and 'betrayed disregard of relevant material' for arriving at a fair price. Therefore, the Court overruled the sale of the steel mills, holding that the government had 'violated its fiduciary responsibility to its citizens' and the Court had to 'rectify the wrong when assets of the nation were at stake'. The Court was therefore willing to substitute its assessment for the government's estimation of a fair price for the selling of economic assets, in service of its conception of the 'national interest'.

The steel mills decision had significant repercussions on the relationship between the judiciary and the military. One lawyer explained that: 'The first real opposition of the judiciary to the military came in 2006. They would not tolerate the Steel Mills privatization. This sent a signal that the court intended to be disruptive.'[41]

In 2007, the terms of both the president and the parliament were expected to expire, creating the possibility of legal challenges to (1) Musharraf's re-election as president, (2) his possible postponement of the parliamentary elections and (3) his authority to remain both president and chief of army staff. Musharraf was less willing to tolerate a potentially unreliable judiciary that could not be expected to guarantee the regime's political stability.

On 8 March 2007, a full bench of the Supreme Court issued notice to the government regarding the recovery of people who had been missing for many months after being detained by intelligence agencies.[42] The following day, Musharraf summoned Justice Chaudhry for a meeting in the military headquarters. Musharraf informed Chaudhry of a series of complaints against him, including charges of corruption and nepotism, and Musharraf asked him to resign from his position; however, Justice

---

[40] Interview L-22, 16 April 2017.
[41] Interview L-62, 26 May 2017.
[42] '199 Persons Still Missing, SC Told', *News*, 9 March 2007.

Chaudhry refused to resign, even after being pressured by military intelligence (Khan 2016). Musharraf sent a presidential reference against Chaudhry to the Supreme Judicial Council, the superior judiciary's internal disciplinary body, levelling a series of allegations against him, including nepotism, abuse of power and issuance of government resources.[43] Video and images of Musharraf ordering a defiant Chaudhry to resign, and later of security officials forcing Chaudhry into a police car, spread across the media and became the catalyst for a backlash against Musharraf's regime (Ghias 2010).

The military regime's treatment of Chaudhry and his refusal to resign brought the entire lawyer's community of the country together in a movement that came to be known as the Lawyers' Movement.[44] The movement began with lawyers protesting in the high courts and boycotting court proceedings. The government responded to the lawyers' protests with heavy-handed tactics, attacking and injuring protesting lawyers in the courtrooms. Images of the black-coated lawyers protesting and braving bleeding wounds captured the headlines week after week (Aziz 2012; Khan 2015). Business in courts around the country came to a standstill.[45] Journalists swooned over the defiance of the lawyers, reporting on the unprecedented and 'unshakeable solidary of the lawyers in raising the banner of the independence of the judiciary and the rule of law'.[46] Lawyers who aligned with the executive or did not throw their full weight behind the movement were thrown out of the bars and the bar councils cancelled their licence.[47] Ahsan Bhoon, the president of the Lahore High Court Bar Association, and a known supporter of the regime, 'came under immense pressure to change his stance and support Iftikhar Chaudhry'.[48] With regular rallies, protest events and boycotts of the courts, the lawyers kept the momentum going for several months. The leaders of the Lawyers' Movement, Muneer Malik, Aitzaz Ahsan Ali Ahmed Kurd and Hamid Khan, turned Iftikhar

---

[43] 'Iftikhar Ceases to Be Chief Justice', *The News*, 10 March 2007.
[44] It also created schisms in Musharraf's own political coalition, as leaders of his party, the PML-Q did not think the confrontation with the judiciary was prudent, and tried to distance themselves from the decision. Interview No. P-2, 7 February 2021.
[45] 'Lawyers to Boycott Courts Today', *The News*, 12 March 2007; Muhammad Faisal Ali, 'Lawyers' Protests Turn Lahore into Gridlock', *Dawn*, 13 March 2007.
[46] Imtiaz Alam, 'The Bar at War', *News*, 20 March 2007.
[47] Ibid.
[48] Interview L-90, 25 January 2017.

Chaudhry into a political campaigner, having him speak to large public rallies of lawyers and supporters around the country (Khan 2019). When he arrived in major cities, such as Lahore, tens of thousands came to watch him and welcome him (Malik 2008).[49]

The Lawyers' Movement had turned the dismissal of the chief justice into a massive public controversy that dominated the headlines for months. In this environment, the movement leaders were able to ensure that the reference before the Supreme Judicial Council, which met and deliberated in private, was shifted to the Supreme Court, making it a public court hearing.[50] In June 2007, the Court began its hearings on the presidential reference against Chaudhry. This was a high-stakes case in which the military took an active interest. The Court banned all unauthorized personnel, including military intelligence, from entering the court and ordered the removal of all bugging decides from the courts and judges' homes (Khan 2016). The judges ruled in favour of reinstating Justice Chaudhry. Justice Ramday, who presided over the bench, announced the decision to widespread celebration within the legal community.[51]

The judgment restoring Chaudhry clearly articulated the Court's new role conception. The Court, in self-assured language, held that '[i]n a system where the people had opted to be governed by a written and federal constitution ... the judiciary was obliged to act as the administrator of the public will'.[52] Justice Ramday defended the interventionist approach the Court adopted under Justice Chaudhry, saying the Court had to defend the rights of the people 'against any violations and encroachments' which included the duty of 'guarding public property and the public exchequer'. He explained that the judiciary overruled the actions and policies of the government because 'it stood commanded by the people through the Constitution framed by them to preserve it'. In short, the Constitution was the manifestation of the will of the people, and the Court was upholding the 'people's will'. In his concurring opinion, Justice Ijaz Ahmed said, '[t]he time has come to put the nation on a right path and this can be done by following the character of the Founder of Pakistan so as to strengthen the country

---

[49] 'Massive Show of Support for CJ', *Dawn*, 6 May 2007.
[50] The Supreme Judicial Council was the disciplinary body of the judiciary and comprised senior judges of the Supreme Court and high courts.
[51] 'Verdict Termed Victory for Nation', *Dawn*, 21 July 2007.
[52] Mr. *Justice Iftikhar Muhammad Chaudhry* v. *President of Pakistan*, 2007 PLD SC 578.

and to remove all excessive and colourable exercise of power in each and every sphere of government'. In this landmark judgment the Court had overturned the actions of the military dictator, upheld its independence with the support of the agitation by the lawyers and articulated a broad mission for the judiciary to save and transform the country.

Musharraf's actions against the chief justice had backfired, triggering a mass movement led by the lawyers and greatly diminishing the regime's popularity and stability. Simultaneously the regime was also rocked by a surge in terrorist activity during the summer, including a bloody confrontation between the military and a militant mosque based in the capital city Islamabad, which left many dead and the regime facing the anger of the religious right. Amid all these crises, the bar associations and the judiciary did not let up in challenging Musharraf. Backed by political parties and civil society, the bar associations now argued that the movement was moving beyond restoring the chief justice to a broader agenda of restoring constitutional democratic rule to Pakistan (Malik 2008; Shafqat 2017).[53] The exiled leaders of the leading political parties, former prime ministers Benazir Bhutto and Nawaz Sharif, were arranging to return back to Pakistan to prepare for the expected elections.

Amid all this political turmoil, the judiciary grew even more assertive. Between August and November 2007, the Supreme Court dominated the headlines daily, as the judges dealt with a range of petitions that struck at the core interests of the military regime.[54] First, the Court overruled Musharraf's deal to keep Nawaz Sharif exiled abroad, allowing Sharif to return to the country.[55] Second, the Court took up petitions challenging the National Reconciliation Ordinance (NRO), a US-brokered deal between Musharraf and Bhutto's PPP under which corruption charges against dozens of political leaders and bureaucrats would be lifted, allowing these leaders to return back to Pakistan and participate in elections on the condition that they accepted that Musharraf remained president. Third, the Court ordered the government to open the militant mosque (Lal Masjid) that had been besieged by the government and pay compensation to all those who died during

---

[53] 'SCBA Pledges to Start Pro-democracy Drive', *Dawn*, 25 July 2007.
[54] 'Even Detractors Beginning to Admire Iftikhar Chaudhry', *Dawn*, 21 July 2007.
[55] 'SC Summons Senior Officials in Nawaz Case', *The News*, 18 October 2007; 'Nawaz Can Come Back Anytime: SC', *The News*, 31 October 2007.

the military operation against the mosque.[56] Fourth, the Court resumed proceedings of missing persons and declared that there was 'irrefutable proof the missing persons are being detained by the military's secret agencies' and ordered their release by 13 November 2007.[57] Most importantly, in October 2007, all eyes were set on the Court as it heard petitions challenging the candidacy of Musharraf in the presidential elections, particularly while he still remained chief of army staff. The judiciary decided to allow Musharraf to run for president but barred the Election Commission from announcing official notification of the results until it had finally disposed the petitions challenging his candidacy.[58] By 20 October 2007, the political system was at a standstill and parliament did not meet, as it awaited the Court's word.[59] The offices of judges were bugged and members of military intelligence visited judges to offer them deals and pressure them to rule in Musharraf's favour.[60]

Anticipating that the Court would rule against Musharraf's candidacy, the regime decided to pre-empt this by taking drastic action. On 3 November 2007, a state of emergency was declared and the Constitution was suspended once more. Lawyers and activists around the country were arrested and detained, and curbs were placed on the media. A new PCO was announced, and judges were once more asked to take a new oath under the new PCO. This time an overwhelming majority of judges in the high courts and Supreme Court refused to take the oath. In the Supreme Court, only four out of seventeen judges agreed to take the oath. In the Sindh High Court, only four out of twenty-eight judges took the oath. In the Lahore High Court, only thirteen out of thirty-one judges took the oath. In the Peshawar High Court, ten out of sixteen judges took the oath. Only in the Balochistan High Court did all five judges take the oath. The result was that most judges were removed from the superior judiciary after

[56] 'SC Orders Lal Masjid Re-opening', *News*, 3 October 2007.
[57] 'Agencies Holding Missing Persons: CJ', *News*, 30 October 2007.
[58] 'SC Resumes Hearing in Pleas against Musharraf Today', *The News*, 17 October 2007.
[59] 'Verdict in Musharraf Case Likely in 10–12 Days: SC', *The News*, 19 October 2007; 'Musharraf Not Eligible to Contest: Justice Falak Sher', *The News*, 4 October 2007; 'Next 48 Hours Crucial as Fear Grips Country', *The News*, 1 November 2007; 'SC Verdict: Govt Mulls Options', *News*, 25 October 2007; 'Chief Justice, SC Judges Still Being Shadowed', *The News*, 3 November 2007.
[60] Interview J-75, 23 November 2016.

refusing to take the oath.[61] The regime scrambled to appoint and promote new judges who were willing to take the oath, and members of the judiciary under the new chief justice, Abdul Hameed Dogar, were known, derogatorily, as the PCO judges.

Musharraf was then re-elected president while still in uniform. The Court of the PCO judges upheld the new PCO and Musharraf's emergency declaration.[62] However, the regime did not last long. Agitation on the streets grew, as lawyers, civil society activists and political parties resisted curfews and arrests and continued to pour out onto the streets calling for a return to democratic rule. Lawyers refused to attend the courts of the PCO judges, and most legal activity remained at a standstill.[63] Musharraf lifted the state of emergency after six weeks, after issuing a series of decrees to ensure the regime's actions in November would not be legally challenged. In December 2007, Benazir Bhutto, the leader of the PPP and the country's most prominent political leader, who had returned to Pakistan in October, was assassinated. Her assassination proved to be the final blow to the regime. In February 2008, elections were held, and her party, now led by her husband Asif Zardari, swept to victory, and the former Prime Minister Nawaz Sharif's PML-N came in second, while Musharraf's own party, the PML-Q, was wiped out. Musharraf remained president for a few months, but as the new parliament prepared grounds to impeach him, he decided to avoid the ignominy of impeachment and resigned, bringing an end to his regime. Thus, Musharraf, who's regime seemed so stable a year earlier, was forced out of power. His downfall was not triggered by his political rivals, but by his high-handedness with an activist judiciary that had established its independence and relevance, encouraged and supported by an organized and independent bar.

Even with the resumption of democracy, however, the judicial crisis remained unresolved. The judiciary was now populated by Musharraf's PCO judges, and the judges appointed by the PPP. The PPP's leadership had returned to Pakistan under the NRO that had removed corruption

---

[61] 'Majority of Judges Refuse to Take Oath under New PCO', News, 4 November 2007; 'Provisional Constitutional Order', Dawn, 4 November 2007; 'PCO and Its Victim Judges', Dawn, 7 January 2008.

[62] Tikka Iqbal Muhammad Khan v. Federation of Pakistan, 2008 PLD SC 178.

[63] 'No Lawyer Appears before PCO Judges in Pindi', Daily News, 13 November 2007; Syed Faisal Shakeel, 'Martial Law in Garb of Emergency: Bar', Dawn, 11 November 2007; '340 Lawyers Sent on Judicial Remand', Nation, 7 November 2007; 'LHCBA Members Enforce Boycott of PCO Judges', Dawn, 12 February 2008.

charges and convictions against much of its leadership.[64] Justice Chaudhry had already accepted petitions challenging the NRO while he was still chief justice, and if he was reinstated the government faced the possibility that the judiciary would overrule the NRO. Further, the military had ostensibly returned to the barracks but still remained engaged in fighting the war on terror and would have preferred not having activist judges intervening in these security operations.

The PPP government allowed the PCO judges to remain, expanded the number of judges in the high courts and Supreme Court and incrementally reinducted the judges who did not take the oath back to the benches, but refused to reinstate Justice Chaudhry himself.[65] The bar associations continued their agitation, demanding that Justice Chaudhry be reinstated, disrupting court proceedings, locking courts and protesting in the streets.[66] By March 2009, the bar associations in an alliance with the leading opposition party, the PML-N, organized a Long March from Lahore to Islamabad to demand the reinstatement of Justice Chaudhry.[67] Under pressure, the PPP government conceded, and agreed to reinstate Chief Justice Chaudhry. By March 2009, nearly all the judges who had not taken Musharraf's second oath, and who were still below retirement age, had returned to the courts, under Chief Justice Chaudhry.

In the short period between 2005 and 2009, the judiciary engaged in high-risk activism, challenging the military regime on its core interests and prerogatives. As the cases discussed here indicate, the judiciary was intervening in all matters of state and justifying this expansion on the grounds of representing the public interest, and this new role placed it at odds with the military regime. A majority of judges were willing to lose their jobs and their authority to promote this agenda, indicating how deeply the new activist norms had been entrenched in the judiciary. The mobilized support provided by the bar associations for the judiciary's activism highlighted the close synergy that had developed

---

[64] This had included the late Benazir Bhutto and her husband, Asif Zardari, who was now the president.

[65] Nasir Iqbal, 'Sharif's Candidature Case: PCO Judges' Position Questioned', *Dawn*, 16 January 2009.

[66] 'PCO Judges to Be Punished', *Dawn*, 26 March 2008; 'Lawyers Turn Their Back on Courts', *Dawn*, 19 September 2008; 'Long March if Judges Not Reinstated: Aitzaz', *Dawn*, 4 April 2008; 'Lawyers Have Power to Uproot PPP Govt: Bar', *Nation*, 24 September 2008.

[67] '"N" to Fully Support "Long March"', *Nation*, 26 February 2009.

between the two institutions. Just as the bar associations had chided the judges when they collaborated with Musharraf's regime, the bar associations mobilized in support of the judges when they challenged the regime.

The New Democracy and the Restored Judiciary (2009–2017)

During the new democratic dispensation, the military carefully managed its withdrawal from power to ensure it could protect its core interests and continue to more covertly involve itself in the politics of the state. Shah (2014b) writes that the military maintained its internal and legal autonomy, control of military budgets, autonomy in relations with the executive and legislature, and control over foreign policy, defence policy and intelligence.

The country lurched from crisis to crisis during this period, ensuring the military remained in a central policymaking role. The primary crisis was the threat of Islamist terrorism and the military-led war on terror. By 2008, large swathes of the country's North-West Frontier Province came under de facto control of the religious militants of the Taliban, and cities around the country faced a relentless stream of terrorist attacks (Abbas 2008). Perhaps the most decisive event was the Taliban's brutal attack on an Army Public School in the city of Peshawar in 2014, in which over a hundred children were killed.[68] The military had already launched several operations against the militants, but after the attack on the school, an operation of unprecedented scope and size was launched. The military demanded more powers and autonomy to carry out the operation, and the legislature readily granted it these powers. This included expanded discretion in detention powers and the use of force, military-run committees determining security policies in the different provinces and the expansion of the jurisdiction of military courts to include those accused of religion-based terrorism.[69] Thus, in the fight against terrorism the military gained powers it had not even been given during Musharraf's dictatorship, including the creation of a parallel judicial system unseen since Zia's era.

Beyond the war against the Taliban, Karachi also witnessed a surge in violence. The war against the Taliban in the north sent a flood of

---

[68] Ismail Khan, 'Taliban Massacre Schoolchildren: Principal among 141 Dead in Attack on Army Public School, Peshawar', *Dawn*, 17 December 2014.

[69] Owen Bennett-Jones, 'Does the Military Still Control Pakistan?', BBC, 28 September 2015, www.bbc.co.uk/news/world-asia-34333470.

refugees into Karachi, triggering ethnic tensions between the different ethnic groups in the city. The Taliban also increased their presence in the city, adding to the mix of violence and insecurity. The military was given powers to take the lead in bringing peace to the city. The military's paramilitary organization, the Rangers, took the lead in policing responsibilities in the city, sharing and often superseding the authority of the civilian police and provincial government (Waseem 2021).[70] Thus, during this period of violence and insecurity, the military was deeply embedded in internal policing around the country.

In 2010, the country also faced the biggest natural disaster in its recent history, with a flood that spread across much of the provinces of Punjab and Sindh, leaving millions homeless. Once again, the military played a central role in carrying out disaster relief, assuming civilian roles that civilian institutions simply did not have the organizational and administrative capacity to undertake.[71] Thus, through a series of crises the military maintained a wide degree of autonomy and assumed a range of roles typically managed by civilian institutions.

The civilian political parties largely acquiesced to military autonomy and authority over defence and foreign policy, but there was still contestation between the two sides over the extent of the military's authority and autonomy. The PPP government tried to bring the military intelligence service, the ISI, under more civilian control in 2008 and create a parliamentary committee on national security to determine rules of engagement and agreements with foreign militaries in 2011. However, the military continued to apply pressure through its political allies and media connections to ensure that such efforts yielded few substantive results, and the military's prerogatives remained largely intact (Shah 2014b).

In 2009, the US government signed a new law that expanded civilian aid and redirected military aid to the Pakistani army through the civilian government, making it conditional on certification that the military was operating under civilian control and keeping out of political and judicial processes (Shah 2014b). This generated tension between the government and the military, as the military had previously benefitted from direct control over military ties with the USA and the military believed that the civilian ambassador to the USA, a

---

[70] 'Rangers' Powers Extended by Another 90 Days', *Dawn*, 12 October 2017.
[71] Saeed Shah, 'Pakistan Floods: Army Steps into Breach as Anger Grows at Zardari', *Guardian*, 8 August 2010.

close aid of the PPP government, had orchestrated this change. The military was not willing to lose this prerogative, and in 2011 a story emerged in the media about an alleged memorandum sent by the Pakistani ambassador to the USA, asking for US help against a military coup in exchange for meeting American demands regarding Pakistan's national security policy. The director-general of the ISI claimed he had verified the story, and soon the military leadership and the political opposition used the scandal that came to be known as 'memo gate' to apply pressure on the government to fire the ambassador and permit the military to retain its control over military assistance. The government fired the ambassador, and the military retained effective control over US military assistance. Thus, during this period, there was considerable contestation between the government and the military over military prerogatives, but the military adapted its methods for preserving prerogatives and largely succeeded.

At the same time, even as the military maintained its prerogatives, the parties learned some lessons from the 1990s and reduced the levers the military had to intervene in the political process. Under the 18th constitutional Amendment, parliamentary supremacy was restored, the president was turned into a figurehead and the president's powers to dissolve the assemblies were removed.

The PPP government served its entire five-year term from 2008 to 2013, the first civilian government in Pakistani history to do so, and elections were held on schedule. This was in spite of the fact that the military did actively consider ousting the PPP president.[72] And in 2013, Nawaz Sharif, the political leader whom Musharraf ousted in the coup in 1999, returned to power in a landslide victory for his party, the PML-N. Sharif and the military did not see eye to eye on several issues, particularly over the questions of relations with India and trying Musharraf for subverting the Constitution (Shah 2019). Relations between Nawaz Sharif and the military continued to grow strained over the course of his term. In the aftermath of the attacks on the Army Public School, as the military's role in internal policing grew, so did its interest in advancing its role in shaping national policy, further straining relations with Sharif's government. As the military embedded itself within private media, media outlets aligned with the military gave increasing coverage to allegations of corruption that dogged Sharif and his family. In 2014,

---

[72] Declan Walsh, 'Pakistan Army Chief Considered Plan to Oust President', *Guardian*, 30 November 2010.

two opposition parties, Pakistan Tehreek-Insaaf (PTI) and the Pakistan Awami Tehreek organized a sit-in in the centre of the capital city for a hundred days in 2014, to protest against alleged rigging of the 2013 elections by the PML-N. Imran Khan, the leader of the PTI, used his pulpit to excoriate the PML-N and PPP for corruption, gaining widespread media coverage, and there was general recognition that Imran Khan's sit-in had the support of the military (Shah 2019).

Thus, during this period, Pakistan's political parties and military were locked in a tense and volatile relationship, as political parties sought to protect their electoral turf, and establish themselves as independent centres of power, while the military adapted its methods and utilized opportunities to preserve and expand its prerogatives under civilian rule. By 2017, when Nawaz Sharif was famously disqualified from political office, it was clear that civil–military relations had plunged to new depths of antagonism.[73] And, as discussed in the next section, the judiciary played a critical role in shaping the trajectory of this civil–military confrontation.

The Populist Judiciary, the Military and the Civilian Government
In the aftermath of the Lawyers' Movement and the restoration of Justice Chaudhry, the judiciary achieved a level of visibility, authority and popularity that was unprecedented in its history. The judiciary was rewriting its role in the political system, stepping into the domains of the executive and legislature. Petrol prices, sugar prices, private and public sector corruption, the cutting down of trees, land allotments, bureaucratic appointments: all these issues invited *suo moto* interventions by the Supreme Court. Judges summoned public office holders to the court rooms and then rebuked them for not carrying out the Court's orders (Waseem 2012). The restored judiciary had little support for elected governments, and the courts were willing to use all the tools at their disposal to assert their will over the government in all matters of politics and policymaking.[74]

In comparison to the judiciary's relentless focus on the actions of the civilian governments, and routine contestation of executive and legislative authority, there were fewer confrontations between the military and judiciary during this period than between 2005 and 2007, leading

---

[73] Haseeb Bhatti, 'Nawaz Sharif Steps down as PM after SC's Disqualification Verdict', *Dawn*, 28 July 2017.
[74] Anil Kalhan, 'Courting Power', *Herald*, November 2013.

TABLE 5.2 Comparison of reported judgments pertaining to
military prerogatives (1989–1999 and 2009–2015)

	Security prerogatives	Economic prerogatives	Political and policymaking prerogatives
Proportion of decisions contesting the military (1990–1999) (%)	42.5	37.8	44.2
Proportion of decisions contesting the military (2009–2015) (%)	35.9	55.7	76.5

to criticisms that the judiciary served the interests of the military in
constraining the electoral branches and democratic consolidation
(Shah 2014b). However, this does not accurately characterize the
relationship between the two unelected institutions during this period.
As shown in Table 5.2, when we compare the judiciary's reported
judgments towards the military during the two democratic periods
(1988–1999 and 2009–2015) we see that while the judiciary was
slightly more deferential on security prerogatives during this period, it
was more assertive in contesting the military's economic prerogatives
and political and policymaking prerogatives, indicating that the
increased judicial assertiveness towards civilian and military state institutions was a new, durable feature of Pakistan's jurisprudence, and was
not a temporary fixture of the final years of Musharraf's rule or Chief
Justice Chaudhry's leadership.

A closer reading of these decisions further highlights how the judiciary continued to challenge the military. During this period, the courts
made salient judgments challenging the special prerogatives provided
to military-affiliated commercial enterprises. I discuss two cases that
highlight the judiciary's more assertive approach to the military's commercial interests during this period. In *Army Welfare Sugar Mills
Workers Union* v. *Army Welfare Sugar Mills*, the Court overturned a
longstanding precedent upholding a ban on union activities in industrial units run by the Army Welfare Trust.[75] The Court ruled that

---

[75] *Army Welfare Sugar Mills Workers' Union* v. *Army welfare Sugar Mills*, 2009
SCMR 202.

under the Industrial Workers' Ordinance, industrial workers had a right to unionize. In the past, the judiciary had held that the Army Welfare Trust, being an army welfare foundation, had a direct connection to national defence, and therefore was exempt from upholding statutory rights granted under the Industrial Workers' Ordinance. However, the Court now decided that the Army Welfare Trust Sugar Mills did not possess a direct connection to national defence work, and therefore the Industrial Workers' Ordinance applied to the sugar mills, granting workers the right to unionize. The Court narrowed its interpretation of work related to national defence and reduced the scope of this exemption provided to military-affiliated companies.

Another similarly significant judgment was the *Suo Moto Case No. 10 of 2009*, also known as the *Makro-Habib* judgment.[76] In this decision the Court cancelled the lease of land by the Army Welfare Trust to build a shopping centre. The Army Welfare Trust had 'purchased' a large segment of prime real estate from the government for a nominal fee, and then leased the land to a Belgian retail chain to establish a shopping centre on the land.[77] In 2009, the Court received a letter from a civil society activist that was published in the newspapers, urging the Court to look into the matter, as this land was previously used as a playground. The Court converted the letter into a petition, and justified its intervention into this issue of the acquisition and repurposing of land, by saying that this fell within the Court's original jurisdiction, as it pertained to the fundamental right to 'access parks and playgrounds'. One of the members of this civil society organization challenged the acquisition of the land, asking: 'The property was given to the Army Welfare Trust for only Rs. 6,000. Why is the Army Welfare Trust being favoured so much if it is just a regular NGO [non-governmental organization]?'[78] The Army Welfare Trust claimed that it possessed a special relationship with the military, which justified the favourable terms of its land acquisition and opaque nature of the land transfer. But the Supreme Court ruled against the Army

---

[76] *Suo Moto Case No. 10 of 2009 in Re*, 2010 SCMR 885.

[77] At the time General Musharraf was president, and, as chief of army staff, he was also the president of the Army Welfare Trust. Petitioners challenged the lease of land and construction of the shopping centre before the Sindh High Court, but in 2008, a bench of PCO judges ruled in favour of the Army Welfare Trust, allegedly without even providing notification about the hearing to the petitioners. Interview No. L-7, 10 March 2017.

[78] Interview No. L-7.

Welfare Trust, arguing that the lease of land was illegal, as the Army Welfare Trust was a private organization that did not possess a special relationship with the state, and therefore was not permitted any special privileges in the process of land acquisitions. One of the judges who decided this case explained that 'big money was involved in the decision. But these institutions were expected to act in the public interest. They just did not do it.'[79] The Court judgment emphasized the need for '[s]tate functionaries to act in furtherance of the public interest' and said the civil and military offices involved in this deal had not done so. Thus, the Court designated the Army Welfare Trust a private organization exempt form special privileges. The decision drew considerable military interest and concern. The Army Welfare Trust has repeatedly asked the Court to review its decision, and the chief of army staff, General Kayani, issued a statement to the Court that the 'military is beholden to defend each and every square inch of its property'.[80] The military was concerned about the domino effect on its other property acquisitions. Justice Khawaja, who had authored the judgment and challenged military land acquisitions in other cases as well, faced a backlash, 'including death threats and TV programmes against him and his wife'.[81]

These two cases show that judges were less willing to accept the argument that military-run commercial organizations possessed special privileges and were more willing to scrutinize military acquisitions, activities and exemptions than before, even in salient cases where the military was invested in the outcome and tried to influence the court's proceedings.[82] Thus, the judiciary continued to increase its scrutiny of the military's economic interests, challenging and even overturning military land acquisitions and other special privileges previously afforded to the military.

The judiciary was even more assertive on the military's political and policymaking prerogatives. The courts heard a series of petitions against

---

[79] Interview No. J-50.
[80] Interview No. L-7.
[81] Interview No. J-50.
[82] Former judges explained that in disputed land claims, where the ownership claim was made by an organization with connections to the military leadership, the military often sent members of the ISI to the court proceedings. The presence of these intelligence officers was intended to convey a message to the judges of the interest of the military leadership, and thus influence their decision-making. Interview No. J-19; Interview No. J-4, 18 June 2017.

the former military regime, challenging the state of emergency and the issuance of the PCO in November 2007, charging Musharraf with treason for suspending the Constitution and overruling Musharraf's right to stand for subsequent elections.[83] In *Sindh High Court Bar Association* v. *Federation of Pakistan* (2009), the Court ruled that the PCO was illegal and unconstitutional. The judgment was a statement by the judiciary about its past history and its new role and legitimacy.[84] The Court went through a detailed history of the judgments, upholding military usurpations of power on the grounds of the doctrine of necessity before rejecting the doctrine of necessity as a justification for extra-constitutional interventions. The Court stated:

> It is held and declared that the doctrine of necessity ... were not applicable to all or any of the unconstitutional ... actions taken by General Pervez Musharraf on and from 3rd November 2007 until 15th November 2007 ... because they were not taken ... for the welfare of the people. It is further held and declared that the doctrine of necessity ... absolutely has no application to an unconstitutional and illegal assumption of power ... not provided for in the constitution.

The Court's statement revealed the judiciary's guiding priorities and self-conception. The Court wanted to divorce itself from a past of complicity with military rule, and also highlight that, in separating itself from military rule, it was looking out for the welfare of the people. Thus, in this statement both pillars of the judiciary's new role conception were clearly articulated: an opposition to military rule, and a populist mission to uphold the welfare of the people. The Court congratulated itself for being the court that 'for the first time in the history of Pakistan ... instead of accepting or acquiescing in the situation ... acted boldly and independently', and also discussed popular support from the bar associations and from local and global media for the actions of the judiciary, to demonstrate popular legitimacy for the judiciary. After this verdict, Musharraf became liable for treason charges, and his lawyers submitted multiple petitions contesting the maintainability of treason charges against him, but the courts

---

[83] It is noteworthy here that the judiciary did not accept petitions challenging Musharraf's original assumption of power in 1999 or the PCO of 2000, since a majority of judges on the bench had taken oath under the 2000 PCO.

[84] *Sindh High Court Bar Association* v. *Federation of Pakistan*, 2009 PLD SC 879.

repeatedly upheld the treason charges against him and allowed the treason case against him to proceed.[85,86]

Finally, the judgment also aimed to set a red line for judges on collusion with any actors outside the judiciary attempting to undermine the judiciary, by declaring all actions taken by the ousted Chief Justice Dogar since November 2007 would be voided, which included the appointments of all the judges he appointed over that two-year period. The action led to the largest purge in judicial history, as all judges who took the oath, both under Musharraf's PCO and during the first year of PPP's democratic rule, were removed from the Court. This dramatic move served both to underscore the judiciary's position against collusion with the military, and to consolidate the control of Justice Chaudhry and his closest allies over the judiciary.

In 2012, the Court reopened and finally issued a verdict on a petition challenging military interference in elections that had remained undecided since the 1990s. As discussed in Chapter 4, the Court had admitted a petition challenging alleged rigging of the 1990 election by the ISI for hearing in 1994, but did not pursue the case any further.[87] The case was picked up again by the Court in 2007 before Musharraf dismissed Justice Chaudhry. Finally, in 2012, the Court reopened the case and determined that the army and ISI had acted in an unlawful manner, stating that the functions of the military are only to 'defend Pakistan against external aggression of threat of war' and 'act in aid of civil power when called upon to do so'.[88] The judgment held that the former chief of army staff was liable under the Constitution and was required to uphold the Constitution not subvert it. The Court ordered an investigation into the rigging of the elections to charge and try both the conspirators and beneficiaries of the rigging plot. The actual verdict was an unambiguous statement about the limited constitutional role of the military and affirmed the judiciary's stance against political manipulations by the military. As one of the lawyers involved in the case explained:

---

[85] *Pervez Musharraf* v. *Nadeem Ahmed* 2013 SC 585; *Federal Republic of Islamic Republic of Pakistan* v. *Pervez Musharaf*, 2014 PCrLJ 684.

[86] The courts also did not allow Musharraf to stand for subsequent elections. See *Pervez Musharraf* v. *Election Commission of Pakistan* 2013 CLC 1461; *Pervez Musharraf* v. *Appellate Tribunal for General Elections* 2013 PLD Peshawar 105.

[87] The ISI's political cell had allegedly supplied millions of rupees to an alliance of right-wing parties led by Nawaz Sharif to oppose Bhutto's PPP in the 1990 elections.

[88] *Muhammad Asghar Khan* v. *Mirza Aslam Baig, Former Chief of Army Staff*, 2013 PLD SC 1.

From 1996 to 1998, the case was not really going anywhere. The courts were humming and hawing. [Chief Justice] Sajjad Ali Shah ran into his own problems. [Chief Justice] Saeeduzzaman Siddiqui was simply not going into it. The case just hung around. Then in 2012, the Court decided to take on the case ... and now we have a judgment criticizing the role of the ISI. This was not just a private decision, but an institutional indictment.[89]

Judicial criticism of the ISI's political engineering during the proceedings and in the judgment irked the military leadership. General Kayani, in published comments from his meeting with army officers, issued a warning to the Court, advising it to 'pause and examine if it was actually strengthening or weakening institutions'. He warned the Court that 'no individual or institution has the monopoly to decide ... the ultimate national interest'. Justice Chaudhry, in response, held a special full court event, in which he invited the media and held forth on the Supreme Court's achievements; he also made a statement that 'gone are the days when stability and security of the country was defined in terms of missiles and tanks'.[90]

Thus, the judiciary took a clear and unambiguous stance in outlawing the military's political interventions. The judiciary's own repeated interventions in the activities of the civilian and executive legislature, coupled with its stance against military interventions, were part of the judiciary's jurisprudential strategy to carve out its own role as the legitimate intervening authority, co-opting the military's own self-serving anti-corruption rhetoric and using both constitutional and popular support to legitimize itself in this new role as a tutelary power within Pakistan's political system. The consequent back-and-forth demonstrated the willingness of the Court to confront the military leadership when its new role as an intervening authority in the political system was challenged.

As one lawyer explained:

The judiciary sees itself as performing a function so that the army does not. What Iftikhar Chaudhry did was create an environment where the court acted as the political arbiter instead of the military. This was part of the judicialization of politics. The judiciary has grabbed a suprademocratic role from the army. The judiciary's role is not to hold the military

[89] See Interview No. L-62.
[90] Salman Masood, 'Top Pakistani Generals and Judges Trade Barbs', *New York Times*, 5 November 2012, www.nytimes.com/2012/11/06/world/asia/pakistan-generals-and-judges-trade-barbs.html.

186

accountable, but it is to take over some dominance or some space from the military, such as the macro-level anti-corruption agenda.[91]

On questions of the military's security prerogatives, the judiciary remained largely deferential to the military's interests, but the judiciary used these cases as opportunities to expand its own national security role and authority. The Court intervened in the 'memo gate' scandal discussed earlier and appointed its own commission of judges to inquire into the case and then began its own fact-finding proceedings against the former ambassador, summoning him for questioning before the Court.[92] The Court sided with the military in undermining the civilian government's foreign policy objectives and personnel, but in doing so it gave appellate courts the power to conduct investigations and gather evidence and establish its role in the preservation of national security.[93]

Similarly, in light of the growing violence in Karachi, the Supreme Court decided to begin *suo moto* proceedings to inquire into what needed to be done to improve law and order in the city. The chief justice began a series of wide-ranging hearings, turning the court into an inquiry commission in which public officers and stakeholders from the commercial capital were brought before the court to face questions and criticism from the judges for their mismanagement of the city. There was little consideration for precedent and procedure during the proceedings, as one lawyer involved with the proceedings explained: 'Iftikhar Chaudhry was doing whatever he wanted. Whatever came to his mind, that was popular with his following.'[94]

After the hearings, the Court ordered the paramilitary Rangers to take over some policing responsibilities in the city, granted the Rangers the authority and discretion it needed to secure parts of the city that had become violent 'no-go areas' and ordered the Rangers to report to the Court about their progress.[95] The Court empowered the military with internal policing powers, but in doing so it ordered the first ever judiciary-mandated national security operation, and gave itself an oversight role, thus extending its reach into the area of national security. Throughout this period, the judiciary tried to expand its oversight role

---

[91] Interview No. L-36, 23 May 2017.
[92] *Watan Party* v. *Federation of Pakistan*, 2012 SCMR 584.
[93] Ather Naqvi and Farah Zia, 'Leaders of All Kinds Disappeared or Went Quiet', *The News*, 11 March 2012.
[94] Interview No. L-60, 13 April 2017.
[95] Suo Moto Case No. 16 of 2011 along with CMAs PLD 2013 SC443.

in the conduct of national security, establishing special benches to hear cases regarding detentions and enforced disappearances during security operations. Thus, even where the judiciary upheld the military's security prerogatives, it used these decisions as opportunities to begin to 'play a national security role of its own'.[96]

In the Karachi 'Law and Order' judgment, the Court defended its decision to assert jurisdiction over the formulation of security policy in Karachi by citing newspaper articles regarding crime, violence and corruption in the city. The Court determined that this violence was undermining the ability of people to exercise their fundamental rights, chastised the government for its failure to address the problem and thus claimed the Court was compelled to intervene. The Court also authorized a judicial bench to continue to monitor the law and order situation, and to manage the implementation of the Court's orders. This bench would then produce interim orders on the implementation of the Court's judgment, and issue directives to different state authorities regarding their compliance with the Court's directives. The implementation proceedings were open-ended and judges had wide discretion to determine what issues they considered, which officers they summoned and what discussions they had in the courtroom. This routine would become a familiar routine across the Court's *suo moto* interventions into public policy questions, as it would oversee other security and bureaucratic institutions through interim orders and open-ended implementation hearings.

In January 2015, the judiciary confronted the most significant test of its willingness to challenge an expansion of the military's security prerogatives. In January 2015, after the heinous attacks on the Army Public School, the parliament amended the Constitution to establish military courts for trying civilians suspected of terrorist offences, expanding the prerogative of the military's internal judicial system to also try this class of civilians. Several bar associations petitioned the Court, challenging the expanded jurisdiction of military courts through the 21st Amendment. The petitioners argued that this amendment could be struck down because it violated the *basic features* of the Constitution pertaining to fundamental rights and the independence of the judiciary.[97] The petitioner Hamid Khan argued that the

---

[96] Interview No. L-36.

[97] The doctrine of basic structures is a judge-made Indian principle stating that a country's constitution has certain features that cannot be amended by its legislative body. Hence amendments to a constitution must not be in conflict with the basic

extension of the powers of the military courts 'abridged the fundamental right of access to justice; that independent court, independent procedure and right to engage counsel of choice are the essential elements of a fair judicial system, which are denied to those to be tried by the military courts'.[98] The Court therefore could choose between upholding the establishment of special military courts on the grounds that the judiciary could only interpret and uphold the Constitution but not challenge it, or overturning or returning the constitutional amendment on the grounds that the military courts violated the most salient features of the Constitution by denying fundamental rights and granting judicial powers to the executive branch.

The Court's plurality opinion, instead, chose a third option: it held that the 21st Amendment did not violate the most salient features of the constitution, and therefore could be upheld. The Court argued that since the judiciary still maintained limited powers of judicial review over the transfer of cases to military courts and the decisions of military courts, the judiciary held that 'it is difficult to hold that the essential nature of the Salient Features of Fundamental Rights as applicable in the Country has been repealed, abrogated or substantively altered'. Thus, a majority of the Court decided that the Court *did* have the power to overturn constitutional amendments passed by the legislature if they violated the 'basic structure' of the constitution.[99]

This decision showed the Court's delicate balancing act. On the one hand, as one of the judges who upheld the decision explained, the judiciary recognized that the 'people were supportive of' the new military courts.[100] Indeed, the new courts were even popular with large

---

structure of the constitution. The Pakistani judiciary has extensively debated this doctrine and had, until 2015, only partially borrowed it for the Pakistani context.

[98] Whereas military courts are expected to follow the same rules of evidence as civilian courts, in practice these courts were lax on questions of the admission and verification of evidence. In particular, civilian courts typically did not admit prior confessions as evidence given that they could easily be extracted or coerced by security officers behind closed doors. Yet, confessions were frequently admitted by military courts and were often used as dispositive evidence. Further, while defendants were granted access to legal counsel, they were given little choice in the legal counsel they were granted. Thus, military courts were staffed with officers from the military hierarchy with no legal training or regard for rules of evidence, in opaque procedures behind closed doors. Also see Newberg (2016).

[99] *District Bar Association, Rawalpindi and others v. Federation of Pakistan*, PLD 2015 SC 401.

[100] Interview No. J-9, 14 November 2016.

segments of the bar.[101] Another former judge further explained why the courts were willing to tolerate procedural leniency in these cases. He said, 'procedure has a significant place but the endeavour is to save somebody', and this class of accused 'deny nothing, glorify what they have done' and will return to their practices if released, and endanger people once again.[102] There was a presumption of guilt shared by both the military and the judiciary that underlay the exceptional status judges were willing to grant those accused of terrorism. Thus, a plurality of the judiciary shared the military's sentiments about this class of accused and recognized the overwhelming public support for military courts. On the other hand, the judges did not want public support for military courts to lead to a significant reduction in judicial authority. Therefore, they chose to uphold the constitutional amendment, but in a way that advanced the judiciary's broader authority. The Court bestowed itself with the power to determine whether procedurally valid constitutional amendments comported with the Court's interpretation of the basic structure of the constitution, a significant advancement of judicial authority. Hence, the judiciary balanced its interest in expanding its authority with its interest in preserving popular support.

An important caveat here is that the judiciary has not pushed for the implementation of military-related judgments the way it has in cases pertaining to the civilian government. There has been little progress in the investigation ordered in Asghar Khan, and the courts even allowed Musharraf to leave the country while treason proceedings were ongoing. This was especially apparent in security-related cases, including cases of enforced disappearances.

After Musharraf's regime fell, the practice of enforced disappearances persisted, as did the judiciary's interest in placing limits on this practice. In many of these cases the courts would ask for the production of those who had been disappeared, but the military showed little interest in complying. In a strongly worded verdict in 2013, the Court held that armed forces personnel responsible for the enforced disappearances should be dealt with 'strictly in accordance with law'.[103] The civilian

---

[101] Several major leaders of the bar challenged the establishment of military courts both inside the court room, but a bar association leader who brought one of the petitions told me that 'we challenged the military courts, but in reality we were for it'. Interview No. L-14, 5 November 2016.

[102] Interview No. J-33, 21 March 2017.

[103] Human Rights Case no. 29388-K of 2013, in the Matter of, PLD 505 SC 2014.

government was asked to produce all the remaining missing persons, and act against those civil and military officers involved in these enforced disappearances. Justice Khawaja threatened to hold high-ranking functionaries of the government in contempt of court if they did not act against those responsible.[104] He soon became the subject of a malicious campaign questioning his integrity and patriotism. Mysterious banners appeared all along Constitution Avenue, the most securitized road in the capital city Islamabad upon which all the major government buildings were constructed. These banners questioned the patriotism and reputation of Justice Khawaja (Khan 2016). After Justice Khawaja's retirement, the interest of the judiciary in seeing its judgments on missing persons implemented seemed to wane.

The lack of initiative in pursuing implementation indicates the judiciary's reluctance to push the military too far, particularly in security-related cases, but it remains apparent that the judiciary expanded its reach over military prerogatives, subjected (at least some of) its interests and assets to judicial scrutiny and narrowed the military's permissible role in the political system.

However, the judiciary's contestation of military prerogatives did not mean this was a pro-democracy judiciary committed to upholding elected civilian supremacy. Instead, judges actively pursued an agenda of judicial supremacy, taking on the role of the key overseer of Pakistan's political order, and the judges challenged what they saw as the excesses and corruption of Pakistan's other power centres, justified by an apparent interest in ensuring the welfare of the people. This was evident under both Justice Chaudhry and successive chief justices, who used their powers to override and even remove elected leaders. Judicial interventions into electoral, bureaucratic and policymaking processes helped constrain and undermine the elected governments of the time (Waseem 2015). There was an apparent alignment of interests between the military and the superior judiciary in weakening and delegitimizing elected governments, and the tacit support of the military was likely to have further emboldened judicial interventions into elected government.

Under the 18th Amendment, the president's power to dissolve elected assemblies had been removed, but the judiciary's power to oust parliamentarians for not fulfilling vague standards of morality and sagacity, under Articles 62 and 63, remained, and they became vehicles for

---

[104] Reema Omer, 'Produce Missing Persons, or Face Contempt of Court: SC', *Pakistan Today*, 18 March 2014.

the unelected judiciary to manipulate the arrangement of elected power, ostensibly to target and eliminate political corruption. In 2010, the Court overturned the NRO, described earlier in the chapter, reopening corruption cases against political leaders and bureaucrats, including then President Zardari. The judgment was a foregone conclusion, as the Court had made its opposition towards the NRO evident throughout the proceedings. A lawyer who closely followed the case narrated how the Court itself disseminated reports from the 1990s, discussing the alleged corruption of Benazir Bhutto and her husband, President Zardari, in the 1990s, to all those present in the courtroom.[105] Incidents like this revealed that the target of the Court's judgment was President Zardari, and also highlighted the willingness of the Court to bypass judicial conventions in pursuing this target. Justice Chaudhry ordered the PPP Prime Minister Gilani to write a letter to Swiss authorities to reopen corruption cases against his president, and continued to spar with the government over the writing of the letter. In 2012, the Supreme Court convicted Gilani for contempt of court for refusing to write a letter to the Swiss authorities, and then, based on that conviction, ousted the prime minister for violating the morality standards under Article 62 and 63.[106] Several years later, the Court used the same powers to remove a second prime minister, Nawaz Sharif, in 2017, under Article 62, on charges of corruption (this case is discussed in more detail in Chapter 6).

The Court justified these actions against the elected leadership based on a scathing critique of political corruption. In his judgment striking down the NRO, Justice Chaudhry stated that the Constitution represents the 'will of the people', and claimed that the 'constituents' have made a 'case to strike down such a law' and called upon the court to do so. His colleague, Justice Ijaz Ahmed, articulated an even broader, and more populist, interpretation of the judiciary's power of judicial review, stating that 'validity of any law can be tested by its results . . . any legislation which hurts the welfare of the people should not be allowed to stand among the people'. It is noteworthy that Justice Chaudhry positively cited sections of the *Zafar Ali Shah* judgment, which validated the military coup in 1999 as necessary for eliminating the 'eruption of corruption'. This highlighted the ideological alignment between the military and judiciary on the question of expanding the powers of unelected institutions to target the perceived corruption of elected officeholders.

---

[105] Interview No. L-85, 2 February 2021.
[106] PLD 2012 SC 553.

Beyond targeting political corruption, judges issued policy directives directly from the court on a range of issues, including bureaucratic appointments and the development of socio-economic policies. The superior judiciary significantly expanded the meaning of the 'right to life' protected under Article 9 of the constitution, to convert questions of socio-economic policy into justiciable questions of fundamental rights.[107] The high courts and the Supreme Court also applied and expanded the doctrine of 'structured discretion' to intervene in the administration of the bureaucracy and constrain executive discretion in bureaucratic appointments. Between 2009 and 2018, about a quarter of public interest litigation pertained to scrutinizing executive appointments and promotions. Repeated judicial interventions into political leadership selection, bureaucratic structures and socio-economic policymaking, which continued even after Justice Chaudhry retired in 2013, weakened the authority of political parties, paralysed governance processes and undermined elected civilian supremacy.

Thus, the judiciary's increased confrontations with the military did not mean that the judiciary saw itself as an ally of elected civilian supremacy. In fact, it was seeking to expand and consolidate its role as an independent power centre with a tutelary role in Pakistan's newly reconfigured political order, leaving Pakistan's new-found democracy fragile and unconsolidated.

Summary of Judicial–Military Relations (1999–2017)
In this period, the judiciary emerged as a powerful stakeholder in the political system, pursuing an expanded independent role protecting middle-class socio-economic interests, blurring the boundaries between the executive, legislature and judiciary, and challenging the military's political interventions and economic excesses and impunity. Even in periods of relative deference to the military, the judiciary continued to preserve its independence and assert an expanded role. The judiciary pursued an independent agenda of judicial supremacy backed by a populist rationale, confronting both military dominance under Musharraf and the political authority of elected governments after Musharraf's downfall. Where the institutional agendas of the military and judiciary aligned, the two institutions supported each other, but where their interests did not align, the two institutions clashed, and these clashes transformed Pakistan's political order. In the next section

---

[107] Interview No. L-30.

I outline how the shift in judicial audiences over the previous thirty years shaped the judiciary's pursuit of judicial supremacy and its increasingly confrontational relationship with other state institutions during this period.

UNDERSTANDING THE CONFRONTATIONAL COURT

The previous section outlined how the judiciary pursued an agenda of judicial independence and supremacy, legitimized by a middle-class focused populist rationale, that frequently placed it at odds with the military, as well as civilian governments. How do we explain the judiciary's new role in the political system and approach to the military during this period?

Judicial Leadership

Scholars of judicial politics focus on the attitudes and preferences of individual well-placed judges within the judicial hierarchy to explain trends in judicial behaviour across judicial institutions (Mate 2013; Hendrianto 2016; Abeyratne and Porat 2021). Chief Justices of courts, in particular, tend to wield considerable power and discretion over fellow judges and thus can affect the decision-making of their courts, which is why their attitudes and preferences tend to merit especially close attention. This is particularly the case in Pakistan, with its highly centralized judicial structure, where chief justices appoint and transfer judges, organize benches for hearings and make other key decisions regarding the institutional management of the judiciary and its personnel.

The popular narrative regarding the clash between the judiciary and the military in 2007 presents the events of 2007 as a profound rupture from a past characterized by submission and stagnation, and the most popular explanation for this apparent rupture was the activism of Chief Justice Iftikhar Chaudhry (Ghias 2010; Siddique 2013; Gilani and Cheema 2015). Justice Chaudhry crafted a new and expansive rights-based jurisprudence through the use of public interest litigation, to win popularity and build a momentum for increased judicial activism, ultimately challenging both the military and civilian governments in a bid for judicial supremacy.

There is no doubt that Chaudhry's activism transformed the judiciary, but, as the previous section demonstrates, the high courts were already expanding the role of the judiciary and intervening in socio-economic issues, including regulating the growing economic holdings and interests of the military before Chaudhry was appointed chief justice. Going back to 1988, with the *Benazir Bhutto* decision, we see the judiciary, with several interruptions, gradually expanding its jurisdiction, intervening in more governance issues and regulating the economy. In *Zafar Ali Shah* (2000), the Supreme Court emphasized the role of the judiciary in protecting socio-economic rights. Between 2002 and 2005, before Iftikhar Chaudhry became chief justice, there was an unprecedented surge in decisions challenging the military's economic prerogatives. Thus, the judiciary certainly grew more assertive under Chaudhry's leadership, but the judiciary was already expanding its role, and challenging more military interests at the high courts before Chaudhry became chief justice, indicating his leadership alone could not explain the rise in judicial contestation.

Variation in Regime Structure

Changes in the political environment and the nature of the military regime also played a role in shaping judicial assertiveness towards the military. Courts are strategically deferential when confronted with a strong, stable unified government, and will be more assertive when the political system is more fragmented, particularly when there is meaningful party competition (Chavez 2004), or when political institutions are not unified (Ferejohn et al. 2007). Khan (2015) argues that the Court remained deferential as part of a strategy of self-preservation during the early period of Musharraf's rule when his authority was at its height. A Supreme Court judge who took the oath under the PCO in 2000 and validated Musharraf's seizure of power in the *Zafar Ali Shah* case defended his decision saying:

> Some judges resigned, but others kept working in order to save the judicial system. Therefore, we decided to take the oath under the PCO. There were three main questions:
>
> 1. Whether the judges should resign en bloc? If this path had been adopted, it could have resulted in anarchy. And then there would have been military courts and no rule of law or dispensation of judges. So the court rejected that course. Therefore, we decided to take the oath under the PCO.
> 2. Should we have accepted the PCO? This meant we would be subordinate to the extra-constitutional order. We adopted a middle ground. We would take the oath but after taking the oath, courts will still have the power to make decisions according to the constitution. We upheld the power of the judiciary.

3. Should we have halted the takeover? We decided to give what we did, in order to save what we could.[108]

The judge's statement reveals how strategic concerns about preserving the authority of the judiciary in the face of a strong stable military regime with unfettered powers governed the decisions of the courts in the early years of the regime.

Musharraf's regime was less closed and repressive than Zia's regime, creating more space for the judiciary to assert itself than under the previous military regime. The resumption of constitutional rule in 2002 also opened up more opportunities for the judiciary to accept petitions challenging the military. However, the amended Constitution in 2002 was a vehicle for the military to establish a long-term political arrangement with the military at the helm, and thus did not significantly dilute Musharraf's authority.[109] Between 2002 and 2006, there was no noteworthy reduction in the strength and stability of the regime, nor were there any political challengers to the regime (Jaffrelot 2015). Up till 2005, there was little evidence of mass popular opposition towards the regime, outside the peripheral regions of the state.

However, by 2007, there was some evidence of differences within the military itself. Musharraf's ambition to hold on to the offices of both chief of army staff and president beyond 2007 likely created tensions between Musharraf and the officers, who also aspired to the position of chief of army staff, particularly the ambitious head of the ISI, General Kayani. While it is difficult to credibly comment on internal divisions within the military's institutional leadership, given the opaque nature of the institution, there are some indications of differences between Musharraf and Kayani. During the hearings challenging the suspension of Justice Chaudhry, Kayani avoided signing the regime's affidavit substantiating the charges of corruption and nepotism against Chaudhry, indicating his differences with Musharraf over the removal

---

[108] Interview No. J-16.
[109] The civilian constitutional arrangement was also influenced by Musharraf's interest in maintaining international legitimacy. However, in the era of the war on terror, the government did not have to make significant concessions to democratic constitutional rule in order to maintain international legitimacy and ensure the continued provision of aid, and only had to demonstrate a façade of constitutional democracy, while continuing to preserve authority with the military leadership (Grewal and Kureshi 2019).

of Chaudhry. Given that Chaudhry was expected to rule against Musharraf's power to hold both offices, it was in Kayani's interest to tacitly allow Chaudhry to stay in place and issue this ruling. Chaudhry's knowledge of this fragmentation within the military leadership would have emboldened him to challenge Musharraf on this key question.[110]

Hence, it is likely that strategic considerations regarding regime unity and authority certainly played a role in shaping the judicial behaviour during this period. However, these considerations were by no means decisive, since, as Chapter 4 shows, judicial assertiveness towards the military's prerogatives began well before internal differences emerged in 2007. High courts were increasingly challenging the military's economic prerogatives after 2002, and the Supreme Court expanded its public interest litigation and challenged key policies of the government from 2005 onwards. In fact, the Court's confrontational jurisprudence may have provided an opportunity *for* Kayani, rather than vice versa. Therefore, the judiciary was not only responding to changes in the political environment and any weakening in the military's unity when it started confronting the military regime.

The Rise of Electronic Media

The proliferation of private electronic media during Musharraf's rule also provided the Supreme Court with an opportunity to build public support and legitimacy for an activist judiciary (Ghias 2010; Gilani and Cheema 2015). Judges picked up cases from newspaper articles and championed causes they believed would generate positive coverage and be well received, building a reservoir of public support.

But positive media coverage clearly did not hold the military back from acting against the judiciary. If anything, the positive media coverage of the judiciary led to both a judicial and media crackdown by the regime. In November 2007, when the military regime had decided the activist judiciary posed a threat to the regime's interests and needed to be curtailed, the regime declared a state of emergency, and both the judiciary and media paid the price. Therefore, favourable media coverage did not deter the military from undermining the judiciary.

Instead, the growth of private media had a more indirect role to play in increasing judicial willingness to contest the military regime, even in

---

[110] At least one judge admitted that Justice Chaudhry was aware of Kayani's differences with Musharraf at the time he made the decision to defy General Musharraf. Interview No. J-2.

the absence of new political openings. The growth of private media closely connected the judiciary with audiences that judges cared about and gave these audiences a platform through which they could engage closely with and form and express opinions about judicial decisions. Judges were now especially concerned with how the media covered their decisions and shaped their reputation with their respective social networks. Thus, the new electronic media increased judges' motivation to build esteem with social networks with which these judges identified, and this impacted the judiciary's approach to other state institutions, including the military. The effect of the proliferation of private electronic media and increased media coverage of the judiciary was therefore to reduce the distance between the judiciary and the audiences that it cared about, and thus increase the importance of building and maintaining a reputation as a key aspect of judicial behaviour. Therefore, when discussing the impact of private media, what matters most is: what audience did judges care most about?

The urban middle class was the primary consumer of new private media coverage, and these urban middle-class social networks primarily populated the bar associations from which judges were recruited, and were the audiences to which judges sought to project themselves. The growth of private media did not encourage judicial assertiveness by deterring military retaliation, but by connecting the judiciary more closely with urban middle-class social networks that favoured an assertive, populist judiciary.

Thus, shifts in the unity and authority of the military, the proliferation of private electronic media and the leadership of an activist chief justice all played roles in explaining the emergence of an assertive judiciary confronting both military regimes and elected governments. But the process and timing of the surge in judicial assertiveness indicate that this surge was also guided by a change in judicial preferences that preceded the change in judicial leadership and emergence of significant political openings. Therefore, in order to understand the actions of the judiciary during this period, it is necessary to examine the normative and utilitarian interlinkages that entrenched the legal and policy preferences of the judiciary during this period.

The New Judicial Audiences

I argue that the legal and policy preferences generated by this shift in audiences described in Chapter 4 best explains the emergence of a more independent and confrontational judiciary. I first discuss the utilitarian interlinkages between the bar and the bench, then the normative interlinkages between the bar and the bench and the norms being transmitted from the bar to bench. Finally, I demonstrate that these interlinkages shaped the institutional preferences underlying judicial behaviour during this period.

Utilitarian Interlinkages: Judicial Careers and Reputations
By 1999, the judiciary's institutional interlinkages with the military had been reduced, as the chief justices gained formal primacy in the judicial appointment process, and the majority of judges were recruited from the politically active bar, although there were still a number of High Court and Supreme Court judges who were appointed during Zia's regime. The military could not assume that the judiciary would collaborate with or acquiesce to its political agenda as it did under Ayub and Zia. Musharraf's strategy with the judiciary, therefore, was to first use the oath-taking to oust the most independent-minded judges, place more pliable judges in positions of authority in the judicial hierarchy and then bargain with these judges to incentivize them to support his political agenda.

A senior lawyer explained that before the *Zafar Ali Shah* decision validating Musharraf's coup, 'judges were given a promise that their retirement age was being extended from sixty-five to sixty-eight'.[111] This would mean that senior judges already in positions of authority would get to extend their tenures in exchange for upholding Musharraf's political agenda. In 2002, Chief Justice Irshad, who had upheld the coup, was appointed as Musharraf's chief election commissioner after he retired as chief justice, and the next chief justice, Sheikh Riaz Ahmed, had a reputation for corruption, including accepting money from parties to decide cases (Khan 2016).[112] Justice Iftikhar Hussain, who became the chief justice of the Lahore High Court, was also inclined to cooperate with the regime and he remained chief justice of the court for five years, ensuring that the 'court had no impact' (Huq 2004).[113] Justice Saiyed Ashad, the chief justice of the Sindh High Court, was also known to be a 'pro-Musharraf judge'.[114] Thus, through the oath-taking and subsequent bargains the regime

---

[111] Interview No. L-88, 5 June 2017.
[112] Interview No. L-15, 20 May 2017.
[113] Interview No. L-62.
[114] Interview No. L-2, 23 June 2017.

ensured that the judiciary was led by 'judges who had been corrupted and were cooperating with the regime'.[115] In 2002, the government announced the constitutional package of the LFO. Along with amending the Constitution to shift powers from the parliament to the presidency, the LFO also extended the age of retirement of judges from sixty-five to sixty-eight.[116] When judges agreed to accept the age extension, they also had to accept and legitimize Musharraf's constitutional amendments. Thus, Musharraf used incentives to ensure these judges cooperated with the regime.[117]

Musharraf successfully bargained with senior judges to ensure they did not confront the regime, but he was not able to control the judiciary and fragment its authority the way Zia had; nor did he intervene as directly in the internal workings of the judiciary as previous dictators had, leaving many of the internal norms of the judiciary that had developed after the *Al-Jihad* case intact. Under Musharraf, barring the PCO and a few key interventions, seniority was largely respected.[118]

During Musharraf's regime, the formal rules of appointment that were established after the *Al-Jehad* decision largely remained in place. After the *Al-Jehad* decision the chief justices of the high courts and Supreme Court had the primary say in the selection of judges. The high courts, and especially the Supreme Court, were largely populated by judges appointed from the bar. The few judges who were promoted from the judicial bureaucracy were usually a lot older by the time they moved through the entire bureaucracy and were promoted to the bench, and, barring a few notable exceptions, rarely spent more than a few years as High Court judges before they had to retire. In appointing

---

[115] Ibid.

[116] The extension in the age of retirement was meant to benefit the judges.

[117] Other tactics to soften judges' attitudes towards the regime included the allotting of plots of land to judges, a practice and continues till today, although evidence of its actual impact on curtailing judicial assertiveness is, thus far, limited. See Sultan Mehmood and Bakhtawar Ali, 'Judicial Capture by Favour Exchange', Working Paper.

[118] Two notable exceptions were Justice Najm-ul-Hasan Kazmi and Justice Iftikhar Hussain. Justice Najm-ul-Hasan Kazmi was known to challenge the regime, and was forced out. Interview No. L-84. Justice Iftikhar Hussain served as chief justice of the Lahore High Court for five years, while junior judges were promoted to the Supreme Court before him, to keep the Lahore High Court leadership in the hands of a pro-regime judge.

a judge from the bar, judges typically selected lawyers who had developed two types of reputation:

1. With the judges themselves. Justice Khawaja explained his selection as a judge of the Lahore High Court:

> I had formed an impression with Chief Justice Ajmal Mian, and with Justice Rashid Aziz Khan. How did Rashid Aziz select my name? Rashid Aziz heard me a few times arguing the cases. What helped me was two key players had had exposure to me as a lawyer.[119]

2. With senior and influential lawyers with which the judges had ties. Judges do not talk to the whole bar, they just 'talk to prominent lawyers, who will consider their number of reported cases, and if the lawyers have ever appeared against them or with them, as well as their level of professionalism, i.e. if they enjoyed a reputation of being a tout or not'.[120] This allowed bar politics to influence the judicial appointment process, particularly in the Lahore High Court.

> Before becoming a judge, in Lahore, you belonged to or identified with a group or groups within the bar. After becoming a judge, you pick judges accordingly, from the group to which you belonged. Bar politics entered [the appointment process] that way.[121]

Thus, ambitious lawyers seeking promotions built relationships with senior lawyers and political groups in the bar in order to move forward. A senior lawyer explained to me how the appointment process played out in the Lahore High Court:

> After the Judges' case, in terms of appointments ... there is pressure from the bar. The judges ask the bar groups: what are your objections to my nominees? People aligning themselves with groups enhance their chances of becoming judges. Hamid Khan had a monopoly over bar politics (in Lahore) for seventeen years. He was the key stakeholder from the bar and could ensure members of his group were selected. He was always very harsh on the bench. But generally, he placed emphasis on ... more independent-minded judges.[122]

---

[119] Interview with Justice Jawwad Khawaja.
[120] Interview No. L-84. The number of reported cases means those that had been reported by the courts, in which those lawyers had appeared as counsels.
[121] Interview No. L-27, 28 May 2017.
[122] Interview No. L-36.

The military-run executive was not entirely removed from the appointment system. Musharraf's attorney general did play an influential role in the appointment process, to ensure the judges appointed would 'not be the type to upset the apple cart'.[123] However, the attorney general also wanted to maintain good relations with judges, and therefore 'would want the kind of people who the judges wanted as judges'.[124] As one lawyer explained, under Musharraf 'it was still the chief Justice who had the final say. Makhdoom Ali Khan [Musharraf's attorney general] is not a bully. Really, he also wanted to appoint judges who were competent.'[125] The extent to which the military-led executive involved itself in judicial appointments depended on the extent to which each High Court's chief justice was willing to cooperate with the government, and shortlist their recommendations for nomination. For example, according to a senior lawyer, Musharraf's legal team closely consulted with Justice Iftikhar Hussain in the Lahore High Court on nominations, as he was amenable to placing their preferred judges on his shortlist for appointments.[126] Thus, during Musharraf's era, judicial appointments still remained primarily in the hands of the judiciary, while Musharraf's attorney general and advocates-general remained the regime's primary institutional interlinkages with the judiciary, with their influence over the appointment process depending on the cooperation of the relevant chief justice. The regime did not overturn the new norms of judicial appointment in the judiciary, and primarily ensured that more radical judges were not appointed to the bench. Judges appointed during this period were mostly professional lawyers who maintained close relationships with senior lawyers and groups in the bar. After the restoration of the judiciary in 2009, both political parties and the military played a more limited role in the judicial appointment process. As one politician explained:

> In the 1990s [before Al-Jihad], it was a game between the judiciary and the executive. Chief ministers, chief justice all involved themselves, the CJs would put their foot down for one or two people, but normally they would go along with the executive because they thought if they go along, they can get favours they need from the chief minister. After 2008, governments could not get their people appointed.[127]

123 Interview No. L-30, 12 June 2017.
124 Interview No. L-70, 18 June 2017.
125 Interview L-2, 23 June 2017.
126 Interview No. L-5, 7 February 2021.
127 Interview No. P-5.

Another member of the PPP lamented the lack of influence his party had in judicial appointments to the Sindh High Court, and claimed the PML-N only fared somewhat better with judges in the Lahore High Court because of familial and kinship-based relationships between senior politicians and some judges of the Lahore High Court.[128]

In *Sindh High Court Bar Association* (2009), the Court ousted all the judges who had been appointed between Justice Chaudhry's suspension in 2007 and restoration in 2009. With many new judges to appoint, Chaudhry's primary criterion was loyalty. As one senior lawyer explained, 'after the PCO, loyalty to the Lawyers' Movement was the sole criterion for appointment. Tehreeki [movement] lawyers as they were called were selected.'[129] Thus, judges were appointed from the groups within the bar that had actively been engaged in the Lawyers' Movement. The result was that the role of bar association leaders who had led the Lawyers' Movement became especially significant in the appointment process. As one lawyer from the Lahore High Court explained, 'today the judiciary in Lahore is 60 per cent under the control of the bar'.[130]

The new civilian government attempted to restructure the judicial appointment system to make it a collaborative process involving multiple political institutions. There was a concern across political parties that, over the last decade, the chief justice had wielded too much control over judicial appointments, and the 18th Amendment attempted to change that (Khosa 2018). The 18th constitutional Amendment, passed in 2010, established two new forums for judicial appointments: the Judicial Commission and the Parliamentary Committee.[131] The Judicial Commission was headed by the chief justice of Pakistan and consisted of senior judges of the Supreme Court and high courts, the attorney general, law ministers and a representative of the Bar Council. The commission was to nominate judges for each vacancy in the high courts, and the nominations were then sent to the Parliamentary Committee, composed of representatives from the two houses of the legislature and including members

---

[128] Interview No. P-9.
[129] Interview No. L-88.
[130] Interview No. L-40, 28 May 2017.
[131] The 18th Amendment to the Constitution did not only amend the judicial appointment process, it also elevated parliamentary supremacy over the presidency, and devolved federal powers to the provincial governments.

from both the ruling party and the opposition, for confirmation. This new process was challenged before the Supreme Court for infringing upon the independence of the judiciary by including the elected government and parliament in the process of judicial appointments.

A legislator involved with drafting the 18th Amendment stated, 'we were mindful that this would be too radical a change for the judiciary to accept', as 'right now judges are in their own little cocoon and from there being called up for interviews and confirmations before parliamentary committees might be too much for them to swallow'.[132] The Court admitted the petition challenging the constitutional amendment and advised that the legislature alter the 18th Amendment to increase the number of judges on the Judicial Commission, ensuring that judges comprised a majority on the commission, and to restrict the power of the Parliamentary Committee to reject a recommendation of the commission. The same legislator explained to me, 'privately, we were told that the judges told the government that if you do not make amends then the entire 18th Amendment will be scuttled, federalism and everything'.[133] These alterations were made in the 19th Amendment. Then two separate Court decisions made the Parliamentary Committee almost redundant, and the chief justices maintained the steering role in appointments.[134] Thus, the constitutional amendments made almost no significant change to the balance of power in the judicial appointment process, and only further entrenched the formal control that judges had in the process of judicial appointments (Mehmood 2021).

The chief justices of the high courts and the Supreme Court were therefore the primary authorities in judicial appointments.[135] When there were vacancies for the High Court to fill, the High Court chief justice would typically informally consult with the lawyers and judges who had most access to the chief justice, namely fellow High Court judges, senior lawyers (possibly from the judge's former law firm), leaders of the bar (particularly the leaders from the bar group with which the judge was previously affiliated), government lawyers with

---

[132] Interview No. P-5.
[133] Ibid.
[134] *Nadeem Ahmed v. Federation of Pakistan*, PLD 1996 SC 234; *Munir Hassan Bhatti v. Federation of Pakistan*, PLD 2010 SC 1165.
[135] The one role the military continued to have was that any nominated judge had to pass a screening by the ISI, to ensure there were no security concerns regarding the judge.

whom the chief justice interacted and Supreme Court judges (specifically the chief justice and judges who had been elevated from the same High Court).[136] As a journalist explained, 'references are everything, and people will lobby judges and bar leaders so that they can ensure the chief justice puts their name on the list'.[137] These names are then sent to the chief justice of the Supreme Court who will discuss the shortlist informally with his fellow Supreme Court judges, particularly the ones who also sit on the Judicial Commission, and they finalize a list. The chief justice then presents the names before a meeting of the Judicial Commission, but since the judges have agreed beforehand on the names they would approve, and they outnumber the non-judicial members of the commission, inevitably those names are finalized with little discussion or deliberation. Hence, the process was dominated by the chief justices of the High Court and Supreme Court, and the lawyers, bar leaders and judges they informally consulted with. Political parties had a limited role in the judicial appointment process, and could only influence it to the extent that individuals within the political party had personal relationships with individual judges.

Hence, the judicial appointment system was one in which judges had primacy, the role of executive institutions including the military was reduced and the bar had an informal but significant role in the appointment process, cementing the utilitarian interlinkages between the bench and the bar.

Normative Interlinkages: Judicial Esteem and Reputations
From the 1990s onwards, and especially after 2007, the relationship between the bench and the bar grew closer. As one former judge explained, 'before the judiciary was held in awe. There was distance between the bar and the bench. Now this distance has disappeared.'[138]

Initially, when Musharraf ousted the Sharif government, many in the lawyers' community favoured Sharif's removal.[139] However, the expectation was that this constitutional deviation would be temporary and that

---

[136] The few judges elevated from the lower courts were usually selected at the discretion of the chief justice, from among those lower-court judges who had reached the requisite level of seniority.

[137] Interview No. J-7, 23 February 2021.

[138] Interview No. J-44, 28 November 2017.

[139] Waseem Ahmad Shah, 'Justice Siddiqi Remains Focus of Attention', *Frontier Post*, 5 July 1999.

democracy and constitutional rule would be restored swiftly. Therefore, there was little support for sustained military rule. Khan wrote:

> The military assumed that the action to oust Mr. Sharif symbolized their (lawyers') distaste for democracy itself. This was a wrong assumption. When the regime announced that all judges would have to take the oath to the PCO to remain judges, bar associations around the country responded with condemnation.[140]

Over the next two years, bar associations mobilized in opposition to Musharraf's regime. During the 1990s, the Supreme Court Bar Association (SCBA) had been established and became the leading forum within the national hierarchy of bar associations. The leadership, resolutions and decisions of the SCBA came to de facto represent the views of the bar. Between 2001 and 2004, the SCBA challenged Musharraf's legislative and electoral actions in the courts, including his referendum, his assumption of the office of the presidency while remaining chief of army staff and his amendments to the Constitution, and even appealed to the United Nations.[141] Other bar associations held rallies from the high courts to protest against Musharraf's legislative actions, and ousted members who had joined the government's legal team.[142] Thus, from the early days of the Musharraf regime a norm of activism against the military regime was established in the bar.

In 2002, the bar activist Hamid Khan won the presidency of the SCBA, and he launched a concerted campaign to resist legislation empowering the military regime.[143] In subsequent SCBA elections, support or opposition for the actions of the regime typically dominated elections, and candidates who had established a reputation for opposing the regime were more successful. In the Lahore High Court Bar Association, the Professionals Group that had been formed by Hamid Khan, and which was largely led by lawyers opposed to the regime, regularly won the bar elections.[144] Thus, across major bar associations, lawyers won elections campaigning on a platform that opposed the regime, and large segments of

---

[140] Shujaat Ali Khan, 'Drive for Bar Polls Kicks off', *Dawn*, 15 November 2000.

[141] Rafaqat Ali, 'SCBA Challenges Referendum', *Dawn*, 18 April 2002; 'Lawyers to Convince Legislators against LFO', *Dawn*, 27 December 2002; Sajid Zia, 'Lawyers Vow to Resist Amendments with Full Force', *Nation*, 16 July 2002; 'SC Bar Approaches UN on LFO', *Nation*, 19 February 2003.

[142] 'LHCBA to Launch Anti-Musharraf Drive', *Pakistan Times*, 26 November 2004.

[143] 'Lawyers to Convince Legislators against LFO', *Dawn*, 27 December 2002.

[144] 'Uniform Issue Dominates SC Bar Poll Campaign', *Dawn*, 18 October 2004.

the lawyers' community continued to pursue oppositional politics challenging the regime, just as it had against Zia.

However, there was an important difference between the bar's opposition to the Zia regime and the Musharraf regime, as now judges became the targets of the oppositional campaign as well. A veteran of the bar's movement against Zia explained that 'we never agitated against the judges. We never shut down the courts throughout our time … We were active but we never fought a fight against the judiciary.'[145]

However, this time judges who cooperated with the regime were not spared. After the *Al-Jihad* decision the bar had grown more vocal about judicial appointments and the conduct of judges. Bar associations condemned judges who took the oath under the PCO, and the chief justice for administering the oath of office of president to General Musharraf.[146] In 2002, the SCBA criticized Musharraf's LFO, and especially the proposed extension of the retirement age of judges, and advocated for the Supreme Court to strike down the LFO.[147] When the Court upheld Musharraf's referendum and LFO, including the extension in the retirement age, judges came under harsh criticism from the bar. The extension in the retirement age divided the bar and the bench, because it benefitted senior judges, but therefore delayed promotions of junior High Court judges, and reduced the numbers of vacancies for lawyers to fill. An alliance formed between junior judges and the bar against the retirement extension. Hamid Khan, as president of the SCBA, accused the judges of the Supreme Court of sharing power with the military rulers for which it was being rewarded.[148] The SCBA announced that they would not argue any constitutional matters before the Supreme Court as they could not expect justice from the compromised Court.[149] The bar's campaign against the judges who were willing to cooperate with the regime and accept the age of extension intensified.[150] The Pakistan Bar Council then released a White Paper on the judiciary, which called out judges who had bad reputations, discussed corruption among senior judges, and

---

[145] Interview No. L-9.
[146] 'CJ Violating Constitution: SCBA', *Dawn*, 5 August 2001.
[147] 'LHCBA Slams Amendments, Increase in Judges' Retirement Age', *Daily Times*, 26 June 2002; 'Judiciary Helping Military Government: SCBA', *Dawn*, 7 November 2002.
[148] Ibid.
[149] Mohammad Kamran, 'Hamid Khan Not Guilty of Contempt: SCBA', *Daily Times*, 8 November 2002.
[150] Javed Rana, 'Lawyers May Take Extreme Course', *Nation*, 12 April 2003.

shamed judges for upholding the powers of the regime.[151] Thus, bar associations exercised their power over the reputations of judges to pressure the judiciary into acting in line with the preferences of the bar.

The judiciary's response demonstrated how sensitive judges were to the pressure campaign being waged against several senior judges by the bar. Chief Justice Riaz accused Hamid Khan of contempt of court for his statements against the judiciary.[152] The Supreme Court also tried to defend its decisions upholding the regime's authority and actions, by trying to show that they had the support of senior lawyers. As the leading lawyer Farhatullah Babar wrote:

> Never before has the Supreme Court sought to defend oath taking by judges of superior courts under the Provisional Constitutional Order (PCO) as it did last week. The Supreme Court said that senior lawyers like Khalid Anwar and SM Zafar welcomed the oath taking by the judges of the Supreme Court. One hopes that the honourable judges are guided solely by law and the Constitution and not by *certification of some members of the bar*. If such certification is accepted as a guiding principle it would be difficult to counter the statement of the bar which it is claimed represents the collective wisdom of the lawyers' community.[153]

Clearly, the judges were acutely concerned about the viewpoint of the bar, and the ability of bar leaders to shape their reputations. A senior lawyer explained:

> Once you become a judge, you ask who do I please? Start off as a judge, the judge cares about senior leaders of the bar. Then they care about how the Supreme Court views them and how other judges are viewing them. Once they go up to the Supreme Court they care about the bar leaders again because at that stage they will be viewed closely by the bar and the legal community.[154]

One former judge explained his experience of building a reputation. He said:

> When I became a judge, I did not know bail, criminal procedure or any other aspect of criminal law ... I was only a very typical tax lawyer. But

---

[151] 'SCBA to Publish White Paper on Judges', *News*, 11 June 2003.

[152] Naveed Ahmed, 'SC Dismisses SCBA Statement as Contemptuous', *News*, 31 October 2002; 'Law Minister Unhappy at SCBA Chief's Remarks', *Dawn*, 23 October 2002.

[153] Farhatullah Babar, 'SC and the Bar', *Nation*, 5 November 2002.

[154] Interview No. L-60.

> I always sat with an open mind towards any one appearing before me. I never talked down to any lawyer who was appearing before me. I always tried to give relief so I got a reputation as a relief giving judge among lawyers.[155]

Another judge complained about how challenging reputation-building was, particularly as a junior High Court judge, saying: 'An additional judge is like a naked woman on the streets, everyone loves watching her, but also loves calling her names.'[156].

Why is it that reputation with the bar had become so much more important? First, most judges coming from the bar were conscious about their reputations with groups in the bar. Leading lawyers, who had helped these judges get appointed, now felt the judges were indebted to them and expected them to make decisions in line with their preferences. As one bar leader explained in a speech to a lawyers' rally at the Sindh High Court: 'what were these judges before? All these judges were lawyers first here in the bar, we enrolled them, and gradually with our help they became judges, and when they retire they will come back here to us lawyers.'[157]

Second, with the proliferation of private media, judges grew 'a lot more concerned about self-aggrandisement and cared about how they were projected'.[158] But their primary spokespeople were senior lawyers who appeared on television channels to discuss the decisions of the judges, elevating the importance of bar leaders in shaping the esteem of judges with their social networks. As a senior judge explained, 'the bar was the loudspeaker for the judges'.[159]

Third, the bar leader had the capacity to mobilize the bar. As the bar associations grew exponentially, the sheer size of the bar associations added to the power and influence of the leaders of the bar. The bar was filling up with young lawyers with poor training, little money and few employment prospects. These idle lawyers spent their time in the bar-rooms with colleagues looking for opportunities.[160] The unemployed

[155] Interview No. J-65, 14 March 2017.
[156] Interview No. J-58, 10 February 2021. The use of such an analogy by the judge is also indicative of the gendered nature of the judicial profession in Pakistan.
[157] Speech at Sindh High Court, April 2018.
[158] Interview No. L-22.
[159] Interview No. J-41, 1 April 2019.
[160] 'Young Lawyers Face Tough Time in Pakistan', Dawn, 19 October 2010.

and discontented lawyers populating the barrooms were an important resource for bar leaders, who brought these lawyers out to protest and rally and disrupt courts to support demands made by bar leaders. As Saroop Ijaz explained:

> The primary edge that the lawyers possessed over other professional and civil society groups was they were already somewhat organized and politicized. The presence of district and even tehsil (local) Bar associations with elected office bearers meant that the minimum requisite infrastructure was already in place ... Impoverishment, compounded with organization and independence made for a volatile combination.[161]

This mobilization potential was on display during the Lawyers' Movement. During the movement, bar associations kept up a regular cycle of protests for over almost two years, and the lawyers developed a repertoire of contention that included rallies, boycotts, long marches, confrontations with police and the sealing of courts. In interviews, bar leaders described the ranks of their bar associations as troops in battle, and used the language of battle to describe the actions they took on the streets against the government.[162] A former judge explained: 'Iftikhar Chaudhry was revived because of the bar. And not because of the senior elements of the bar but because of the rougher elements of the bar.'[163] The ambition of the bar extended to the point that they operated as an independent political movement, even selecting their own presidential candidate to challenge Musharraf in the presidential elections in 2007.[164]

After the Lawyers' Movement came to an end, the lawyers continued to rely on their mobilization potential to pressure and control judges, and frequently resorted to violent and aggressive tactics against judges and other rival groups of lawyers. Since 2007, there has been a growing number of incidents of lawyers breaking out into gunfights, manhandling journalists, beating up judges and locking up courts, and even attacking hospitals, a practice that came to be known as *vuklagardee* (Khan 2019).[165] Judges grew apprehensive of the consequences of upsetting sections of the bar. Even senior judges were not immune. The offices of Chief Justice Sharif of the Lahore High Court were

---

[161] Saroop Ijaz, 'The Method and the Form', *News*, 11 March 2012.
[162] Interview No. L-16, 29 January 2017.
[163] Interview No. J-19, 23 April 2017.
[164] Sajid Zia, 'Lawyers Come up as Major Stakeholders', *Nation*, 25 August 2007.
[165] Ardeshir Cowasjee, 'Lawless Lawyers', *Dawn*, 24 October 2010; Rana Yasif and Muhammad Shahzad, 'Lawyers in the Dock', *Express Tribune*, 12 December 2019.

locked and stoned by lawyers.[166] A senior lawyer explained that after the Lawyers' Movement:

> The Bar has been emboldened. It has gone way beyond its mandate. The bar has a very inflated view of its own importance. Now the bar is perceived as much stronger. Judges have their primary audience as the bar. Judges have become more sensitive to the esteem with which the bar holds them. The bar has a lot of glamour.[167]

Thus, since 1999, the bar's willingness and ability to pressure judges and tarnish their reputations and standing has grown significantly. This meant that, as one bar leader from the Lawyers' Movement put it, 'we were each other's biggest supporters and each other's worst enemies'.[168] Judges who pursued the agenda of the bar were actively supported by the bar, and judges who fell out of line became its targets. Another bar leader summarized the impact of the change in bar–bench relations:

> Some disruption has been good. Judges get called out when they need to. Judges have historically been so removed from any critical quarter, so they think everything that comes out from them is gold. The disruption has had its extreme effects. We have seen judges play to the gallery.[169]

Bar associations disparaged judges who cooperated with Musharraf's regime, and lionized judges who refused to do so, and after the restoration of democracy, leading bar associations were just as critical of political parties and political leaders as they had been of the military regime.[170] Bar associations rallied in support of Chaudhry overturning

---

[166] Rana Tanveer, 'Lawyers Attack CJ's Court', *Express Tribune*, 1 October 2010.

[167] Interview No. L-50, 18 May 2017.

[168] Interview No. L-99, 28 January 2017.

[169] Interview No. L-2.

[170] This did not mean that divisions did not develop in the bar, as political parties sought to win over factions of bar associations. However, just as it did in the 1990s, the bar maintained a degree of autonomy from political parties, and bar leaders also advocated for the autonomy of the judiciary from political parties, rejecting the 18th Amendment for providing parliament with more influence in the judicial appointment process. Even as political parties supported candidates in bar association elections, electoral candidates had to demonstrate their distance from political parties in order to be deemed credible by the voting lawyers. In 2016, for example, Farooq Naek, a former law minister of the PPP, ran for the Supreme Court Bar Association elections, and he was widely seen as too close to the leadership of the PPP. Rasheed Rizvi, his rival during the elections, attached the label of a party worker to Naek, successfully used Naek's political ties against him

the NRO that withdrew old corruption cases against politicians. Qazi Anwar, the president of the SCBA, described parliamentarians as 'smugglers and cheaters', and the SCBA called for a Long March to ensure the Court's NRO decision was implemented and 'the ruling clique' was exposed.[171] Therefore, gaining the bar's esteem required demonstrating distance from, and if possible defiance of, military and political party elites.

Enforcing Populist Judicial Supremacy

The 2000s was the era of the confrontational court and the judiciary was unwilling to accept a role as merely a collaborator or instrument in upholding another institution's supremacy, and was focused on establishing its own role as an independent power centre and shaping the political and policymaking processes of the state based on its preferences. I argue that this role conception emerged from, and was enforced by, the lawyers' community, the key audience for the judiciary. The populist sentiment that pervaded most of the legal community was that the military and political parties were self-interested elites, and both the bar and judiciary had to be kept independent from party leaders and military generals and given wide latitude to hold them accountable to the people.

As of 2007, only one judge remained who had been appointed during Zia's regime, and the majority of High Court judges had been appointed after the *Al-Jehad* decision. One lawyer explained, 'the relationship between lawyer and judges has become far too cosy. As judge you carry over your prejudices from the bar. Judges come to the bench as fully formed jurists. You become a judge after having ... ideological preferences developed in the bar.'[172] I spoke to two former Supreme Court judges, one recruited from the bar and another promoted from the subordinate judiciary, and the two viewpoints reflect how their prior experiences shaped their understanding of the role of the judiciary. The judge recruited from the bar explained how important his time as a lawyer was in shaping his views as a judge:

and won the elections by demonstrating his own independence from political parties.

[171] 'SCBA President under Fire', *Business Recorder*, 30 March 2010; Dilshad Azeem, 'Lawyers Threaten Long March Again for SC', *News*, 10 March 2010.

[172] Interview No. L-70.

As a lawyer, I always thought lawyers had a leadership role in society. The public is not vocal, lawyers need to be playing a role in shaping public opinion. As general secretary of the bar, I used to be very vocal about these issues. When I was attorney general, I learned that the bench had a role to play to bring about social change. Law can be a catalyst for social change, and this informed my decision-making.[173]

In contrast, the judge promoted from the lower judiciary explained that 'judges have their own sphere of action. To overstep that sphere is unjust. Good fences make good neighbours. Judicial self-restraint is important.'[174]

The emphasis of the judges from the bar on a broad policymaking role for the judiciary is juxtaposed with the emphasis of the judge from the lower courts on respect for the separation of powers, which highlights how much of a difference a background in the more activist bar made.

This does not mean that a judges' viewpoints are static and entirely defined by their time as lawyers, and that once they join the judiciary these views do not change. As one judge explained, 'after becoming a judge, you carry the ideas about the law you developed as a lawyer, but you also realize the importance of the state's ideology, which you have to protect'.[175] Another senior lawyer said, 'once lawyers become judges, particularly when they become senior judges, they interact more with senior state officials as well, bureaucrats and military people, and this influences them'.[176] Further, judges are especially influenced by their seniors, who they interact with and who guide them through the early years of their career.[177] Thus, judges' perspectives evolve based on their understanding of their role within a state institution, their increasing interactions with other state officers and their relationships with fellow judges. But with a growing majority of judges arriving from an increasingly activist bar, the preference for a more independent and public interest–minded judiciary that had developed among many lawyers also moved with these lawyers to the bench.

The bar was also able to enforce its preferences, as judges sought to please the bar through their decisions. As one former judge explained, while describing an incident he witnessed in court:

---

[173] Interview No. J-2.
[174] Interview No. J-6, 20 November 2016.
[175] Interview No. J-70, 5 February 2021.
[176] Interview No. L-64, 2 February 2021.
[177] Interview No. J-65.

Today the maverick judge is favoured who does not consider himself bound by procedure and promises to do substantive justice ... You put on a show, you have to be seen to be bold. In a case the judge said 'procedure and all is clear but tell me the issue and I will do substantive justice'. I said to the judge, 'sir you cannot do that in this case you will be out of jurisdiction'. He said, 'but I will do substantive justice'. Why did the judge do this? He is creating an impression. There will be lawyers in attendance and this way a positive view is formed of the judge.[178]

Another judge explained his process of preparing court decisions, saying:

I always think about choosing the right angle or lines that I know will generate applause from the people in the courtroom. You see, it is important to see the effect your words will have on the young lawyers, then your judgment will have the most impact.[179]

The more unified the bar was on a particular issue, the less likely the judges were to go against the consensus within the bar.[180] The events of the Lawyers' Movement in 2007 highlight how the bar can use its interlinkages to affect the actions of the bench, even among judges who were not necessarily predisposed to the preferences upheld by the bar. Initially, in March 2007, when Justice Chaudhry was forced out by the regime, his case was referred to the Supreme Judicial Council (SJC), which carried out its proceedings in private. Chaudhry's junior, Justice Javed Iqbal, headed the SJC. He was known to be sympathetic to the military and was willing to act through the SJC against Chaudhry.[181] However, after the lawyers unified behind Justice Chaudhry, and the Lawyers' Movement took off, the Court accepted the demand of the lawyers and altered the proceedings against Chaudhry from a private disciplinary proceeding before the SJC to a public court proceeding hearing challenges to Chaudhry's dismissal. One lawyer explained that 'many of Chaudhry's fellow judges were hostile towards Iftikhar

---

[178] Interview No. J-33, 21 March 2017.
[179] Interview No. J-70.
[180] One leading figure in the Lawyers' Movement explained that it was hard to get judges to join the bar in defying the regime in 2002 because there was less unanimity within the bar regarding condemning judges who collaborated the regime than there was in 2007. Interview No. L-7.
[181] Interview No. L-94.

Chaudhry. But then they saw lawyers started coming out on the streets and ... the bench followed suit.'[182]

Thus, judges who were recruited from the bar would endorse many of the preferences of their former colleagues in the bar, either because they shared the same preferences from their time as lawyers, or because they wished to gain the esteem of their former colleagues. As judges who endorsed these norms for sincere or strategic reasons, moved upwards in the judicial hierarchy and became senior judges, these preferences became dominant. New and junior judges would be more inclined to adopt similar preferences, not just to gain the esteem of their former colleagues, but also to build their reputations with senior judges in order to advance their careers. The urban middle-class lawyer community had converged around opposing the hegemony of both military and political party elites, criticizing judges who supported or participated in this hegemony and celebrating judges that used whatever institutional tools they could to disrupt it, and through the interlinkages between the bar and the bench, these preferences became increasingly hegemonic within the judiciary.

The career of Chief Justice Iftikhar Chaudhry exemplifies the close ties between judges and the bar, and how the bar's linkages with the bench shaped the decision-making of the bench. Chaudhry did not come from a privileged background, and he got his law degree from a less renowned law school in Sindh before practising law in Balochistan. He was elected president of the Balochistan High Court Bar Association in 1986, where he gave speeches opposing military rule, and he was also twice elected as a member of the Balochistan Bar Council, before becoming a judge. Once Chaudhry became chief justice, he paid close attention to cultivating a relationship with the bar. In 2006, a dispute grew in the SCBA over the election for its president, as the outgoing president of the bar who had close ties with the regime sought to ensure that Muneer Malik, the activist presidential candidate who opposed military rule, could not win the election.[183] As chief justice, Chaudhry intervened and upheld Munir's victory in

---

[182] Interview No. L-66, 28 May 2017.
[183] 'Qayyum Quotes Musharraf: Decision on Uniform Issue Soon', *Dawn*, 21 September 2006.

215

the bar election.[184] In this way Chaudhry, unlike his three predecessors during Musharraf's rule, won the support of the bar (Ghias 2010). One lawyer explained that 'Iftikhar Chaudhry preferred to be under the glare, among the people. He gave much access to the bar, and judges were seen more clearly by lawyers.'[185] Therefore, when Musharraf ousted Chaudhry, the bar with which he had established a close relationship mobilized to resist the military and demand his reinstatement. Chaudhry's history as a bar leader and emphasis on strong ties with the bar were vital in building an assertive judicial campaign against the military regime.

Chaudhry's approach to jurisprudence also highlights the impact of his years as a lawyer and, as a judge, the importance he paid to gaining the support of the bar. As Supreme Court justice, Chaudhry used his *suo moto* powers to intervene in a range of issues that affected discounted sections of the middle class. From dealing with questions of high commodity prices and petrol prices, issues that hit the urban middle class the hardest, to pursuing cases of elite political and military corruption, Chaudhry's policy preferences closely mirrored the middle-class anti-corruption agenda that had become the consensus in the bar (Waseem 2012). As one judge explained, 'Chaudhry was one of the bar, and he always played to this gallery. Judges like him played to the bar, and projected populism with the bar.'[186] Chaudhry bypassed procedural norms to turn his courtroom into a public spectacle where he intervened in issues generating widespread attention, guided by what the popular sentiment in the bar would support.

However, just as reputations are built in the bar so are they brought down. After reinstatement, Chaudhry had the support of the bar as he championed a range of causes that were popular within the bar. But he also grew increasingly intrusive in the affairs of the bar and consolidated his control over judicial appointments. A close group of lawyers and judges tied to Chaudhry and the Lawyers' Movement were strongly favoured in judicial appointments, and this alleged favouritism caused the alienated sections of the bar to lash out (Khan 2019). By 2010, a new grouping of lawyers formed within the bar on a platform to reassert

---

[184] Adnan Adil, 'Legal Remedies', *The News*, 17 December 2006.
[185] Interview No. L-80, 22 July 2017.
[186] Interview No. J-19.

the bar's separation from Chaudhry's Court and break the hold of this group of lawyers and judges over the bar after the Lawyers' Movement.[187] Championed by the famous human rights lawyer Asma Jahangir, the new group organized to win a series of bar association elections, and then used these platforms to criticize Chaudhry and his actions (Khan 2019) .[188] Former judges and political parties, who had been targeted and humiliated by Chaudhry in court, cooperated with this group, and levelled allegations of corruption against Chaudhry and his son, which further fuelled the campaign of criticism against Chaudhry within the bar.[189]

By 2013, once Chaudhry retired, he had become a far more controversial and divisive figure than he had been in the aftermath of his reinstatement. Thus, Chaudhry's rise and fall exemplifies how vital the bar can be in making or breaking the reputations and fortunes of judges, and how time spent in the bar and relations with the bar shaped a judicial agenda of pursuing judicial supremacy legitimized by a middle-class populism that opposed and distrusted both military rule and political parties.[190]

Chaudhry was not the only influential judge echoing populist preferences developed within the bar, and the agenda of judicial supremacy did not start or end with him. Chief Justice Saqib Nisar, when questioned about judicial interventions into the functions of executive institutions, expressed the same ideas, stating:

> Only this way will the government officials have to improve the system. I will not back down. I will not sit quietly. If I have to stage a sit-in

---

[187] 'Bar Not to Be Made "A-Team" of Anyone, Says Asma', *Dawn*, 31 July 2010; 'Asma Wants Distance between Bar, Bench', *Dawn*, 19 October 2010.

[188] 'Asma Criticizes SC over Suo Motu Notices, *Dawn*, 21 May 2011; Mohammed Hussain Khan, 'Asma Criticizes Court Verdict on PCO Judges', *Dawn*, 19 May 2011.

[189] Amir Riaz, 'Musharraf Cronies, PCO Judges Back Asma', *News*, 27 October 2010.

[190] It is also worth noting that this very tactic of targeting judges' reputations based on allegations of financial improprieties committed by judges or their families, which was used to such effect against Justice Chaudhry towards the end of his career, has also became a useful tool for the military to use to bring judges into line. As judges became increasingly prominent public figures, military intelligence agencies recognized the utility of targeting the reputations of several High Court judges to ensure they could be more pliable. Interview No. L-80, 10 April 2017. This tactic of gathering intelligence to target judges' reputations was used increasingly frequently after 2017, as I detail in Chapter 6.

protest against the government I will but I will ensure that the bureaucracies and politicians get their jobs done.[191]

Chief Justice Khosa opined that the judiciary had the power to 'cleanse
the fountainhead of authority of the State so that the trickled down
authority may also become unpolluted. If this is achieved then the
legislative and executive limbs of the State are purified at the top.'[192]
Thus, judicial opposition to both military and political party dominance shaped judges' repeated interventions into regime structure, electoral processes, bureaucratic appointments and policymaking, as
detailed in the first section. As one politician lamented, 'what can we
do, when all these judges all think they are messiahs now, all come to
save the people'.[193]

CONCLUSION

Thus, while strategic considerations regarding openings in the political
environment, and support from private media and civil society, certainly played important roles in shaping judicial behaviour during this
period, these factors alone are not enough to explain the increase in
judicial assertiveness seen in Pakistan during this period, the targets of
this assertiveness and the new role the judiciary was carving out for
itself within Pakistan's political system. I argue that the diminishing
role of the military and the increasing role of the politically active bar
as audiences shaping the preferences of the judiciary best explain
judicial behaviour during this period. As the utilitarian and normative
interlinkages between the judiciary and the military weakened, more
independent-minded judges who were appointed from networks more
attuned to middle-class priorities and less wedded to military supremacy
came to populate the benches. With increasing normative and utilitarian interlinkages between the judiciary and the bar, the dominant
preference within the bar for an activist judiciary, unrestrained by
procedural limitations, regulating the political system to check both
military rule and political corruption and pursue a middle-class populist

---

[191] 'I Pray My Verdicts Bring to Fore Pious, Honest Person: CJ,' *The News*, 23
March 2018.
[192] See *Imran Khan Niazi* v. *Nawaz Sharif*, PLD 2017 SC 265. Justice Khosa was quoted
in Chapter 4 during his time as a lawyer in the 1990s advocating for the judiciary to
assume wide powers to check the corruption of the legislature.
[193] Interview No. P-5.

agenda, became increasingly hegemonic within the judiciary, leading to greater confrontation with military and civilian governments.

As one lawyer explained, 'the judges now see themselves as playing the same role as the military . . . an institution beyond corruption that can bring governance to the country'.[194]

---

[194] Interview No. L-36.

CHAPTER SIX

EPILOGUE

A Judiciary Fragmenting?

INTRODUCTION

Ten years after the high point of judicial assertiveness in 2007, 2017 was another critical juncture in the evolution of Pakistan's judiciary. In this chapter, I briefly discuss the messy politics of the judiciary since 2017, as it has both contributed to, and been compromised by, autocratization processes in the country. First, I will briefly discuss the trajectory of relations between the judiciary, military and political leadership during this period, as a new, more authoritarian political structure emerged. The military is once more in a position of political dominance, but the de jure leadership of the state lies with an elected political party, the Constitution remains unsuspended and unamended, and the superior judiciary retains its authority and broad jurisdiction. The judiciary itself appears polarized: divided over its role and relationship with other state institutions.

I suggest that two parallel dynamics are apparent in the internal culture of the judiciary. First, the institutional preferences underlying judicial interventions against previous civilian and military governments continue to motivate the judiciary's efforts to expand its authority and regulate civilian governments. However, the efforts of the military and affiliated elites to build closer institutional interlinkages with certain sections of the judiciary have also fragmented the judiciary on the question of rising military dominance. As judges of the superior courts find themselves split over the audiences they are responding to, their jurisprudence reflects these differences. However, the period under scrutinty in this epilogue is too limited for discerning patterns in judicial behaviour and identifying enduring shifts in the judiciary's internal culture. Without the benefit of hindsight to analyse the path the judiciary may be taking, this chapter's findings are tentative at best.

REVIVAL OF AUTHORITARIAN POWER

In 2017, the Supreme Court disqualified the elected prime minister, Nawaz Sharif, from holding elected office, due to corruption allegations and a misdeclaration of financial assets. When the so-called Panama papers (leaked documents containing personal financial information about wealthy individuals and public officials) were made public, they tied Sharif's children to offshore companies that owned prime real estate in London (Cheema 2018a). A petition was moved before the Supreme Court by the opposition party, the PTI, calling for Sharif's disqualification from office, based on allegations that these properties were purchased using unexplained and ill-gotten income. Sharif's assets and financial dealings came under judicial and media scrutiny, and the issue of political corruption became increasingly salient in the build-up to the 2018 elections (Cheema 2018a). The judgment came down in two stages. In the first stage, two judges ruled there was adequate circumstantial evidence of corruption to disqualify Sharif, while three judges constituted a Joint Investigation Team of civilian and military investigative officers to provide confirmed evidence of Sharif's financial misconduct.[1] The investigation unearthed considerable information about potential corruption and ill-gotten wealth, information that merited further investigation and scrutiny (Cheema 2018a). But the Court, rather than allowing the process of investigation, confirmation and conviction to go through before disqualifying Sharif, relied on the one minor source of income that Sharif had admitted to not declaring on his election papers, as adequate evidence to disqualify him under Article 62 of the Constitution (Cheema 2018a). Thus, the Supreme Court significantly expanded its original jurisdiction, first by directly taking up a trial case of corruption as a case of 'fundamental rights', rather than allowing it to work its way through the trial courts, and then finding that a relatively minor proven misdeclaration of assets was adequate to

---

[1] *Imran Khan Niazi v. Nawaz Sharif*, PLD 2017 SC 265.

disqualify an elected prime minister, without the prospect of appeal. In subsequent cases, the Supreme Court further expanded the potency of its power, ruling that a disqualification from elected office under Article 62 of the Constitution was a lifetime ban, and also rendering the disqualified individual ineligible to hold a leadership position within a political party. The Court could now purge individuals from political life, on the basis of civil charges.

Over the next few months, in the build-up to the 2018 elections, high courts were invited to apply the same standards articulated in the Panama decision against others running for political office. Prosecutions and disqualifications were primarily targeted against the ruling PML-N, while other parties seemed to be handled with greater restraint (Javid and Mufti 2020). The mechanics of the Panama decision revealed an apparent cross-institutional synergy that would undermine the electoral prospects of the PML-N. First, the PTI played a key role as the petitioner and instigator. Led by the charismatic leader Imran Khan, and organized around a platform of anti-corruption populism, the PTI had considerable support in the country's urban middle classes and a proven capacity to mobilize people. Imran Khan and his party pushed this anti-corruption manifesto both inside and outside the courts, petitioning the judiciary to act against leaders of the two long-standing political parties, PPP and PML-N, and mobilizing a vocal constituency demanding decisive action from the judiciary against the allegedly corrupt traditional parties. Second, the military played a key role in the Joint Investigation Team, as military intelligence officers unearthed evidence to disqualify Sharif, enabling the military to once more shape leadership selection in the name of combating political corruption. Finally, the Supreme Court read its powers widely in order to weed out corruption, enabling it to disqualify PML-N leaders. Thus, the military, Supreme Court judges and the PTI played different roles in a campaign of selective accountability that ultimately derailed the PML-N's electoral prospects, by rendering several PML-N leaders ineligible to run for elections, and motivating other members of the PML-N to defect to the PTI in order to avoid the axe of accountability (Shah 2019). This effort engineered the electoral landscape to ensure the PTI won the elections.

Once the PTI came to power in 2018, the military's authority and influence across state institutions grew substantially. Khan's new cabinet was full of politicians and policymakers who had served in Musharraf's government several years before, and an increasing number of formerly uniformed officers were now managing key governance portfolios.[2] This combination of elected governments with widening military involvement in governance led local analysts to call the new governing arrangement a 'hybrid' regime.[3] Within the first year of the PTI's government, the anti-corruption drive became an instrument for crippling political opposition and dissent, and silencing any criticism of the military. The NAB was weaponized against the political opposition, as leaders of the PML-N and PPP and allied bureaucrats were arrested on corruption charges.[4] There has also been a significant drop in freedom of expression in Pakistan, with Freedom House citing actions taken by the state to curtail media freedom (Freedom House 2020).

Thus, the military has been able to re-establish its position of dominance within Pakistan's political system, in coordination with civilian partners. The Supreme Court's judgment against Sharif set the stage for this incremental autocratization, but the institution grew increasingly divided over the role it would play in the emerging system.

Judicial Polarization between 2017 and 2020

By the time of the 2018 elections, constitutional courts were regulating the functioning of political institutions and influencing the selection of the state's political leadership. The judiciary justified its intervention in the electoral process as necessary to save the country from the menace of the corruption and deceit of oligarchic politicians. In a judgment dismissing Sharif's petition to review his criminal conviction, Justice Ejaz Afzal's words exemplified this anti-corruption rhetoric when he stated that Sharif 'tried to fool the people ... without realizing that ... you cannot fool all the people all the time'.[5] As the judiciary's regulation of electoral processes expanded, so did its interventions in policymaking and administration, bolstered by the same rhetoric of tackling political incompetence and vested interests.

During the tenure of Chief Justice Saqib Nisar (2016–2019), the Supreme Court used its *suo moto* powers to intervene in governance to

---

[2] Abbasi, 'Majority of PTI Minister, Advisers Served under Musharraf', *The News*, 19 August 2018.
[3] Nadeem Paracha, 'Hybrid Regimes and Their Discontents', *Dawn*, 11 October 2020.
[4] Sana Jamil, 'Pakistan's Prison Politics: Who Was in and Who Was Out in 2019', *Express Tribune*, 30 December 2019.
[5] See Hasnaat Malik, 'Sharif Tried to Fool the Nation: SC', *Express Tribune*, 7 November 2017.

an extent that had never been seen before. It is hard to do justice to Justice Nisar's whirlwind of on-bench and off-bench interventions, as he sought to fix all of Pakistan's socio-economic problems: water purity and distribution, milk production, public sector corruption, hospital management, educational disparities and population control, through the striking of the gavel.[6] Within the first three months of 2018 alone, Nisar launched thirty *suo moto* cases, often prompted by news articles he read, headlines he watched on the evening news or even posts he saw on social media.[7] In one case, Nisar took *suo moto* notice of a photograph circulating on social media that showed a funeral procession passing over sewage in a narrow street.[8]

Upon taking *suo moto* notice, Nisar would then order public officials to present themselves before the Court. During these proceedings, he would typically reprimand public officers and comment on state mismanagement, and in interim orders, he would direct public officers to remedy the issue and report back to the Court, dismiss officers who did not adequately address his concerns and sometimes even issue contempt of court charges against public officials who did not satisfactorily comply with his orders. Perhaps the most controversial example of Justice Nisar's *suo moto* jurisprudence was his order to construct new dams to resolve Pakistan's water shortages, 'for the collective benefit of the nation'.[9] Nisar launched a fundraising scheme for donations to pay for the multi-billion dollar dam-building project, authorizing televised ads and newspaper articles to openly solicit funding, and even ordering convicted parties in cases to do with assault, land acquisitions and environmental damage to deposit funds into the fund for the dam for the Court's new project.[10] Off the bench, Nisar also transformed the role of the chief justice, donning the hat of government inspector and international fundraiser, showing up at hospitals, schools and water plants to assess their conditions, followed by news cameras.[11] After Nisar's term ended, the Supreme Court walked back some of the most

---

[6] Saroop Ijaz, 'Chief Justice Saqib Nisar: Judging too Much', *Herald*, February 2019.

[7] 'Pakistan's Top Court is Eager to Take on Any Brief', *Economist*, March 2018.

[8] 'CJP Takes Suo Moto Notice', *Geo News*, 20 March 2018.

[9] *Barrister Zafarullah Khan* v. *Federation of Pakistan*, Constitutional Petition no. 57 of 2016.

[10] Murtaza Ali Shah, 'CJP Says Dams' Funds Initiative a Movement for Humanity', *The News*, 26 November 2018; Khaled Ahmed, 'The Caliph of the Court', *Indian Express*, 17 August 2019.

[11] 'CJP Visits National Hospital', *The News*, 1 October 2018.

egregious aspects of his jurisprudence. However, while Nisar's tenure was particularly jaw-dropping for the dizzying frequency of judicial interventions and disregard for legal procedure, his populist instinct to combat corrupt political interests and save the country from his courtroom was shared by other judges.

Why did Justice Nisar not face more political pushback from other state institutions during his tenure? The targets of Nisar's actions were primarily the federal and provincial government institutions, but he showed no appetite to contest military prerogatives. The populist jurisprudence of this period facilitated autocratization in Pakistan and the revival of military power, by delegitimizing the governance and governments of Pakistan's elected parties, limiting political discretion in the state administration, chipping away at the authority of provincial governments and inviting the interventions of unelected federal institutions into the management of politics and policymaking. After the military-backed PTI came to power, high courts permitted state institutions to arrest and detain members of the political opposition and civil society activists, denying bail applications for arrests based on often flimsy charges.[12] The courts were also largely silent on the practice of enforced disappearances, and regularly delayed hearings in cases pertaining to military interests.[13] The selective nature of these judicial interventions meant Justice Nisar was unlikely to face pushback from the most powerful state institution, but it also prompted concerns that the superior judiciary had come under the control of the military.

However, the judiciary was not returning to the subordinated role it had played during previous dictatorships. There were significant pockets of the judiciary that did not want to shy away from confronting military power and restraining authoritarian power. The Islamabad High Court provided several arrested opposition members and activists with legal relief, and sought to place constraints on the powers of the NAB.[14] The Peshawar High Court set aside the sentences of seventy-four people convicted by military courts, on the grounds that these trials did not meet the evidentiary standards required for conviction.[15]

---

[12] Ishaq Tanoli, 'SHC Dismisses Bail Plea of PTM Leader Ali Wazir', *Dawn*, 1 June 2021.

[13] Interview No. L-60.

[14] Interview No. 102, 15 February 2021. See Saqib Bashir, 'IHC Asks NAB to Not Violate Legal Provisions', *Express Tribune*, 24 January 2021.

[15] Sirajuddin, 'PHC Sets Aside Sentences', *Dawn*, 18 October 2018.

The Balochistan High Court ruled that the DHA could not acquire property or perform municipal functions.[16] A Special Court declared General Musharraf guilty of high treason for suspending the constitution. In spite of Musharraf's non-attendance and repeated requests for delays (he has been living in self-exile in Dubai since 2014), and significant pressure to abandon the case, the Special Court issued a verdict providing a strongly worded repudiation of Musharraf's actions. The Court convicted Musharraf and even called for government action against his military collaborators (Kureshi 2021). The treason judgment revealed both the continuing enthusiasm for confrontation within sections of the judiciary, and the growing polarization, as soon after the Special Court judgment, a three-member bench of the Lahore High Court accepted an appeal against the verdict of the Special Court.

Pakistan's representative institutions and electoral process had been significantly weakened, largely as a result of the alignment of interests of its two premier unelected institutions, but it was less clear that there was consensus between the two institutions regarding the role the judiciary. In November 2019, Chief Justice Khosa issued an interim order suspending a three-year extension granted to the chief of army staff by the PTI government, finding the government had not identified a legal instrument that enabled the granting of extensions, nor provided adequate justification for granting the extension. Chief Justice Khosa rebuked the lawyers of the government for mishandling the question of the extension, and public figures who were aligned with the military publicly criticized Justice Khosa's comments, raising concerns that the two institutions were barrelling towards a major confrontation.[17] However, ultimately, the Court stepped back, providing the government time to issue the necessary legislation for authorizing an extension, and granting the chief of army staff a temporary extension until this legislation was passed (Nazar 2021). The Court justified its actions as an 'exercise of judicial restraint' that was 'essential to the continuance of rule law', language that was a far cry from the confrontational discourse of the interim order.[18] Speculation abounds as to what transpired, but the contrast between the interim order and the final judgment was revealing of the potential for a serious confrontation

---

[16] Saleem Shahid, 'BHC Declares DHA Act Unconstitutional', *Dawn*, 18 December 2020.

[17] Interview No. J-48, 11 February 2021.

[18] *Jurists' Foundation* v. *Federal Government*, 2020 PLD SC 1.

between the two institutions, and the process of interinstitutional bargaining that plays out over the course of interim orders in the build-up to the final court verdict – bargaining that remains largely hidden to outside observers.

Perhaps the issue that most clearly highlights the friction over the role of the judiciary in this regime structure was the controversy of the Faizabad sit-in. In 2017, a protest sit-in in the area of Faizabad in the capital city Islamabad by the Tehreek-e-Labbaik Pakistan (TLP), a newly founded Islamist political party, against allegedly blasphemous actions by the PML-N government, led to a violent confrontation between the government and protesters, and invited intervention by the two major unelected institutions.[19] The military, which was widely suspected to have provided covert support to the TLP to weaken the PML-N government, chose to mediate between the government and the protesters.[20] The Supreme Court initiated *suo moto* proceedings, ostensibly to ensure the protest did not disrupt people's fundamental rights. Both unelected institutions deemed it their prerogative to intervene and manage the government's handling of the TLP. In the 2018 election, the TLP participated in the elections, in spite of questions regarding its funding sources, and managed to peel off votes from the PML-N, thus helping ensure the PTI's victory.[21]

A two-member bench of the Court continued hearings into the handling of the TLP's sit-in and subsequent participation in elections, and, in its final judgment in 2019, held that the approach taken by the military's intelligence agency, the ISI, towards the TLP indicated that the ISI was providing support to the TLP, and called on intelligence agencies to stop interfering in electoral politics and curtailing freedom of speech.[22] The judgment challenged the political role of the military's intelligence agencies at a time when military power was rising. The judge that authored this judgment, Justice Qazi Faez Isa, became the subject of a concerted campaign to have him removed from the Court, a campaign that exposed fault lines within the judiciary over its relationship with the military.

---

[19] 'After Crackdown on Faizabad Dharna: Army Called Out in Islamabad', *The News*, 26 November 2017.
[20] 'Only Negotiated with Army Officials', *Dawn*, 29 November 2017.
[21] Waseem Abbasi, 'TLP Inflicts Losses to PML-N', *The News*, 30 July 2018.
[22] *Suo moto* case no. 7/2017.

In April 2019, the government initiated an inquiry into properties held by members of Justice Isa's family, and alleged that Justice Isa was the undeclared owner of these assets. On the basis of this inquiry the government filed a reference with the SJC, alleging that Justice Isa was guilty of judicial misconduct and had to be removed. Isa denied the allegations, and petitioned the Supreme Court to quash the government's reference as *malafide*, motivated by government anger against Isa's judgment in the Faizabad case. Justice Isa's petition was joined by petitions from bar councils and bar associations, and resolutions from bar associations across the country questioned the wisdom and motives behind the references.[23] The case was divisive, as some lawyers were concerned that the reference posed a grave threat to judicial independence, but others worried that quashing this reference meant judges could not be held accountable.[24] The debate over independence and accountability continued, but it was clear this reference was an attempt at purging the judiciary of judges willing to confront the military. The future of the confrontational court was on the line.

As the case moved forward, outside the court, government sources 'leaked' details of Justice Isa's alleged financial misconduct and a malicious campaign of misinformation was carried out through media outlets and a web of social media accounts with links to the government, aimed at discrediting and vilifying Justice Isa.[25] In response, Justice Isa chose to wage an equally public campaign. Backed by bar association leaders, Justice Isa disclosed his written responses to the government's allegations, publicly revealed details of his assets, and used the Court proceedings to address audiences outside the courtroom.[26] In words designed for public consumption, he called out executive institutions for surveilling judges, suppressing the media and threatening his family, and declared he was 'fighting for the future of Pakistan'.[27] Thus, Justice Isa combated the anti-corruption populism

---

[23] Hasnaat Malik, 'Bar Council Opposes Reference against Isa', *Express Tribune*, 12 June 2020.

[24] Interview No. J-50, 20 February 2021.

[25] Hasnaat Malik, 'References and Vendettas', *Express Tribune*, 2 May 2021; Nasir Iqbal, 'Onslaught against Judiciary Shocks Senior Lawyers', *Dawn*, 13 May 2021.

[26] Hasnaat Malik, 'Justice Isa Seeks Clarity on Reference Reports', *Express Tribune*, 29 May 2019.

[27] Nasir Iqbal, 'Justice Isa Says He's Fighting for Future of Judiciary', *Express Tribune*, 3 March 2021.

of the military-backed PTI by adopting a populist idiom as well, casting himself as a figure of resistance.

Within the courtroom, Justice Isa's fate split the judiciary. The Court ruled unanimously in favour of Justice Isa's petition. However, the Court was split over the motive behind the reference and the future of the reference. The majority judgment was designed to avoid any confrontation with executive institutions. It upheld the importance of both judicial accountability and independence, criticized civilian government officials for filing the reference but remained silent on the military's role, and sidestepped the questions of surveillance of judges and the intent behind filing the reference. The order also directed taxation authorities to verify the assets of Justice Isa's wife and family to see if there were any concerns meriting resuming the SJC proceedings.[28] On the other hand, the dissenting note of Justice Mansoor Ali Shah was far more confrontational, finding that the reference against Justice Isa was a product of malicious intent. He stated that 'the vengeance and resentment against the … Judge … is more than visible', condemned the unauthorized surveillance of judges, called for criminal proceedings against executive officers involved in the reference and objected to the majority judgment's initiation of an investigation by taxation authorities.

Justice Isa did not relent, and he went on to file a review petition, challenging the need for, or legality of, the court-ordered investigation by the taxation authorities of his family, once again joined by several bar associations. The proceedings proved especially heated, as Justice Isa and his wife repeatedly pleaded with judges to acknowledge the harassment they were facing from government and military officers, and Supreme Court judges openly confronted and chided each other during oral proceedings.[29] Justice Isa's review petition prevailed, and, in a split verdict, the Court quashed the reference against Justice Isa and the investigation of his family. The majority opinion held that, in directing the taxation authoritarites to initiate an investigation into Justice Isa's wife's financial assets, the Court had violated her right to a fair hearing, whereas the minority held otherwise.[30] Both the majority and dissenting opinions discussed public confidence in the judiciary and the reputation of judges. The majority held that stifling 'independent

---

[28] *Justice Qazi Faez Isa v. Federation of Pakistan*, PLD 2020 SC 346.
[29] Hasnaat Malik, 'Clash of Top Court Judges', *Express Tribune*, 22 April 2021.
[30] *Justice Qazi Faez Isa v. The President of Pakistan*, PLD 2022 SC 118.

judges' like Justice Isa would 'erode public confidence in the judiciary'. It went on to state that 'the members of all Bar Associations across the country hold Justice Isa as an honest, independent and impartial judge ... and [the bar associations] are the main stakeholders in the judicial system and are best suited to express their opinion about ... a Judge'. The minority verdict responded by saying that judges should be held to the same standards of accountability as 'public servants', for 'if aspersions cast against judges are not dispelled', the judges' 'credibility is dispelled' and the Court's '[m]oral authority is eroded'. The opinions indicated how individual and institutional reputational concerns shaped jurisprudence in publicly salient decisions. The case and its aftermath signal the growing tensions over what role the judiciary should have within the political system, both between the judiciary and other state institutions, and between the judges themselves.

Thus, over the last three years, the courts remain largely committed to playing an expansive and authoritative role in politics and in governance. The disdain for party-based government, and a willingness to regulate the actions of political branches, also persists. But the willingness to confront military institutions seems to have diminished, and varies across sections of the judiciary.

SHIFTING JUDICIAL AUDIENCES?

Why are we seeing a diminished appetite for confrontation? One reason is the so-called 'hybrid' regime. In an increasingly autocratic political system, with the revival of military dominance, expansion in the role of military intelligence agencies and repression of the political opposition and civil society, judicial assertiveness became costlier. However, strategic deference in an increasingly authoritarian political environment is not the only explanation for increasing judicial restraint, as the judiciary has played an important role in facilitating this autocratization. Further, as the previous section shows, friction between the judiciary and civilian and military executive institutions persists.

Understanding the current fragmentation within the judiciary over its relationship with other state institutions and role within the political system requires paying attention to the audiences of the judiciary. As the judicialization of politics and governance has accelerated, judges have become more public figures, whose actions from day to day are covered by electronic and print media and debated in bar rooms, law firms, talk shows and Facebook and WhatsApp groups. The surveillance of judges and their families by intelligence officers and journalists has also increased. Thus, building and maintaining reputations has become a more complex and precarious challenge, and executive institutions can constrain judges by threatening to damage their reputations. Several lawyers and judges have highlighted the growing concern about the surveillance of judges. As one former judge explained, 'all judges have skeletons ... either their own, or those of family members, and intelligence agencies keep a tab on these skeletons'.[31] The military-backed government uses the information they keep on judges and their families to damage their standing and esteem with their professional and social networks. Justice Isa said, when imploring his fellow judges to take a stand against unauthorized surveillance against judges, 'I can honestly say that files are ready against each of you and it could be the turn of any one of you'.[32] Surveillance has indirectly helped the military and affiliated elites enhance utilitarian and normative interlinkages with the judiciary.

In terms of utilitarian interlinkages, intelligence files can be used to impact the appointment, promotions and disciplining of judges. Surveillance of Justice Isa's family was used to frame Justice Isa as corrupt and initiate removal proceedings against him. Strong executive opposition to judges can also be used to prevent their promotion. Justice Waqar Seth, chief justice of the Peshawar High Court and the lead judge in both the Musharraf treason trial and the overturning of the military court convictions, saw his elevation to the Supreme Court delayed repeatedly, until he tragically died of Covid-19. On judicial appointments, intelligence agencies would prepare intelligence reports on candidates for judicial appointments, which the Judicial Commission would then consider in confirming appointments, and these reports could be used to scuttle appointments.[33] Thus, concerns about military influence in judicial appointments, promotion and removal persist. However, the interventions today are not direct in the way they used to be. Judges are still preeminent in the appointment and promotion of judges, and the impact of the military on judicial careers is more indirect and covert, as one senior lawyer explained: 'In the 1980s, the establishment did not have to use covert methods to control judges, because they had

---

[31] Interview No. J-13, 11 January 2021.
[32] Nasir Iqbal, 'Justice Isa Cautions Judges', *Dawn*, 18 March 2021.
[33] However, chief justices frequently disregarded the intelligence reports, if they favoured the nominee. Interview No. L-52.

direct control over their careers. Today it relies on its ability to surveil judges.'[34] In short, across Pakistan's history, the military has shifted from appointing judges, to bargaining with judges, to surveilling judges, in order to influence judicial behaviour.[35]

In terms of normative interlinkages, the increased public visibility of judges, and the expansion of social media, has made the esteem in which judges are held more vulnerable to leaked surveillance *as well as* misinformation that is spread via social media accounts covertly linked to the PTI government and the military.[36] Damaging stories of judicial corruption, nepotism or anti-national activities, some true and some false, are planted and spread across social media, and these stories impact judges' standing with their professional and social networks.[37] The leaked reports were circulated across social media, and discussed and validated by pro-government journalists. Judges, fearful of potentially damaging stories, both real or manufactured, grew increasingly cautious about antagonizing the military and military-backed government. As one lawyer who recently considered becoming a judge explained, 'the problem is, as a judicial nominee or judge, you have to stay silent and keep a low profile. So, when fake stories spread about you, there is little or nothing you can say or do to defend yourself.'[38] Thus, through intelligence agencies, pro-government journalists and an army of social media accounts, the military has built informal interlinkages with the judiciary.

However, the military is not the dominant audience for the judiciary the way it was several decades ago. Judges still monopolize control over the judicial appointment process, and the bar remains a critically important audience for judicial careers and esteem. In 2020, the Judicial Commission decided not to entertain unsigned reports by intelligence agencies in the process of appointments and confirmation of judges, and also resolved that it would not consider reports that lack

---

[34] Interview No. L-71, 15 December 2020.

[35] The military has also built inroads into other key offices of the judicial system, namely by co-opting the registrars of the courts, an important bureaucratic office within the judiciary that, among other issues, plays a role in deciding when cases will be heard, and which cases will be delayed. Interview No. L-60.

[36] Saad Sayeed, 'Facebook Removes Accounts Linked to Pakistani Military Employees', *Reuters*, 1 April 2020.

[37] Anonymous social media accounts would 'leak' government reports that maligned Justice Isa and his family, and were designed to damage his credibility.

[38] Interview No. L-52, 2 February 2021.

supportive materials, making it harder for intelligence reports to influence judicial nominations.[39] Bar leaders continue to maintain an informal stake in the judicial appointment process, and the opinions of the bar leaders remained important in judicial appointments.[40]

Bar associations around the country have denounced the revival of authoritarian power in Pakistan,[41] commended judges who defied the military and civilian executive branches and criticized judges who were deemed too closely aligned with the military.[42] As the government pursued its case against Justice Isa, bar councils and bar associations voiced solidarity with him, organized protests to support him and filed petitions joining Justice Isa's own petition to quash the reference against him.[43] Thus, Justice Isa's fate became wired into bar politics, and bar support for Justice Isa significantly influenced the bench. As a senior lawyer explained, 'the Court would not have even accepted Justice Isa's petition challenging the Supreme Judicial Council proceedings against him, had it not been for the pressure from the bar'.[44] Judges were sensitized to bar criticism and support for judicial defiance, and Chief Justice Gulzar Ahmed objected to prominent figures in the bar commenting that some judges were bold while others were not, as this was creating divisions in the bench.[45] Thus, just as military pressure for deference grew, bar support for a more confrontational and defiant judiciary has persisted.

Political parties and the military are aware of the growing importance of the bar, and its role in shaping judicial behaviour, and have sought to establish closer ties to bar associations, through the provision of opportunities and patronage. As the stakes in bar association elections grew higher, bar elections grew more expensive. Political parties saw the expensive electoral process as an opportunity to gain influence in bar elections, by providing finances to fund bar elections in exchange for future support for the party.[46] Parties also recognize the importance of

[39] Hasnaat Malik, 'Judicial Commission of Pakistan Reviews Agencies' Role', *Express Tribune*, 21 April 2020.
[40] Interview No. J-90, 13 February 2021; Interview No. R-4, 20 February 2021.
[41] See Pakistan Bar Council Resolution, 8 February 2021 regarding how the 'government has gone against democratic, constitutional and ethical grounds'.
[42] 'Creating Divisions among Judges Amounts to Contempt', *The News*, 7 November 2020.
[43] Haseeb Bhatti and Syed Ali Shah, 'SCBA, Lawyers Protest', *Dawn*, 14 June 2019.
[44] Interview No. L-52.
[45] 'Creating Divisions among Judges Amounts to Contempt'.
[46] Interview No. L-101, 3 February 2021.

the bar as a critically important constituency, and have given important political positions to party members who are active in bar politics. In the 2021 Senate elections, all three leading parties – the PTI, PPP and PML-N –awarded senate tickets to prominent members of the bar. The military-backed government also provided funding to the bar councils to win their support, cultivated sections of lawyers within the bar, and even offered assistance to bar associations on the condition that they supported the government's reference against Isa.[47] As one lawyer explained, 'once lawyers won elections to local bar councils, they would often be visited by people with the agencies, who would then discuss potential career opportunities, in order to get their support'.[48] Thus, the government, military and opposition have all recognized the importance of the bar as a critical audience for the judiciary, and have sought to build inroads.

These efforts have had an impact on bar culture. As the authority and influence of leadership positions in the bar have grown, aspirants to these positions are willing to make deals with the military, politicians and judges to ensure victories and maximize their access to resources. And this has compromised the willingness of bar leaders to unite on critical issues, or hold judges and generals accountable. One reason why Justice Nisar's reign of judicial overreach did not face the same level of opposition from within the bar that other overreaching chief justices faced, is that he cultivated the support of selected senior bar leaders, particularly from Lahore, by providing them with opportunities to boost their professional careers.[49] Further, in 2021, the Lahore Bar Association's Executive Committee announced its support for the government's reference against Justice Isa, in exchange for budgetary allocation of funding for the bar association.[50] Patronage and professional opportunities have helped the military and affiliated political elites influence the bar's relationship with the judiciary.

Thus, over the last few years the military and affiliated elites have adapted to the emergence of the confrontational court by supporting the judiciary on issues where their preferences align, and by establishing new interlinkages with the judiciary to influence the legal and

---

[47] 'All Judgments Are SC's Judgments', *Dawn*, 8 November 2020; Interview No. L-99, 29 December 2020.

[48] Interview No. L-96, 5 February 2021.

[49] Interview No. L-51, 22 January 2021.

[50] Lahore Bar Association Executive Committee Resolution, 29 May 2021.

policy preferences underlying judicial behaviour. As explained in Chapter 5, the preferences that motivated judges of the superior courts to confront unfettered military dominance under Musharraf also motivated judges to confront and seek to establish supremacy over the elected civilian governments. Between 2017 and 2019, the super-ior courts, particularly the Supreme Court, expanded their authority over governance and electoral processes, motivated by the conviction that politicians were either too incompetent or corrupt to meaningfully act in the public interest. This anti-corruption populism permeated through Court hearings and judgments, as evidenced by the increased usage of the word 'mafia' to describe politicians and interest groups who, judges claimed, stood in the way of good governance.[51] The disdain for politicians was a consensus across the judiciary, but the splits that emerged within the judiciary were over (1) how far judges were willing to align with the military in regulating political govern-ments, and (2) how far judges were willing to extend their own powers to regulate political governments.

On the first question, the split within the Court become increasingly apparent. Some judges invited military intervention in the task of regulating the political branches, as was evident in the formation of the Joint Investigation Team against Nawaz Sharif. A lawyer and former Supreme Court clerk explained that, 'for these judges, the real problem was political corruption, and there was nothing wrong with the military helping ... curb political corruption'.[52] These judges, therefore, were willing to align with the military in regulating the political branches, and the military was happy to see the courts expand their powers, as long as they exercised those powers against the political branches. Unfortunately, these judicial interventions enabled the auto-cratization of the state and the revival of military power. And with the revival of military power and the expansion of intelligence surveillance, the military and affiliated elites have been able to exert pressure over other judges, through an increased ability to impact their reputations, with repercussions for their careers, credibility and esteem. Thus, a combination of an alignment of interests between the judicial and military elites in opposition to Pakistan's traditional parties, as well as

[51] Sohail Khan, 'Government Has Become Mafia: Justice Azmat', *The News*, 2 June 2017.
[52] Interview No. L-15, 20 March 2021.

increased military influence over judicial reputations, has produced a sizeable faction of judges unwilling to confront the military, for sincere and strategic reasons.

Yet, another group of judges remains both sceptical of political and military power, and is unwilling to collaborate in enabling authoritarianism. A lawyer close to this group of judges explained, 'it is hard for these judges to sit with the other group of judges, when they [believe] that those judges are speaking to the military on the side'.[53] The strategy of many judges who chose to defy, rather than collaborate with or defer to, the military and the military-backed government, has been to court the support of bar associations. Thus, a different populist idiom, directed against the concealed power of the military and aimed at gaining the support of segments of the bars, permeates the off-bench statements of these judges, as we see in the explosive speech of Justice Shaukat Siddiqui of the Islamabad High Court to the Rawalpindi Bar Association, in which he accused intelligence agencies of meddling in judicial affairs in connivance with Supreme Court judges, a speech for which he was later removed from the judiciary.[54]

The second split is over the extent of judicial populism, as some judges grow increasingly concerned about how populist judicial interventions have negatively impacted democratic stability in the country. There are growing differences between judges over how the Supreme Court should use its *suo moto* powers after Justice Nisar's excessive reliance on this power. Justice Mansoor Ali Shah, in a judgment criticizing judicial overreach, stated that 'when the judiciary starts interfering with the proper functioning of the legislative or executive organs of the government' this amounts to 'judicial imperialism'.[55] However, many, if not most, judges feel that the corruption of politicians and the tyranny of the military compel the judiciary to intervene in the other branches of government, and there remains sizeable constituencies across the legal complex that support the judiciary intervening in the affairs of other institutions.

Thus, today, the pattern of limited but significant confrontations with the military, juxtaposed against extensive interventions into the electoral and governance process of civilian governments, reveals a

---

[53] Interview No. L-82, 15 February 2021.

[54] Sohail Khan, 'Controversial Speech at Rawalpindi Bar', *The News*, 12 October 2018.

[55] *Mian Bashir v. Deputy Commissioner*, CP 446-L/2019.

judiciary that is at once strategically cautious in confronting a military that has seen its powers revived, ideologically aligned with the military in regulating party-based government and ideologically opposed to letting the military define or limit the role the judiciary will play in shaping the state's trajectory. I suggest that shifts in institutional inter-linkages between the judiciary, military and bar associations are grad-ually disrupting the internal consensus regarding legal and policy preferences, but it is too early to determine how far these changes will go, and thus what durable impact they will have.

There are two sobering takeaways from the experience of the last three years. First, it not inevitable that a judiciary with few interlin-kages connecting it to a politically powerful military will prevent the accumulation of political power by the military, or entrench democratic institutions, although it can place key outer limits on the military's power-seeking aspirations, and that impacts the structure of the regime. Second, just because the previous institutional interlinkages between authoritarian elites and the judiciary have diminished, does not mean new interlinkages cannot emerge, and the formal and informal rela-tionships between the judiciary and external institutions, organizations and networks are not fixed but remain in flux.

However, these last three years reinforce the overall argument of this book: that judicial reputations matter, and they shape internal judicial culture, the choices judges make and the values they uphold.

CHAPTER SEVEN

CONCLUSION AND COMPARATIVE PERSPECTIVES

INTRODUCTION

Since the third wave of democracy there is a growing recognition of the critical role the judiciary plays in the establishment and consolidation of democracy (Huntington 1991; Schepelle 2003; Gloppen 2004; Hirschl 2008). Today independent courts are seen as a critical component of liberal democracy and a necessary antidote to the rise of illiberal populism and authoritarianism (Bogg and Freedland 2018; Gardbaum 2015; Lacey 2019). But this commitment to judicial independence from external interventions, as a necessary check on the authoritarian instincts of political and military leaders, must be informed by a deeper understanding of the forms that external interventions into the judiciary can take, and the meanings judges ascribe to institutional independence. When will formally independent judges uphold liberal and democratic norms or challenge powerful authoritarian militaries? Similarly, when will independent judges wield their authority to undermine and displace democratically elected authorities? To answer these questions, we must pay attention to the processes that lead to the formation of hegemonic discourses and preferences within judicial institutions (Ocantos 2016).

The audience-based framework, presented in this book, highlights how external actors do not just shape the space for judges to act upon their preferences, but also shape hegemonic discourses within the judiciary and influence the formation and evolution of judges' legal and policy preferences. In this framework, judges are attentive to the preferences of the authorities and organizations who can advance their careers, and the social and professional networks with whom they seek to build esteem. Judges who express the preferences of these institutions and networks, or audiences, move upward in the judicial hierarchy and build esteem as judges, and through this process, over time, the preferences of these audiences become hegemonic within the judicial system, thus entrenching new institutional preferences. Simply put, judicial legal and policy preferences form in response to the preferences of the institutions and networks, or audiences, that determine the career trajectories and esteem of judges. Applied to the context of judicial–military interactions, I argue that the judiciary's affinity to the military diminishes as authorities and networks from which judges seek approval, to advance careers and build esteem, grow independent from the military. By properly embedding the judiciary in its political, social and institutional environment, this theory can explain how external institutions, organizations and networks shape the legal and policy preferences underlying judicial behaviour.

In Pakistan, the book has brought to bear evidence that, without dismissing altogether the relevance of other factors that contributed to variation in judicial contestation of military prerogatives, a change in judicial audiences is crucial for explaining the judiciary's shift from collaborating with, to confronting, military domination. Over the course of Pakistan's history, a shift in the external audiences shaping the judiciary's legal and policy preferences caused a shift in the judiciary's relationship with the military. The military and its affiliates were gradually displaced as the judiciary's most crucial audience for career advancement and esteem building, through processes that disrupted the institutional interlinkages between the military and the judiciary, and ensured the bar of activist lawyers became an increasingly significant audience, causing a shift in the legal and policy preferences underlying judicial behaviour. What emerged was a politically ambitious judiciary, which eschewed the constraints of a positivist jurisprudence in a state where the formal legal framework is designed to secure executive discretion, and reinterpreted its constitutional ambit to include resolving questions of politics and policymaking, ostensibly in the public interest. The judiciary went from limiting its own powers of judicial review and suspending fundamental rights in order to give the military-led executive the widest possible discretion, to challenging key military prerogatives and confronting a powerful military regime as it established its own role as a centre of political power. However, the judiciary's increasingly confrontational relationship with the military did not translate into a commitment to elected civilian supremacy, as the very institutional ambitions that motivated the judiciary to confront the military also led the judiciary to challenge and undermine elected governments, in its bid to establish judicial supremacy.

The transformation of Pakistan's judiciary yields important lessons for our understanding of the role of judicial institutions in securing democracy. Formal judicial independence is not an adequate guarantee that the judiciary will play a democracy-enhancing role, if judges seek to craft reputations with authoritarian elites to advance their careers or gain esteem. The values propounded by these authoritarian elites will then be manifested in court judgments. Therefore, in constructing judicial institutions, we must also pay attention to the preferences of the networks from which judges are recruited, and the actors who facilitate the careers of judges. If these audiences are inclined towards a more authoritarian and militaristic state, these preferences will work their way into the dominant norms and preferences within the judiciary, shaping institutional understandings about the political system judges should uphold, the role they should play in upholding that system, and their approach to legal principles, precedents and interpretations in playing that role. A judiciary that is less deferential to military supremacy will be one where formal and informal institutional rules and recruiting norms do not privilege the military and pro-military elites as critical audiences.

However, the Pakistan case also shows that simply cutting interlinkages between the military and the judiciary may increase the judiciary's willingness to confront and contest the military, but it is also no guarantee that the judiciary will uphold democratic norms. In a judiciary with limited interlinkages either to the military or to political society, the dominant legal and policy preferences that emerge may put courts in conflict with both. In Pakistan, as the military's linkages to the judiciary diminished, political parties were largely unsuccessful in filling the gap. Instead, a largely autonomous and oppositional bar developed close interlinkages with the judiciary, and the judiciary that emerged from this shift in audiences was opposed to unfettered military rule and also antagonistic towards political parties and electoral supremacy, and it was willing to use its authority to undermine both. The lesson here is that judges will always be responsive to different elites, for material and non-material reasons, and therefore the ideal institutional configuration would be one that ensures that judges are responsive to a diversity of audiences, that is, recruited from multiples networks and by multiple stakeholders.

The next section explores the generalizability of the audience-based explanation to other country cases. The third section considers this study's implications for debates in public law and comparative politics.

GENERALIZING THE AUDIENCE-BASED APPROACH

The audience-based explanation for variation in judicial contestation of military prerogatives can be applied to judicial–military interactions beyond Pakistan. Although the process of reshaping judicial preferences towards the military in Pakistan through a change in judicial audiences was based on institutional processes unique to Pakistan, the impact of audiences on judicial norms and preferences underlying judicial behaviour towards the military is not. To demonstrate the generalizability of the audience-based approach, I first outline the significance of audiences in shaping the judiciary's approach to the military in Egypt under the regime of General Mubarak (1981–2011). I select Egypt because, similar to Pakistan, the military was the preeminent institution shaping the political order of the state, with deep penetration into the state's economy as well. I then provide two shorter case studies of judicial–military relations in Turkey's military-led tutelary political system after 1961 and before the rise of Erdogan and the Justice and Development Party (AKP) in 2003, and judicial–government relations in India from independence till the 1990s. I discuss Turkey because, as shown in Table 7.1, Pakistan, Egypt and Turkey are all located at different points in the typology of judicial–military relationships developed in this book, and thus help show how variation in institutional interlinkages can explain variation in judicial assertiveness towards politically powerful militaries. I then discuss India, to demonstrate the utility of the audience-based framework for explaining judicial behaviour beyond the context of judicial–military relations and authoritarian and post-authoritarian states, with a discussion of the role of audiences in shaping the judiciary's approach to elected governments.

Egypt
In 1952, a group of military officers led by Colonel Nasser overthrew the Egyptian monarchy and established a socialist republic. The state was ruled by Nasser's official party, the Arab Socialist Union, but

241

TABLE 7.1   Cross-national variation in judicial relationship with the military

Country		Utilitarian interlinkage	Normative interlinkage	Type of court
Pakistan	1950s and 1960s	Yes	Yes	Loyal court
	1980s and 1990s	Yes	No	Controlled court
	2000s and 2010s	No	No	Confrontational court
Egypt	1990s	No	No	Confrontational court
	2000s	Yes	Yes	Loyal court
Turkey	1960s	No	Yes	Collaborative court
	1980s	Yes	Yes	Loyal court

Egypt's rulers came from the military, and the military remained the most powerful institution. Mubarak, Egypt's third leader since the 1952 revolution, was also from the armed forces, and under him the military's penetration of both Egyptian state and society grew, as the economic, institutional and judicial autonomy of the military increased (Arafat 2017).

Egypt's judiciary, unlike most judiciaries in the Middle East, had a history of comparative independence.[1] Mubarak ruled from 1981 till 2011, and during the first two decades of Mubarak's regime the Supreme Constitutional Court (SCC) and the administrative courts accumulated a large body of rulings seeking to limit the power of the regime. Just as in Pakistan, the judiciary pursued an agenda of judicializing politics and leaving its own imprint on the political landscape and trajectory of Egypt. In the economic sphere, the SCC overturned Nasser-era nationalization laws and pursued economic liberalization (Moustafa 2007). In the political sphere, the SCC also issued strong

---

[1] The Egyptian judiciary is divided into hierarchical structures with differing jurisdictions. The national courts are a hierarchical arrangement with courts of appeal and the Court of Cassation at the apex, and these courts primarily deal with civil and criminal matters. The administrative courts primarily deal with administrative matters, and the State Council is the court at the apex of this judicial structure. The Supreme Constitutional Court, which was established by Nasser's successor, Anwar Sadat, under the 1971 Constitution, primarily deals with constitutional matters.

rulings in favour of the political oppositions' rights and pushed for a restructuring of the electoral system for local and national elections. Moustafa (2007: 1) writes that by the turn of the century, the SCC had become the 'most important venue for political activists to challenge the regime' and expose its repressive nature.

The SCC was not alone in this increased activism, as the other courts increasingly challenged some of the regime's security interests and prerogatives of the military. The administrative courts defended political and civil rights of individuals and groups. In 1978, the High Administrative Court significantly limited the application of the emergency law by narrowing the legal definitions of 'suspicion' and 'sedition' (Rutherford 2008). In 1993, courts acquitted all defendants in the assassination of the speaker of parliament, rejecting confessions obtained through torture (El-Ghobashy 2016). In 1992, the Council of State struck down Mubarak's referral of civilians to military tribunals on grounds that this violated the constitution's guarantee of a fair trial. In the mid-2000s, the administrative courts overruled the military's expulsion of the residents of a mid-Nile island. Thus, administrative courts became an important venue for challenging the regime and the prerogatives of the military. As the regime produced ever more intrusive statutes to empower state authorities to take more repressive coercive actions, more Egyptians turned to the courts to contest arbitrary and unfair decrees. The number of petitions increased sixfold and this included important impact litigation meant to hold the government publicly accountable for its' actions (El-Ghobashy 2016). The Court of Cassations, the supreme appellate court for Egypt's courts of general jurisdiction, also asserted itself on questions of civil liberties, issuing rulings that limited state policing and surveillance powers over citizens (Hamad 2019).

By the early 2000s, the clash between executive institutions and increasingly assertive sections of the judiciary reached its height. In 2000, the SCC passed a landmark transformative judgment holding that the judiciary should monitor all national elections. Shortly after the ruling, Justice Al-Ghiryani issued a ruling invalidating the 2000 parliamentary election results in East Cairo (Aziz 2016). This decision went too far for Mubarak, and prompted him to act to rein in the judiciary and end this streak of activism. What was the source of the growth in judicial activism during the 1990s?

Egypt's modern legal system was shaped in the first half of the twentieth century and reached its utmost degree of independence in the 1940s, with the codification of the Law of the Independence of the Judiciary (Rutherford 2008). Lawyers and judges had been at the forefront of the anti-British nationalist movement in the 1930s and 1940s and were heavily influenced by ideals of classical liberalism (Rutherford 2008). This included an emphasis on the separation of powers and judicial independence, and the judiciary sought to protect and promote some level of autonomy since then, limiting the inter-linkages with Egypt's executive institutions, including the military. The limited interlinkages between executive and judicial institutions mani-fested themselves in limited but consequential confrontations between the judiciary and military under Mubarak's regime

Utilitarian Interlinkages
At the highest levels of Egypt's judicial structure, the executive branch exerted some influence over judicial appointments, but did not domin-ate them. Egypt's Higher Judicial Council has been the governing body responsible for the administrative affairs of the ordinary judiciary. Its members are primarily the presidents and vice-presidents of the leading courts of appeal at the apex of the judiciary. When a vacancy occurs for the presidency of a court, the senior members of the court involved develop a list of candidates (IBAHRI 2014). The president then chooses a judge from this list. The only judge President Mubarak could choose unilaterally was the president of the SCC. For all other pos-itions the president was expected to choose a candidate from the ones selected by the judges (Rutherford 2008). Other than the presidents of the courts, most other judicial appointments remained in the hands of the judges.

However, the executive institutions did maintain some links to the judicial system. The Higher Judicial Council primarily comprised the presidents of the leading courts and these presidents were selected by the president, ensuring the judges of the Higher Judicial Council were the ones not expected to challenge the regime (Bernard-Maugiron 2016). Also, the minister of justice played an important role in deter-mining the geographical assignment and discipline of judges. Further, judicial candidates, particularly for the superior courts, were vetted by the Ministry of Justice in conjunction with the intelligence services (which was typically run by members of the military) to ensure that judges with ties to opposition parties or societal groups did not populate the judiciary (Bernard-Maugiron 2016). Thus, between a president from the military and intelligences services tied to the military, the military maintained limited but significant utilitarian interlinkages with the judiciary (Brown 1997), but the primary audience for careers remained judges of Egypt's hierarchical judicial system.

Normative Interlinkages
In Egypt, the judicial bureaucracy also formed a distinct community. As a civil law judiciary, all of Egypt's judges undergo the same professional socialization at an early age going through the same cycle of training and advancement, which builds a strong convergence within the judicial corps. Nearly all Egyptian judges in the ordinary court system begin their profession in the General Prosecution Office, and after spending a few years in the office are given the option to pursue a career as a judge. Outside the ordinary and administrative judiciary, the judges of the SCC can, in theory, also be advocates and law lecturers, but these are extremely rare, and the majority of the SCC is composed of judges from other courts.

When law school graduates apply to join the judiciary each year, they go through an evaluation process that examines their academic record, moral character and family background (Rutherford 2008). Historically, those appointed as judges were typically trained in the same law schools, socialized in the same circles, and often married within the same families (Rutherford 2008). Social standing has always been a main criterion for appointment, which meant that most judges came from the upper middle class and elite classes of society who sought to defend their social privilege and opposed radical change in the political system.[2] Thus, judges are typically embedded in this social and professional network.

The distinct identity and the associated preferences of the judicial community are reinforced through the institutions of the Judges' Club and State Council Judges' Club (for judges of the administrative court system). The Judges' Club was established in 1939 in Cairo to enhance solidarity among members of the judiciary, look after their interests and establish a cooperative. It is run by an administrative board whose members are elected by the general assembly of the club, and all judges from the ordinary courts and the public prosecution are represented on the board (Said 2008). The Judges' Club comprises almost 90 per cent of all judiciary personnel in Egypt. Although the Higher Judicial

---

[2] One leading Egyptian judge famously said that children of garbage collectors do not come from a respectable milieu and thus are unqualified to serve as judges (El-Ghobashy 2016).

Council is the primary administrative entity of the ordinary judiciary, the judges' clubs claims to be the true representative entity of the judicial community (Said 2008). Both judges' clubs deliver official statements on political and legal affairs, hold seminars to produce legal proposals and organize conferences to debate and build consensus within the judicial community (Said 2008). In this way, these associations represent and articulate the consensus norms and preferences of the judicial community.

Thus, this community of judges, self-selected from the same socioeconomic strata of society and socialized within the Judges' Club and the State Council Judges' Club, preserved and reinforced the historic preferences of the judicial community. The relative primacy of senior judges in matters of judicial appointments further ensured that the executive branches' authority to alter the institutional culture and preferences of the judiciary were limited. Judges trained and socialized in the historic preferences of the judiciary largely appointed and promoted judges who mirrored these preferences. The relative autonomy and strong corporatist identity enabled the reproduction of a largely similar set of legal and policy preferences, dating back to the era before the military-led revolution of 1952, when the judicial system, its identity and its autonomy were first forged. Multiple judicial traditions from the nineteenth and early twentieth century crystallized into an institutional culture that was associated with liberal constitutionalism, judicial independence and a mandate for the judiciary to protect civil liberties while also projecting state authority. Thus, the judiciary became a bastion for the values of the Egyptian political elite that predated the military-led revolution of 1952. Although different court systems within the elaborate architecture of Egypt's judicial system varied in the extent to which they upheld this distinct brand of political liberalism, by and large judges, seeking to craft reputations to advance their careers and build esteem within this network, would make rulings in line with the defined values of the judicial community.

Judicial Activism under Mubarak
When Mubarak came to power, he was keen on gaining judicial legitimacy for his regime and he conceded to several of the judges' demands. Mubarak undid Nasser's earlier intrusions into the judicial hierarchy, restoring the authority of the Higher Judicial Council over the judiciary, and strengthening the independence of the Council of State, the apex court of Egypt's administrative judicial system (Hamad

2019). Instead, Mubarak used two tactics to gain judicial support while limiting judicial challenges to the regime's interests. First, he tried to co-opt the judiciary, primarily through the use of material incentives, in a similar way to Musharraf in Pakistan. Senior judges who towed the regime's line were given special patronage, including official cars, government residents, subsidized land and housing (Aziz 2016). Those who were perceived as independent could be transferred to less prestigious or lucrative courts by the Ministry of Justice (Bernard-Maugiron 2016). Mubarak, unlike his predecessor Nasser, did not seek to secure favourable rulings by directly reshaping or abolishing the existing judicial system, but focused on bargaining with individual judges using the leverage provided by the limited interlinkages between the judiciary and the executive. Second, where Mubarak could not risk interference by the judiciary, he circumvented the ordinary judiciary through increased reliance on special courts, including the State Security courts and especially the military courts, which fell under executive control. Thus, during the early years of Mubarak's regime, the ordinary judiciary retained its largely independent identity. Mubarak's actions consolidated the role of superior judges as the main audience for the career trajectory of judges. In the absence of significant executive interventions, liberal judges were able to move into positions of authority within different sections of the judicial system, particularly the administrative judicial system.

As more liberal judges were moving into positions of authority within the judicial hierarchy, activist judges were taking up positions of influence within the judges' clubs. During the late 1980s and early 1990s, the Judges' Club for judges of the ordinary courts was led by activist judges who wanted to disentangle the judiciary from any executive influence, reducing the interlinkages between the two branches of government (Bentlage 2010). In 2002, a coalition of judges who pushed for confrontation with the regime took leadership roles within the Judges' Club. The Judges' Club took on both the executive branch and judges who were collaborating with the regime's actions, and even issued a 'Black List' of thirteen judges who allegedly collaborated with the executive branch to engage in electoral fraud (Aziz 2016). Thus, judges who betrayed the liberal activist norms that had developed within the judicial community saw their reputations suffer, as they faced the ire of the Judges' Club. In 2004, when the Higher Judicial Council (now composed of regime loyalists thanks to Mubarak's intervention) reprimanded the activist Justices Al-Ghiryani and Mekky, the Judges' Club publicly criticized

247

the Higher Judicial Council (Aziz 2016). In 2005, the club disseminated reports on the conduct of elections that embarrassed the Mubarak regime. Thus, the Judges' Club advocated for an assertive and independent judiciary that placed checks on executive institutions. In retaliation the regime suspended subsidies provided to the Judges' Club and investigated judges who spoke to the press about electoral fraud. In 2006, judges came out onto the streets in front of the Judges' Club to protest against the regime's actions against fellow judges. The judges' protest was supported by other pro-democracy movements in the country and became a major challenge for Mubarak's regime (Brown and Nasr 2005; Rutherford 2008; El-Ghobashy 2016).

Thus, the liberal ethos guiding Egyptian judicial behaviour in the 1990s and early 2000s was a product of limited utilitarian interlinkages between the military-led regime and the judiciary, and close normative interlinkages between the courts and a liberally inclined Judges' Club that championed activist judges

From Confrontation to Collaboration

The decision of the SCC to monitor the elections, and confrontation between the regime and the Judges' Club, led to Mubarak's determination that the regime had to reshape the judiciary.

First, Mubarak sought to insert regime loyalists into authoritative positions within the SCC. Previously the president of the SCC had always been selected from among the judges already on the Court, but in 2002 Mubarak broke with this convention, and instead placed the second in command at the Ministry of Justice, Fathi Naguib, as president. Naguib then increased the number of justices from nine to fifteen, and handpicked judges who were deferential to executive power, ending the liberal majority on the Court. Thus, Mubarak sought to control this arm of the judiciary by strengthening institutional interlinkages. Naguib handpicked judges who were deferential to executive power, ending the liberal majority on the Court. In the following years, the SCC became increasingly supportive of Egypt's military dictators.

Second, after the mobilization of the Judges' Club in 2006, the regime sought to bring the Judges' Club under control. The government promised financial benefits to the club if government loyalists were elected to the club board. Then more assertive and independent judges were pressured into retirement. Government-controlled media delegitimized the judicial independence movement by accusing movement leaders of having links to the Islamist opposition party, the Muslim Brotherhood. As a result of this campaign to delegitimize or force out activist judges from the club leadership, a coalition of pro-regime judges won the elections of the Judges' Club. This loyalist group then targeted and expelled leading dissident judges within the Judges' Club on grounds of linkages with the Muslim Brotherhood, and decisively started to reshape the judicial community (Aziz 2016). The government also hoped to weaken the Judges' Club by encouraging other judicial associations in the governorates to declare their institutional independence. Most judges who stood up to Mubarak in the late 2000s were purged out of the judiciary and the regime recruited judges from outside the traditional judicial community, including police academy graduates (Aziz 2014, 2016). Thus, by the end of Mubarak's regime, the internal culture of the ordinary judiciary was decisively shifting as the executive built closer interlinkages with sections of the judiciary, although the Council of State and the administrative judiciary maintained its independent character.

By 2013, once Mubarak was removed and General Sisi came into power, overthrowing the short-lived elected government of Mohammad Morsi and the Muslim Brotherhood, the shift in the judiciary became clear, with the close collaboration between the judiciary and the military in consolidating the new regime and repressing its political opponents. As Hamad (2019) explains, a combination of judges' elite backgrounds and liberal values made most judges hostile to the Muslim Brotherhood, seeing them as a danger to society, which made them more willing to enable Sisi's repression. Further, Sisi's minister of justice also launched a campaign against judges with close ties to the Muslim Brotherhood's government, and pro-regime media outlets targeted the more independent-minded judges of the Council of State with corruption charges, smearing their reputation. Thus, a combination of mutual opposition to the Muslim Brotherhood government, increased government interventions in judicial careers and efforts to smear the reputations of judges who weren't aligned with the regime, helped instil a more deferential and collaborative culture within the judiciary. If the entrenchment of liberal constitutionalism as a key feature of the judiciary's legal and policy preferences helped explain the assertive actions of several key judicial institutions in the 1990s and 2000s, since then, a shift in audiences, orchestrated first by Mubarak's, and then by Sisi's regime, has pushed the judiciary towards a more collaborative and deferential approach to executive power and military dominance.

Turkey

Turkey provides an example of a collaborative court under one regime evolving into a loyal court under another regime. Politics in Turkey has been organized around two competing camps: the state elite (including the military) and affiliated political parties that upheld the Kemalist worldview and its top-down agenda of state-driven nationalist modernization, and the political elites that represented large swathes of society opposed to the imposition of the Kemalist agenda (Shambayati 2008). When the military launched its first coup in 1960, it did so to remove and ban the populist Democrat Party from power, which challenged the Kemalist principles of republican state-building. The military was supported by the civilian bureaucracy, the Republican Party (RPP), universities and judiciary, which adhered to the republican principles, and comprised what Belge (2006) calls the Republican alliance. The Republican alliance sought to place limits on majoritarian institutions where ethnic minorities, and left-wing and religious political parties, could undermine the state's political project. Accordingly, the 1961 Constitution empowered counter-majoritarian institutions, including a new Turkish Constitutional Court (TCC), that were expected to uphold the hegemonic status of Kemalism. During brief periods of direct military rule, the military sought to ensure that the judiciary upheld the military's political agenda and interests even after the military receded from power. A look at the audiences shaping the judiciary's preferences explains the regime's confidence in the judiciary.

Normative Interlinkages

In the 1920s and 1930s, after the republican revolution in Turkey, republican elites focused on transforming and modernizing the Turkish legal system, including the process of legal and judicial training, to ensure it upheld Kemalist principles. The Kemalist educational policy called for the reconstruction of educational institutions so they would produce cadres of lawyers and judges socialized in the idea of loyalty to the republican principles shared by the republican elites of the civilian and military bureaucracy (Benvenuti 2011). The judiciary was isolated from political parties and bar associations, who were kept out of both the judicial networks and judicial training. Until 1987, the training of judges was managed by the judiciary and by the military through its supervisory role over the Higher Education Board, and the main venue for the socialization of judges was the courts. Kemalist legal academics and superior judges trained judges for the lower courts of the judicial bureaucracy in the same legal and policy preferences they had learned. The military maintained a role in the training and socialization of judges, even organizing special briefings for judges and prosecutors to ensure they shared the military's priorities (Benvenuti 2011). The judicial bureaucracy ensured that pro-military Kemalist norms and preferences were reproduced in the professional networks staffing the judiciary, and that judges seeking to build esteem within these networks would adhere to these Kemalist norms.

Utilitarian Interlinkages
Under the 1961 Constitution, most of the TCC's judges were elected from the lower courts directly below the TCC, while the remaining three judges were appointed by the National Assembly, Senate and presidency from nominations submitted by the universities and the military courts. Since the lower courts were staffed by Kemalist elites, the universities were run by Kemalist elites and the president was a member of the military, the regime assumed that the Kemalist RPP would win the elections, so the military was confident that the appointment process would be in republican hands. Therefore, the military assumed there were close utilitarian interlinkages between the judiciary and the republican ruling alliance.

However, the utilitarian interlinkages between the military and the judiciary were weaker than the military presumed. The strength of these interlinkages was premised on the assumption that republicans loyal to the military would also win all parliamentary elections. However, this proved to be untrue as, firstly, political parties opposed to the Republican alliance won elections to the National Assembly and Senate, and secondly, the RPP, the leading republican political party, started shifting towards the left, diverging from the military (Shambayati and Kurdis 2009). Thus, parties with divergent norms outperformed military-aligned republicans during the 1960s and 1970s and gained seats in the National Assembly and Senate, where they were able to play a role in judicial appointments. Further, once the presidency shifted into elected civilian hands this removed another crucial utilitarian interlinkage between the military and the judiciary.

From Collaboration to Loyalty
The military's faith in the empowered judiciary was initially well founded. Under the 1961 Constitution, the TCC used its powers expansively, routinely asserting itself against elected governments,

and protecting the autonomy of the state institutions and universities staffed by republicans from political interference and from public accountability (Belge 2006). At the same time, it restricted the civil liberties of religious, ethnic and left-wing political groups, consolidating Kemalism as the only permissible political ideology.

However, as utilitarian interlinkages decreased, limits in the judiciary's commitment to the military emerged. While the judiciary collaborated with the military's political agenda of entrenching a Kemalist republic, it diverged on the military's preference of realizing this agenda through centralized military control. The TCC annulled provisions in the law creating the military-run Board of Higher Education, and declared the law establishing special military tribunals unconstitutional. The military determined that a constitutional court that was more receptive to the military's point of view – not just in upholding Kemalism, but in deferring to the military's preeminent role in directing the state's commitment to these principles – was needed.

In 1982, the military launched another coup, and this time institutionalized a sustained presence at the helm of Turkey's governing system. In the 1982 Constitution, the military ensured the loyalty of the judiciary by consolidating both utilitarian and normative interlinkages between the military and judiciary.

First, judges continued to be trained and socialized in the bureaucratic judicial networks isolated from political parties and civil society, and with close ties to the military and other state elites. The TCC under the 1982 Constitution recruited most of its judges from the civilian and military administrative courts and from among administrative lawyers, ensuring that state judicial bureaucrats dominated the courts (Benvenuti 2011). The military chief of staff sat on the Higher Education Council from 1970 to 2004, shaping the education and training of lawyers and judges.

Second, the new Constitution placed judicial nominations in the hands of the indirectly elected president, who was a military general at the time, stripped the parliament of any role in the appointment of the justices of the TCC and reduced the high courts to nominating bodies, while expanding the nominating role of the military courts and the military-supervised Board of Higher Education (Shambayati and Kirdis 2009). The president also directly appointed members of the High Council of the judiciary and the Council of State, other crucial judicial bodies in the judicial hierarchy.

Thus, the military now had utilitarian and normative interlinkages with the judiciary, as regime supporters populated the bureaucratic judicial networks in which judges were socialized and trained and from which they were recruited, *and* the military president now had considerable control over the judicial appointment process.

After 1982, the superior judiciary acted more predictably in support of the military's mission with little detraction and divergence. The judiciary regulated the political arena on behalf of the military, striking down parliamentary measures and even ousting elected governments and banning political parties. Between 1983 and 2003, the TCC closed eighteen political parties, particularly religious parties, including the Welfare Party and the Virtue Party, which were seen as a threat to Kemalist secularism. The judiciary was 'unfriendly' to elected governments that succeeded the military regime, upheld repression of ethnic separatists and protected secular Kemalist principles within universities (Tezkur 2009; Bali 2012). At the same time, the judiciary did not intervene in military matters, maintaining the autonomy of state institutions.

Thus, the military sought to buttress its normative interlinkages with utilitarian interlinkages, ensuring the judiciary did not simply collaborate in upholding a similar ideological vision, but acquiesced to the military's authority *and* interpretation of this shared ideological vision. If, in the 1960s, there was an 'alliance' between the military and the judiciary, in the 1980s, the judiciary was 'used in the service of the executive (military) branch' (Shambayati and Kirdis 2009; Tuba 2013). This largely pro-military loyal court lasted until the rise of Erdogan? and the AKP in Turkey and his reforms of both the military and the judiciary in 2010.

India

During the 1990s, the Indian superior judiciary expanded its role in governance, clashed with the central government on questions of socioeconomic policy and became known as one of the most powerful judiciaries in the world. As I explain, the audience-based framework helps us understand the emergence of this powerful and confrontational judiciary.

The Indian superior judiciary was historically assertive, initially asserting its authority to protect legal property rights against the land reforms programme of India's ruling party at the time, the Indian National Congress (Moog 2002). Relations between the judiciary and the government deteriorated over time, as high courts overruled several of Prime Minister Indira Gandhi's more radical measures, and even overturned her re-election in 1976 on grounds of electoral malpractice. After Gandhi's short-lived emergency rule, the judiciary pivoted from protection of civil liberties towards the protection of positive rights (Bhuwania 2016).

In the 1980s, the Supreme Court began a new era of public interest litigation. Between 1978 and 1981, the Court gradually laid the foundations for an expansion in the doctrine of standing for public interest claims in a series of decisions that liberalized formal pleading requirements and relaxed the rule of *locus standi* in decisions, enabling 'public-spirited' citizens to bring petitions challenging government actions before the court (Mate 2013, 2015). As Bhuwania (2016) explains, the judiciary shifted from speaking in the language of procedure, as it had done in the early decades post-independence, to speaking in the language of participation, prioritizing a commitment to conceptions of access to justice over a commitment to legal procedure. The Court utilized public interest litigation to take on central government agencies and state and local government actors in a series of cases often focused on socio-economic rights, including cases to do with the environment and urban pollution. In the 1990s, this public interest litigation significantly catalysed the judiciary's expanded role in governance, intervening in cases of high-level corruption, taking over monitoring of key government agencies, appointing commissions to handle welfare and food programmes and closing factories and commercial plants (Mate 2013, 2015).

Thus, over the course of India's first fifty years, the Indian judiciary shifted from prioritizing the protection of civil liberties against government interventions and championing the importance of legal and constitutional procedure, to adopting a new role, bypassing procedural requirements and focusing on socio-economic rights, to actively enter into key areas of governance, overruling, undermining and even supplanting elected executive and legislative institutions. How do we explain this shift?

Utilitarian Interlinkages
India's Constitution initially established a consultative process for judicial appointments similar to the one described in Pakistan. High Court judges were appointed after a consultation between the chief justices (of the Supreme Court and the relevant High Court) and the

government, with the final decision to be made by the president. On judicial promotions, the government could decide which judges were promoted from the lower judiciary to high courts, which judges went from being ad hoc to being permanent, which judges became chief justices and which judges were appointed to the Supreme Court (Chandrachud 2014).

In the first two decades, under Prime Minister Nehru, the government rarely went against the choices of the chief justice on appointments (Narayan 2018). However, the governments of Indira Gandhi and her son Rajiv were keen on using their powers to appoint and promote judges who were either broadly supportive of their policies, or were deferential enough not to stand in the government's way (Chandrachud 2014; Andhyarujina 2018). In the 1980s and 1990s, judges of the Supreme Court also sought to reshape the judiciary according to their own preferences. Justice Bhagwati declared his intent to build a new judiciary, built around a different set of legal and policy preferences, that aligned with his activist social philosophy, leading to considerable tension between the judiciary and the Law Ministry over appointments (Chandrachud 2014). Then the Supreme Court prescribed a new procedure for appointing judges.[3] For judicial appointments, the chief justice of India would have to consult senior judges on the Supreme Court and the relevant high courts, before then submitting an opinion on the appointment to the president, who was now bound to follow the advice of the chief justice. In short, the chief justice formed a new 'collegium' of judges that took over decisive control of the judicial appointment system. Thus, the Supreme Court of India asserted its 'primacy' over the executive, and its power to control its own composition, reducing the institutional interlinkages between the judiciary and the elected government (Chandrachud 2014).

Normative Interlinkages
Through most of India's history, the high courts and Supreme Court were staffed from among lawyers belonging to the urban elite and upper middle class, working in different high courts across the country (Chandrachud 2011; Gadbois 2011). The key constituency for High Court and Supreme Court judges was the network of appellate lawyers

---

[3] *Supreme Court Advocates on Record Association* v. *Union of India*, AIR 1994 SC 268; In re: Special Reference 1 of 1998.

who they worked with, before elevation, and routinely interacted with, both inside and outside courtrooms (Bhuwania 2016). Mate (2014) argues that the new role conception within the judiciary emerged through interactions between the judiciary and the surrounding community of legal elites, including appellate lawyers, legal scholars, intellectuals and civil society activists, who formed the social and professional milieu with which High Court judges interacted and engaged on a regular basis.

As Bhuwania (2016) explains, there was a sociological and professional difference between trial lawyers and appellate lawyers, and civil liberties were usually the concern of trial lawyers who typically worked in lower courts, whereas public interest litigation was the work of the elite lawyers of the appellate courts, who had an interest in shaping government policy, and wanted to incite judges to engage in policymaking. In the 1980s and 1990s, legal scholars and senior advocates attended legal and judicial conferences where they addressed the need to reform the legal system in order to advance the cause of social justice (Mate 2014). Dhavan (1994) wrote that public interest litigation was a product of a movement of middle-class lawyers, judges and activists who wanted to transform the use of the law, in order to find new solutions to problems of socio-economic governance.

Just as in Pakistan, we see a change occurring within the legal networks that judges belong to, and with which they shared normative interlinkages. In both lawyers' communities, a growing distrust of the willingness and ability of other state institutions, elected and unelected, to represent the public interest, led to a growing interest among lawyers to see the judiciary take on that role.

Thus, judges who were recruited from networks of the upper middle-class appellate lawyers took increasing control over the judicial appointment process. The combination of the shift in norms within the legal community, and the shift in appointment process towards empowering the judges who embraced the changing norms, helped entrench a new role conception in India's courts. India's superior judiciary used public interest litigation as a vehicle to intervene in a range of socio-economic governance issues, challenging executive discretion and legislative competence (Bhuwania 2016). Public interest–minded judges bolstered their reputations with senior lawyers, urban activists and large segments of the media, all of whom encouraged this shift in roles for the judiciary.

BROADER IMPLICATIONS OF THE ARGUMENT

Finally, I assess the implications of my findings for broader debates in public law and comparative politics. In this closing section, I make three claims. First, my study of the Pakistani judiciary reinforces the call made by several scholars of judicial politics to expand our study of judicial motivations beyond the application of legal doctrines and the realization of policy preferences (Drahozal 1998; Posner 2010; Epstein and Knight 2012). Second, my findings call for rethinking the sources of judicial legitimacy. Third, this book shows that studies of judicial behaviour and judicial relations with state institutions and society are hollow if the analysis does not embed the judiciary within its surrounding legal complex, and looks to ideas, interactions and incentive structures, within and across the legal complex, to better understand why judges do what they do. Fourth, it demonstrates that ascertaining the ideal institutional setting for securing democracy and the rule of law in a state requires paying attention to both the formal and informal relations between state institutions, which shape institutional autonomy and ideology.

Reconsidering Judicial Motivations

Scholars have emphasized the importance of loosening the assumption prevalent in accounts of judicial politics, regarding judicial motivations and researching how different judicial motivations shape judicial behaviour (Epstein and Knight 2012), whether it is career-building (Hilbink 2007; Kapiszewski 2012), or reputation-building (Baum 2007; Ginsburg and Garoupa 2015). This study shows how judges respond to at least two types of critical audiences with whom they seek to build their reputations: the ones that shape their careers and the ones with whom they seek to build esteem, affirming the need to look beyond policy maximization and doctrinal application in order to understand judicial behaviour. In Pakistan, I show that judges are willing to override legal constraints and political considerations to win the respect and support of these consequential audiences. This is not to say that judges do not also want to realize their policy preferences and preserve or expand the authority of the judiciary in order to realize policy preferences. But the career and esteem motivations help shed light on the directions in which judges choose to expand their jurisdiction, or the issues upon which they fight to preserve their authority.

It is only through recognizing the multiple motivations of judges and studying how audiences effect the ability of judges to realize these goals that we understand the constitution of judicial preferences. The audience-based framework shows that the process of preference formation and evolution of hegemonic preferences and discourses within judicial institutions is partly strategic and partly sincere, as judges who adopt and uphold legal and policy preferences that align with the preferences of the audiences of the judiciary will move forward in their careers and build esteem. The institutional interlinkages that enable these judicial audiences to advance and undermine judges' careers and esteem are the mechanisms by which audiences shape the legal and policy preferences of the judiciary.

Rethinking Judicial Legitimacy

Focusing on the reputational motivations of judges also helps better conceptualize and empirically observe the ways in which judges understand and establish their legitimacy. The legitimacy of the judiciary, as we understand it, depends on the ability of judges to convey the impression that their decisions are driven by the impersonal requirements of legal rights, principles and the demands of justice (Grossman 1984; Scheb and Lyons 2000; Levasseur 2002). Judicial authority can only be secured by the belief that the judges' actions are guided by technical expertise and impartial interpretation and implementation of the law (Landfried 2019). This does not mean that judges must remain apolitical. Judicial systems do not benefit from judges who profess to being apolitical, since being 'apolitical' is in itself a statement of political preferences, as Hilbink (2007) illustrates in her study of 'apolitical' jurisprudence under Pinochet in Chile. However, even a political jurisprudence must be articulated in the impersonal language of the law and rights and grounded in legal precedent and procedure. Yet, as I show, in Pakistan, an outcome-oriented jurisprudence rooted in conceptions of the public interest rather than procedures and precedents has emerged. These judges forsake the legitimacy garnered from cloaking their decisions in the language of legal expertise and impartial enforcement of legal principles, in favour of legitimacy garnered from rooting judgments in the populist language of popular will and anti-elitism.

Judicial populism is by no means a phenomenon unique to Pakistan, and parallels similar developments in India, Brazil and Italy, to name a few. In these states, judges have, at different points in history, justified the assertion and expansion of their powers based on a claim that judges better represent the interests of the public than elected political officeholders, and thus must assume roles typically held by political officeholders (Landau 2014; Bhuwania 2016; Barroso and Osorio 2019; Kumm 2019). The success of, and support for, populist judges in different jurisdictions calls for a reconsideration of how judges secure their legitimacy, showing that legitimacy can come from multiple sources, shaped by the judiciary's political and sociological context, and that these sources impact how judges understand the nature and limits of their authority. In Pakistan, populist judges resisted authoritarian power, expanded their jurisdiction and turned questions that were previously far outside the ambit of the judiciary into justiciable questions, all legitimized by the claim that their interventions were matters of public interest.

However, a populist judge also risks overreaching, blurring the lines between ordinary and constitutional politics and deciding questions that fall outside their area of expertise and which cannot be resolved with the tools at their disposal (King 2012; Rosenfeld 2019). Further, without the cloak of impartiality provided by adherence to precedent and procedure, judges can also find themselves more vulnerable to attack. When it comes to legalistic discourse, the judiciary has an institutional monopoly, but when it comes to populist discourse, the very charge of obstructing the public interest can be lobbed right back at judges from the representative branches of the government. Thus, populist justifications for judicial actions leave judges in a competition with politicians, generals and other political stakeholders over who is the more credible representative of the people. This makes judges more vulnerable to reputational hits on their credibility, and makes institutional clashes more likely, as the elites of different institutions stake their claim to authority on the same bases of representing the interests of the people.

Thus, judicial populism complicates our understanding of the bases of judicial legitimacy and the impact of judicial legitimation strategies on judicial behaviour, judicial power and systemic stability.

Bringing in the Judiciary's External Audiences
The Legal Complex

This book and the 'audience-based' framework shows it is impossible to understand judicial politics without understanding how different sections of the legal complex can project judicial authority or produce judicial ideology. There is a growing agreement among scholars that, without theoretically engaging with the legal complex, theories of judicial politics remain hollow (Karpik and Halliday 2011). The legal profession can be an ally, supporting and encouraging the judiciary to expand and assert its authority (Epp 1998; Moustafa 2007), and a source of ideas that diffuse into the courts, either through the process of litigation, or through academic and professional debates between judges and their reference groups of lawyers and judges (Woods 2009; Mate 2014; Ocantos 2014; Ocantos 2016).

The argument and account presented in this book take the culture and configurations of the legal complex seriously. First, the book provides a historical account of how the assumptions, forms and legal practices that constitute legal culture, emerge and evolve (Zedner 1995; Webber 2004; Arold 2007; Couso et al. 2011; Nelken 2016). I highlight several factors that define the legal culture of Pakistan's legal profession, paying attention to the organization of, and competition within, the legal profession, its relationship with other institutions, the demographic, educational and ideational shifts among lawyers, and the development of a repertoire of political mobilization within the bar. All these factors interact to shape the legal discourses, symbols, practices and role conceptions that define the legal culture within the bar (Chanock 2001). Different sections of the legal complex (including the private legal profession, the judicial bureaucracy, the government's legal department and legal academia) may each develop a distinct legal culture. Variation in the interlinkages between the superior judiciary and the other sections of the legal complex determines which sections of the legal complex shape the internal culture, norms and preferences of the judiciary. By locating the judiciary within the structure of the legal complex, and identifying how this can shape the legal and policy preferences underlying judicial behaviour towards other state institutions, the book connects legal culture to interinstitutional conflicts and democratic outcomes.

The combination of 'internal' and 'external audiences' shapes the way the judiciary approaches its role and relationship with other state institutions. Audiences compete with each other to influence the institutional environment of judges, and this competition will determine the incentive structure for judges and the development of institutional preferences. A judiciary recruited from a specialized judicial bureaucracy shares fewer normative interlinkages with sections of the legal complex outside the judiciary, and thus would be more responsive to 'internal audiences' (Ginsburg and Garoupa 2015). A judiciary that shares interlinkages with sections of the legal complex outside the state, such as the private legal profession or legal academia, would be more responsive to these 'external audiences'. Ideally a judiciary should be responsive to multiple 'internal' and 'external' audiences, but not be beholden to any one audience. Thus, how the judiciary is embedded within the legal complex, and the mix of 'internal' and 'external' audiences it is linked to, shapes judicial strategy and judicial ideology.

The Media

A related concern with audiences is the role of the media in connecting judges with different audiences within and beyond the legal complex. In recent years, in all judicial systems, there has been a subtle shift towards external audiences (Ginsburg and Garoupa 2015). With the trend towards judicializing politics, the focus of building judicial reputations has shifted distinctly outward. In Brazil and Mexico, the Supreme Court has created television channels, and in Pakistan, several judges have called for televising court proceedings. How does the intrusion of media into the courtroom shape strategies for reputation-building? Institutionally, increasing media scrutiny may enhance transparency but diminish collective behaviour on the bench, as judges seeking to enhance their individual reputations and public images may compete to distinguish themselves from each other, undermining collegiality within judicial institutions. This may impact the spirit of oral proceedings, the competition over authoring judgments, the content of judgments and the emphasis on dissenting opinions.

Media coverage can also be a critical way of managing interinstitutional bargaining. Staton (2010) highlights how judges enhance their power vis-à-vis other state institutions, by strategically communicating their actions through the media. In Pakistan, news reports on oral proceedings and interim orders provide judges with opportunities to test out different stances and positions, to see how well they sit with both public opinion and with state institutions. The responses from the public and from other state institutions will also then be transmitted to judges indirectly, through media reports, press statements, talk shows, etc., all of which makes the media a venue for bargaining between the judiciary and other state institutions. Final verdicts will then be the result of this iterative bargaining process. Hence, as the judiciary becomes more connected to external audiences through the refracting lens of electronic, digital and social media, this will critically impact different facets of judicial behaviour, including the content of judgments, judicial behaviour both on and off the bench, and bargaining between the judiciary and other institutions. The future of judicial politics in many parts of the world will depend on the audience the media prioritizes, and the role the media plays in connecting the judiciary to these audiences in different political contexts.

Informality in Interinstitutional Relations

Finally, by studying judicial–military interactions as a distinct relationship within political systems, this study sheds light on the strategies politically powerful militaries use to manage the judiciary, and the conditions under which the judiciary can assert civilian control over the military. The weakness of political parties in much of the developing world means that they are often ill-equipped to bring established powerful militaries under control, which places a greater responsibility on the judiciary to assume this role. Therefore, in the presence of weakly developed political parties and ineffective legislatures, building an effective judiciary is essential to building civilian control over the military.

Designing an effective judiciary requires paying attention to both the formal institutional independence and authority of the judiciary, and the informal relationships the judiciary builds with state institutions and civil society. Judges are embedded in social and professional networks, and the influence of state institutions over the judiciary is not restricted to formal mechanisms of control, but also involves influence through the informal relations between judges and the elites of other state institutions. In Pakistan, in its early years, judges were embedded in social and professional networks that also included military officers and senior bureaucrats, and these close ties influenced judges' choices and preferences. More recently, as the formal role of executive institutions in judicial appointments diminished, the informal role of bar association leaders in the appointment process increased through their relationships with the judges managing the appointment process. Thus, judicial appointments, preferences and behaviour are shaped by informal relations in the social and professional webs to which judges belong (Popova 2012; Urribarri 2012; Butt 2015; Dressel et al. 2017). If judicial authority and autonomy are crucial aspects of the institutional setting for checking powerful militaries and securing democracy and the rule of law, then lawmakers must safeguard judicial autonomy and authority by designing judicial institutions that are secure from interference through formal and informal pathways. This would require ensuring transparency in the process of judicial appointments, appointing judges through multiple streams from different networks and encouraging collegiality within the judiciary.

Thus, this book contributes to a growing literature that seeks to understand the judiciary as a political actor, with a range of motivations and ambitions, and formal and informal relationships with state institutions and society. These different aspects of its politics interact to shape its behaviour in ways that are highly consequential for the political trajectories of authoritarian and post-authoritarian states.

CONCLUSION

Today, Pakistan's superior judiciary is at a crossroads. The courts have never been this consequential, nor this controversial. Front-page headlines discuss major decisions made by the Supreme Court and talk shows bring together lawyers, politicians and journalists to debate the actions and comments of Supreme Court judges. There is a growing chorus of scholars, politicians and civil society members criticizing the judiciary for overextending itself and entering into domains of governance where it is ill-equipped to provide useful solutions to longstanding challenges, weakening elected governments and paralysing governance.

Yet public expectations of the courts have grown to such an extent that judicial retreat may further undermine its legitimacy. Lawyers and politicians continue to turn to the courts for protection from being crushed by the force of an increasingly authoritarian state bearing down on dissenters and marginalized populations, and celebrate the judges who defy the garrison state. Each time the Chief Justice of Pakistan arrives in provincial capitals around the country, large numbers of people throng the courtroom gates, pleading to get some attention and demanding intervention in the issues affecting them, as they see this direct approach as the only way to bypass the seemingly opaque and impossibly complex systems of bureaucratic decision-making and partisan bargaining and lobbying that seem to characterize other governing institutions. Thus, it is hard to imagine the judiciary walking back the role it has assumed, as a central governing institute, shaping political structures and governing policies.

In an oligarchic state, a reputation for defiance carries considerable political currency. Whether judges defy political party elites or military elites, there is always an audience in Pakistan's bar rooms ready to cheer on any display of defiance, even if the defiance is only cosmetic. In this environment, there is little incentive for appearing cautious or restrained, regardless of what the law compels.

The memory of Pakistan's judiciary as both the legitimizer and challenger of military dominance remains alive in the collective memory of the legal community and broader population. As debates rage on in the bar and beyond, regarding the proper role of the judiciary, it will be up to the judges to decide which of these legacies will define its future.

Appendix: Structure of the Pakistani Judiciary

Pakistan's superior judiciary is composed of the Supreme Court, five high courts (four until 2010) and the Federal Shariat Court. These high courts include the Lahore High Court (in the province of Punjab), the Sindh High Court (in the province of Sindh), the Balochistan High Court (in the province of Balochistan), the Peshawar High Court (in the province of Khyber Pakhtunkhwa, formerly the North-West Frontier Province) and the Islamabad High Court (for the capital city region).

Under Article 199(1) of the Constitution of 1973, the High Court accepts five types of writ: the writ of *habeas corpus*, the writ of *mandamus*, the writ of *certiorari*, the writ of *quo warranto* and the writ of *prohibition*. The writ of *habeas corpus* is issued to executive authorities compelling them to release someone from detention and bring them before the courts. The writ of *mandamus* is issued to lower courts or government officials when judicial or executive officers are not following the laws, to ensure that they do. The writ of *certiorari* is issued when a decision made by a lower court is accepted for appeal.[1] The writ of *quo warranto* is issued when the person claims any power without legal authority or when an official does any act without the backing of law. When the lower courts accept a case outside their jurisdiction the higher courts can issue a writ of *prohibition* to stop the lower court's proceedings. Beyond its writ jurisdiction the high courts also have a rights jurisdiction. Under Article 199(2) of the Constitution, high courts can be moved for the enforcement of any fundamental rights that have been abridged.

The Supreme Court has three types of jurisdiction: original jurisdiction, appellate jurisdiction and advisory jurisdiction. Under its original jurisdiction, defined in Article 184, the Court can directly hear cases

---

[1] There is a range of lower courts from which appeals can be made to the high courts, including sessions courts, anti-terrorism courts, labour tribunals and service tribunals, to name a few.

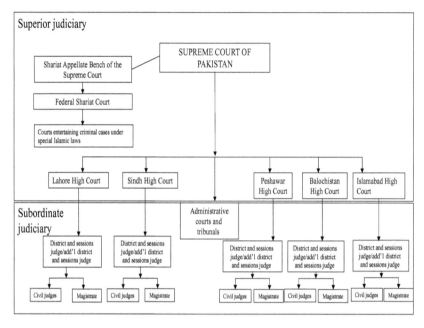

Figure A.1 Structure of the Pakistani judiciary.

pertaining to disputes between two or more governments, that is, the federal and/or provincial governments, and it also can issue orders on questions that it decides are question of public importance involving the enforcement of fundamental rights. Under its appellate jurisdiction, the Court can hear and determine appeals from judgments, decrees, final orders or sentences by the high courts. Finally, the president can gain an opinion from the Supreme Court on any question which he considers of public importance, although this advisory jurisdiction is rarely invoked.

Figure A.1 outlines the structure of the Pakistani judiciary.

REFERENCES

Abbas, Hassan. 'From Fata to the NWFP: The Taliban Spread Their Grip in Pakistan'. *CTC Sentinel* 1, no. 10 (2008).

Abeyratne, Rehan, and Iddo Porat, eds. *Towering Judges: A Comparative Study of Constitutional Judges*. Cambridge: Cambridge University Press, 2021.

Andhyarujina, Tehmtan. 'A Committed Judiciary'. In *Appointment of Judges to the Supreme Court of India*, edited by Arghya Sengupta and Ritwika Sharma, 18–30. New Delhi: Oxford University Press, 2018.

Arafat, Alaa Al-Din. *The Rise of Islamism in Egypt*. Cham: Palgrave Macmillan, 2017.

Arold, Nina-Louisa. *The Legal Culture of the European Court of Human Rights*. Leiden: Martinus Nijhoff, 2007.

Asian Development Bank. 'Private Sector Assessment Pakistan'. 2008. www .adb.org/sites/default/files/institutional-document/32216/private-sector-assessment.pdf.

Azeem, Muhammad. *Law, State and Inequality in Pakistan: Explaining the Rise of the Judiciary*. Singapore: Springer International Publishing, 2017.

Aziz, Sadaf. 'Liberal Protagonists: The Lawyers' Movement in Pakistan'. In *Fates of Political Liberalism in the British Post-colony: The Politics of the Legal Complex*, edited by Terrence Halliday, Lucien Karpik, and Malcolm Feeley, 305–39. New York: Cambridge University Press, 2012.

'The Politics of Anti-corruption'. In *The Politics and Jurisprudence of the Chaudhry Court*, edited by Moeen Cheema and Ijaz Shafi Gilani, 253–80. Karachi: Oxford University Press, 2015.

Aziz, Sadaf, and Moeen Cheema. 'From Nation to State: Constitutional Founding in Pakistan'. In *Constitutional Foundings in South Asia*, edited by Kevin Tan and Ridwan Hoque, 63–90. London: Hart Publishing, 2021.

Aziz, Sahar. *Egypt's Judiciary, Coopted*. Washington, DC: Carnegie Endowment for International Peace, 2014.

'Independence without Accountability: The Judicial Paradox of Egypt's Failed Transition to Democracy'. *Penn State Law Review* 120 (2016): 101–70.

Bali, Asli. 'The Perils of Judicial Independence: Constitutional Transition and the Turkish Example'. *Virginia Journal of International Law* 52 (2012): 235–320.

Barros, Robert. 'Courts out of Context: Authoritarian Sources of Judicial Failure in Chile (1973–1990) and Argentina (1976–1983)'. In *Rule by Law: The Politics of Courts in Authoritarian Regimes*, edited by Tom Ginsburg and Tamir Moustafa, 156–79. New York: Cambridge University Press, 2008.

Barroso, Roberto Luis, and Aline Osorio. 'Democracy, Political Crisis and Constitutional Jurisdiction'. In *Judicial Power: Constitutional Courts Affect Political Transformations*, edited by Christine Landfried, 163–82. Cambridge: Cambridge University Press, 2019.

Baum, Lawrence. *Judges and Their Audiences*. Ann Arbor: Michigan University Press, 2007.

The Puzzle of Judicial Behavior. Ann Arbor: Michigan University Press, 1997.

Belge, Ceren. 'Friends of the Court: The Republican Alliance and Selective Activism'. *Law and Social Inquiry* 40, no. 3 (2006): 653–92.

Bentlage, Bjorn. 'Strife for Independence in Autocratic Regime: The Egyptian Judges' Club 2000–2007'. *Die Welt Des Islams* 50, no. 2 (2010): 243–77.

Benvenuti, Simone. 'Judicial Training in Turkey in Light of Constitutional Traditions and Europeanization'. *Journal of Civil Law Studies* 4 (2011): 309–30.

Bernard-Maugiron, Nathalie. 'A Clash of Institutions: Judiciary vs. Executive in Egypt'. In *Building Rule of Law in the Arab World*, edited by Eva Bellin and Heidi Lane. Boulder: Lynne Reinner, 2016.

Bhuwania, Anuj. *Courting the People: Public Interest Litigation in Post-emergency India*. Cambridge: Cambridge University Press, 2016.

Bogg, Alan, and Mark Freedland. 'Law in the Age of Populism: Towards Sustainable Democratic Engagement'. Max Planck Institute for Comparative Public and International Law, 2018.

Boix, Carles, and Milan Svolik. 'The Foundation of Limited Authoritarian Government: Institutions, Commitment and Power-Sharing in Dictatorships'. *Journal of Politics* 75, no. 2 (2013): 300–16.

Braibanti, Ralph. *Chief Justice Cornelius of Pakistan: An Analysis with Letters and Speeches*. New York: Oxford University Press, 1999.

Braibanti, Ralph, and Joseph LaPalombara. 'Public Bureaucracy and Judiciary in Pakistan'. In *Bureaucracy and Political Development*, 360–440. Princeton: Princeton University Press, 1967.

Brinks, Daniel, and Abby Blass. 2018. *The DNA of Constitutional Justice in Latin America: Politics, Governance and Judicial Design*. Cambridge: Cambridge University Press.

Brown, Nathan. *The Rule of Law in the Arab World: Courts in Egypt and the Gulf*. New York: Cambridge University Press, 1997.

Brown, Nathan, and Hesham Nasr. '*Egypt's Judges Step Forward: The Judicial Election Boycott and Egyptian Reform*'. Policy Outlook – Democracy and Law. Washington, DC: Carnegie Endowment for International Peace, 2005.

Bussiere, Elizabeth. *(Dis)entitling the Poor: The Warren Court, Welfare Rights, and the American Political Tradition.* University Park: Pennsylvania State University Press, 1997.

Butt, Simon. *The Constitutional Court and Democracy in Indonesia.* Leiden: Brill, 2015.

Caldeira, Gregory. 'Neither the Purse nor the Sword: Dynamics of Public Support in the Supreme Court'. *American Political Science Review* 80, no. 4 (1986): 1209–26.

Caldeira, Gregory, and James Gibson. 'The Legitimacy of Justice in the European Union: Models of Institutional Support'. *American Political Science Review* 89 (1995): 356–76.

Carruba, Clifford, and Matthew Gabel. *International Courts and the Performance of International Agreements: A General Theory with Evidence from the European Union.* New York: Cambridge University Press, 2014.

Cass, Roland. 'Judging: Norms and Incentives of Retrospective Decision-Making'. *Boston University Law Review* 75 (1995): 941–96.

Chandrachud, Abhinav. 'An Empirical Study of the Supreme Court's Composition'. *Economic and Political Weekly* 46, no. 1 (2011): 71–7.

The Informal Constitution: Unwritten Criteria in Selecting Judges for the Supreme Court of India. Delhi: Oxford University Press, 2014.

Chanock, Martin. *The Making of South African Legal Culture 1902–1936: Fear, Favour and Prejudice.* New York: Cambridge University Press, 2001.

Chaudhry, Nazir Husain. *Chief Justice Muhammad Munir: His Life, Writings and Judgments.* Lahore: Research Society of Pakistan, 1973.

Chavez, Rebecca Bill. *The Rule of Law in Nascent Democracies.* Stanford: Stanford University Press, 2004.

Cheema, Moeen. *Courting Constitutionalism: Politics of Public Law and Judicial Review in Pakistan.* Cambridge: Cambridge University Press, 2021.

'Pakistan: The State of Liberal Democracy'. *International Journal of Constitutional Law* 16, no. 2 (2018a): 635–42.

'Two Steps Forward One Step Back: The Non-linear Expansion of Judicial Power in Pakistan'. *International Journal of Constitutional Law* 16, no. 2 (2018b): 503–26.

Clayton, Cornell, and Howard Gillman, eds. *Supreme Court Decision-Making: New Institutionalist Approaches.* Chicago: University of Chicago Press, 1999.

Cornelius, A. R., and S. M. Haider. *Law and Judiciary in Pakistan.* Lahore: Lahore Law Times Publishing Company, 1981.

Couso, Javier, Alexander Huneeus, and Rachel Sieder, eds. *Cultures of Legality: Judicialization and Political Activity in Latin America.* New York: Cambridge University Press, 2011.

Couso, Javier, and Lisa Hilbink. 'From Quietism to Incipient Activism: The Institutional and Ideological Roots of RIghts Adjudication in Chile'. In

Courts in Latin America, edited by Gretchen Helmke and Julio Rios-Figueroa, 99–127. New York: Cambridge University Press, 2011.

Croissant, Aurel, David Keuhn, and Seigfried Wolf. 'Beyond the Fallacy of Coupism: Conceptualizing Civilian Control of the Military in Emerging Democracies'. *Democratization* 17, no. 5 (2010): 950–75.

Crouch, Melissa. 'Pre-emptive Constitution Making: Authoritarian Constitutionalism and the Military in Myanmar'. *Law and Society Review* 54, no. 2 (2020): 487–515.

Davis, Sue. 'The Chief Justice and Judicial Decision-Making: The Institutional Basis for Leadership on the Supreme Court'. In *Supreme Court Decision-Making: New Institutionalist Approaches*, edited by Cornell Clayton and Howard Gillman, 135–54. Chicago: University of Chicago Press, 1999.

Dhavan, Rajeev. 'Law as Struggle: Public Interest Litigation in India'. *Journal of the Indian Law Institute* 36, no. 3 (1994): 302–38.

Drahozal, Christopher. 'Judicial Incentives and the Appeals Process'. *SMU Law Review* 51 (1998): 469.

Dressel, Bjorn, Raul Sanchez-Urribarri, and Alexander Stroh. 'The Informal Dimensions of Judicial Politics: A Relational Perspective'. *Annual Review of Law and Social Science* 13 (2017): 413–30.

Dyevre, Arthur. 'Unifying the Field of Comparative Judicial Politics: Towards a General Theory of Judicial Behaviour'. *European Political Science Review* 2, no. 2 (2010): 297–327.

Edelman, Martin. 'The Judicial Elite of Israel'. *International Political Science Review* 13, no. 3 (1992): 235–48.

El-Ghobashy, Mona. 'Dissidence and Deference among Egyptian Judges'. *Middle East Report* 46 (2016). www.merip.org/mer/mer279/dissidence-def erence-among-egyptian-judges.

Eldem, Tuba. 'Guardians Entrapped: The Demise of the Turkish Armed Forces as a Veto-Player'. Doctoral dissertation, University of Toronto, 2013.

Epp, Charles. *The Rights Revolution: Lawyers, Activists and Supreme Courts in Comparative Perspective*. Chicago: Chicago University Press, 1998.

Epstein, Lee, and Jack Knight. *The Choices Justices Make*. Washington, DC: Congressional Quarterly, 1998.

'Reconsidering Judicial Preferences'. *Annual Review of Political Science* 16 (2012): 11–31.

Epstein, Lee, Jack Knight, and Olga Shvetsova. 'The Role of Constitutional Courts in Establishment and Maintenance of Democratic Systems of Government'. *Law and Society Review* 35, no. 1 (2001): 117–64.

Ferejohn, John, Frances Rosenbluth, and Charles Shipan. 'Comparative Judicial Politics'. In *Oxford Handbook of Comparative Politics*, edited by Carles Boix and Susan Stokes, 727–51. New York: Oxford University Press, 2007.

Freedom House. 'Freedom in the World 2020: Pakistan Country Report'. 2020. https://freedomhouse.org/sites/default/files/2020-02/FIW_2020_REPORT_BOOKLET_Final.pdf.

Gadbois, George. *Judges of the Supreme Court of India: 1950–1989*. Delhi: Oxford University Press, 2011.

Gandhi, Jennifer, and Ellen Lust-Okar. 'Elections under Authoritarianism'. *Annual Review of Political Science* 12 (2009): 403–22.

Gandhi, Jennifer, and Adam Prezworski. 'Authoritarian Institutions and the Survival of Autocrats'. *Comparative Political Studies* 40, no. 11 (2007): 1279–301.

Gardbaum, Stephen. 'Are Strong Constitutional Courts Always a Good Thing for New Democracies?' *Columbia Journal of Transnational Law* 53 (2015): 285–316.

Geddes, Barbara. 'What Do We Know about Democratization after Twenty Years?' *Annual Review of Political Science* 2 (1999): 115–44.

Geddes, Barbara, Erica Frantz, and Joseph Wright. 'Military Rule'. *Annual Review of Political Science* 17 (2014): 147–62.

Ghias, Shoaib. 'Miscarriage of Chief Justice: Judicial Power and the Legal Complex in Pakistan under Musharraf'. *Law and Social Inquiry* 25, no. 4 (2010): 985–1022.

Gibson, James, Gregory Caldeira, and Vanessa Baird. 'On the Legitimacy of National High Courts'. *American Political Science Review* 92 (1998): 343–58.

Gilani, Ijaz, and Moeen Cheema, eds. *The Politics and Jurisprudence of the Chaudhry Court*. Karachi: Oxford University Press, 2015.

Ginsburg, Tom. *Judicial Review in New Democracies*. Cambridge: Cambridge University Press, 2003.

Ginsburg, Tom, and Nuno Garoupa. 'Judicial Audiences and Reputation: Perspectives from Comparative Law'. *Columbia Journal of Transactional Law* 47 (2009): 451.

Judicial Reputation: A Comparative Theory. Chicago: University of Chicago Press, 2015.

Ginsburg, Tom, and Tamir Moustafa. 'Introduction: The Functions of Courts in Authoritarian Regimes'. In *Rule by Law: The Politics of Courts in Authoritarian Regimes*, edited by Tom Ginsburg and Tamir Moustafa. New York: Cambridge University Press, 2008.

Gloppen, Siri. 'The Accountability Function of the Courts in Tanzania and Zambia'. In *Democratization and the Judiciary: The Accountability Function of Courts in New Democracies*, edited by Siri Gloppen, Roberto Gargarella, and Elin Skaar. Portland: Frank Cass, 2004.

Goldthau, Andreas. *The Handbook of Global Energy Policy*. Oxford: John Wiley and Sons, 2013.

Grewal, Sharan, and Yasser Kureshi. 'How to Sell a Coup: Elections as Coup Legitimation'. *Journal of Conflict Resolution* 63, no. 4 (2019): 1001–31.

Grossman, Joel. 'Review: Judicial Legitimacy and the Role of Courts: Shapiro's Courts'. *American Bar Foundation Research Journal* 9, no. 1 (1984): 214–22.

Halliday, Terrence, Lucien Karpik, and Malcolm Feeley, eds. *Fighting for Political Freedom: Comparative Studies of the Legal Complex and Political Liberalism.* Portland: Hart, 2007.

    eds. *Fates of Political Liberalism in the British Post-colony.* New York: Cambridge University Press, 2012.

Hamad, Mahmoud. *Judges and Generals in the Making of Modern Egypt.* Cambridge: Cambridge University Press, 2019.

Haq, Anwarul. *Revolutionary Legality in Pakistan.* Lahore: Pakistan Writers' Co-operative Society, 1993.

Hay, Colin. 'Constructivist Institutionalism'. In *Oxford Handbook of Political Institutions,* edited by Sarah Binder, R. A. W. Rhodes, and Bert Rockman, 56–74. Oxford: Oxford University Press, 2006.

Helmke, Gretchen. *Courts under Constraints: Judges, Generals and Presidents in Argentina.* New York: Cambridge University Press, 2005.

    'Regimes and the Rule of Law: Judicial Independence in Comparative Perspective'. *Annual Review of Political Science* 12 (2009): 345–66.

Hendrianto, Stefanus. 'The Rise and Fall of Historic Chief Justices: Constitutional Politics and Judicial Independence in Indonesia'. *Washington International Law Journal* 25, no. 3 (2016): 489–573.

Hilbink, Lisa. 'The Constituted Nature of Constituents' Interests: Historical and Ideational Factors in Judicial Empowerment'. *Political Research Quarterly* 62, no. 4 (2009): 781–97.

    Judges beyond Politics in Democracy and Dictatorship. New York: Cambridge University Press, 2007.

    'The Origins of Positive Judicial Independence'. *World Politics* 64, no. 4 (2012): 587–621.

Hilbink, Lisa, and Matthew C. Ingram. 'Courts and Rule of Law in Developing Countries'. In *Oxford Research Encyclopedias.* Oxford: Oxford University Press, 2019. https://doi.org/10.1093/acrefore/9780190228637.013.110.

Hirschl, Ran. 'The Judicialization of Megapolitics and the Rise of Political Courts'. *Annual Review of Political Science* 11 (2008): 93–118.

    Towards Juristocracy. Cambridge: Presidents and Fellows of Harvard College, 2004.

Hunter, Wendy. *Eroding Military Influence in Brazil: Politicians against Soldiers.* Chapel Hill: University of North Carolina Press, 1997.

Huntington, Samuel. *The Third Wave: Democratization in the Late Twentieth Century.* Oklahoma: University of Oklahoma Press, 1991.

Huq, Aziz. 'Mechanisms of Political Capture in Pakistan's Superior Courts'. *Yearbook of Islamic and Middle Eastern Law* 10, no. 1 (2004): 21–37.

International Bar Association's Human Rights Institute (IBAHRI). 'Separating Law and Politics – Challenges to the Independence of Judges and Prosecutors in Egypt'. 2014. https://issat.dcaf.ch/download/46595/731261/Egypt%20(Feb%202014).pdf.

Iqbal, Javed. *Encounters with Destiny: Autobiographical Reflections*. Oxford: Oxford University Press, 2006.

Jaffrelot, Christophe. *The Pakistan Paradox: Instability and Resilience*. London: Hurst and Co., 2015.

Jalal, Ayesha. *The State of Martial Rule: The Origins of Pakistan's Political Economy of Defence*. Cambridge: Cambridge University Press, 1990.

Javid, Hassan, and Mariam Mufti. 'Electoral Manipulation or Astute Strategy: Explaining the Results of Pakistan's 2018. Election'. *Asian Affairs: An American Review* (2020). https://doi.org/10.1080/00927678.2020.1855033.

Jillani, Tassaduq. 'The Challenge of Judicial Independence and the Experience of Pakistan'. In *The Culture of Judicial Independence: Conceptual Foundations and Practical Challenges*, edited by Christopher Forsyth and Shimon Shetreet, 425–42. Leiden: Martinus Nijhoff, 2012.

Kalhan, Anil. '"Gray Zone" Constitutionalism and the Dilemma of Judicial Independence in Pakistan'. *Vanderbilt Journal of Transnational Law* 46, no. 1 (2013): 1–96.

Kapiszewski, Diana. 'Challenging Decisions: High Courts and Economic Governance in Argentina and Brazil'. Doctoral dissertation, University of California, Berkeley, 2007.

High Courts and Economic Governance in Brazil. Cambridge: Cambridge University Press, 2012.

'How Courts Work: Institutions, Culture and the Brazilian Supremo Tribunal Federal'. In *Cultures of Legality: Judicialization and Political Activism in Latin America*, edited by Javier Couso, Alexander Huneeus, and Rachel Sieder. New York: Cambridge University Press, 2010.

Karpik, Lucien, and Terrence Halliday. 'The Legal Complex'. *Annual Review of Law and Social Science* 7 (2011): 217–36.

Khan, Hamid. *The History of the Judiciary in Pakistan*. Karachi: Oxford University Press, 2016.

Khan, Maryam. 'Empowerment without Accountability? The Lawyers' Movement in Pakistan and Its Aftershocks'. *IDS Bulletin* 50, no. 3 (2019).

'Genesis and Evolution of Public Interest Litigation in the Supreme Court of Pakistan: Toward a Dynamic Theory of Judicialization'. *Temple Journal of International and Comparative Law* 28, no. 2 (2015): 285.

Khosa, Sameer. 'Judicial Appointments in Pakistan: The Seminal Case of the 18th Amendment'. In *Appointment of Judges to the Supreme Court of India: Transparency, Accountability and Independence*, edited by Arghya Sengupta and Ritwika Sharma, 242–54. New Delhi: Oxford University Press, 2018

King, Jeff. *Judging Social Rights*. Cambridge: Cambridge University Press, 2012.

Kumm, Mattias. 'On the Representativeness of Constitutional Courts'. In *Judicial Power: How Constitutional Courts Affect Political Transformations*, edited by Christine Landfried, 281–91. Cambridge: Cambridge University Press, 2019.

Kureshi, Yasser. 'Selective Assertiveness and Strategic Deference'. *Democratization* 28, no. 3 (2021): 604–24.

Lacey, Nicola. 'Populism and the Rule of Law'. Annual Review of Law and Social Science, 15 (2019): 79–96.

Landau, David. 'A Dynamic Theory of Judicial Role'. *Boston College Law Review* 55, no. 5 (2014): 1501–61.

Lev, Daniel. 'Judicial Institutions and Legal Culture in Indonesia'. In *Culture and Politics in Indonesia*, edited by Claire Holt. Ithaca, NY: Cornell University Press, 1972.

Ladinski, Jack. 'The Impact of Social Backgrounds of Lawyers on Law Practice and the Law'. *Journal of Legal Education* 16 (1965): 127–44.

Landfried, Christine. *Judicial Power: How Constitutional Courts Affect Political Transformations*. Cambridge: Cambridge University Press, 2019.

Levasseur, Alain. 'Legitimacy of Judges'. *American Journal of Comparative Law* 50 (2002): 43–85.

Levitsky, Steve, and Lucian Way. *Competitive Authoritarianism: Hybrid Regimes after the Cold War*. Cambridge: Cambridge University Press, 2010.

Malik, Muneer. *The Pakistan Lawyers' Movement: An Unfinished Agenda*. Karachi: Pakistan Law House, 2008.

March, James, and Johan Olsen. 'The Logic of Appropriateness'. In *Oxford Handbook of Political Science*, edited by Robert Goodin, 478–97. Oxford: Oxford University Press, 2011.

Marri, Mir Khuda Baksh. *A Judge May Speak*. Karachi: Ferozsons, 1990.

Mate, Manoj. 'Elite Institutionalism and Judicial Assertiveness in the Supreme Court of India'. *Temple Journal of International and Comparative Law* 28, no. 2 (2014): 361–428.

'Public Interest Litigation and the Transformation of the Supreme Court of India'. In *Consequential Courts: Judicial Roles in a Global Perspective*, edited by Diana Kapiszewski, Gordan Silverstein, and Robert Kagan, 262–88. New York: Cambridge University Press, 2013.

'The Rise of Judicial Governance in the Supreme Court of India'. *Boston University International Law Journal* 33, no. 1 (2015): 170–223.

Mehmood, Sultan. 2021. "The Impact of Presidential Appointment of Judges: Montesquieu or the Federalists?" Working Paper for the Program on Governance and Local Development 40. University of Gothenburg.

Mian, Ajmal. *A Judge Speaks Out*. Oxford: Oxford University Press, 2004.

Milner, Neil. *The Court and Local Law Enforcement: The Impact of Miranda*. Beverly Hills: Sage, 1971.

Mohmand, Shandana. 'Losing the Connection: Party–Voter Linkages in Pakistan'. *Commonwealth and Comparative Politics* 52, no. 1 (2014): 7–31.

Mondak, Jeffrey. 'Institutional Legitimacy and Procedural Justice: Reexamining the Question of Causality'. *Law and Society Review* 27 (1993): 599–608.

Moog, Robert. 'Judicial Activism in the Cause of Judicial Independence'. *Judicature* 85, no. 6 (2002): 268–9.

Moustafa, Tamir. 'Law and Courts in Authoritarian Regimes'. *Annual Review of Law and Social Science* 10 (2014): 281–99.

   The Struggle for Constitutional Power: Law, Politics and Economic Development in Egypt. New York: Cambridge University Press, 2007.

Munir, Muhammad. *Highways and Bye-Ways of Life*. Lahore: Law Publishing Company, 1978.

Narayan, Suchindran Baskar. 'From Kania to Sarkaria: Judicial Appointments from 1950 to 1973'. In *Appointment of Judges to the Supreme Court of India: Transparency, Accountability and Independence*, edited by Arghya Sengupta and Ritwika Sharma, 3–17. Delhi: Oxford University Press, 2018.

Nathan, Barrie. 'Who Judges the Judges? Judicial Appointments and Disappointments: A Comparative Study of Judicial Appointments with Partiocular Reference to England and Wales'. *Journal of Comparative Law* 8 (2013): 405–43.

Nazar, Raza. 'Legislation Is "Required"'. *Oxford University Commonwealth Law Journal* 21, no. 2 (2021): 306–16.

Nelken, David. 'Comparative Legal Research and Legal Culture: Facts, Approaches and Values'. *Annual Review of Law and Social Science* 12 (2016): 45–62.

Newberg, Paula. *Judging the State: Courts and Constitutional Politics in Pakistan*. Cambridge: Cambridge University Press, 1995.

   'Pakistan's Constitutionalism in an Age of Terror'. *Asian Affairs: An American Review* 43, no. 1 (2016): 1–15.

Ocantos, Ezequiel Gonzales. 'Persuade Them or Oust Them: Crafting Judicial Change and Transitional Justice in Argentina'. *Comparative Politics* 46, no. 4 (2014): 479–98.

   Shifting Legal Visions: Judicial Change and Human Rights Trials in Latin America. New York: Cambridge University Press, 2016.

Oko, Okechukwu. 'Seeking Justice in Transitional Societies: An Analysis of the Problems and Failures of the Judiciary in Nigeria'. *Brooklyn Journal of International Law* 31, no. 1 (2005): 9–82.

Patel, Dorab. *Testament of a Liberal*. Oxford: Oxford University Press, 2000.

Pereira, Anthony. *Political (In)justice: Authoritarianism in Brazil, Chile and Argentina*. Pittsburgh: University of Pittsburgh Press, 2005.

Pion-Berlin, David. 'Military Autonomy and Emerging Democracies in South America'. *Comparative Politics* 25, no. 1 (1992): 83–102.

Pion-Berlin, David. ed. *Civil–Military Relations in Latin America: New Analytical Perspectives*. Chapel Hill: University of North Carolina Press, 2001.

Pion-Berlin, David, and Rafael Martinez, eds. *Soldiers, Politicians and Civilians: Reforming Civil–Military Relations in Democratic Latin America*. New York: Cambridge University Press, 2017.

Pompe, Sebastiaan. *The Indonesian Supreme Court: A Study of Institutional Collapse*. Ithaca, NY: Cornell Southeast Asia Program Publications, 2005.

Popova, Maria. *Politicized Justice in Emerging Democracies: A Study of Courts in Russia and Ukraine*. Cambridge: Cambridge University Press, 2012.

Posner, Richard. *How Judges Think*. Cambridge, MA: Harvard University Press, 2010.

Rios-Figueroa, Julio. *Constitutional Courts as Mediators: Armed Conflict, Civil–Military Relations and the Rule of Law in Latin America*. New York: Cambridge University Press, 2016.

'Fragmentation of Power and the Emergence of an effective Judiciary in Mexico'. *Latin American Politics and Society* 49, no. 1 (2007).

Rizvi, Hasan-Askari. *Military, State and Society in Pakistan*. London: Macmillan Press, 2000.

Rosenfeld, Michel. 'Judicial Politics and Ordinary Politics'. In *Judicial Power*, edited by Christine Landfried, 36–65. Cambridge: Cambridge University Press, 2019.

Rutherford, Bruce. *Egypt after Mubarak: Liberalism, Islam and Democracy in the Arab World*. Princeton: Princeton University Press, 2008.

Said, Atef Shahat. 'The Role of the Judges' Club in Enhancing the Independence of the Judiciary and Spurring Political Reform'. In *Judges and Political Reform in Egypt*, edited by Nathalie Bernard-Maugiron, 111–32. Cairo: American University in Cairo Press, 2008.

Scheb, John, and William Lyons. 'The Myth of Legality and Public Evaluation of the Supreme Court'. *Social Science Quarterly* 81, no. 4 (2000): 928–40.

Schepelle, Kim Lane. 'Constitutional Negotiations: Political Context of Judicial Activism in Post-Soviet Europe'. *International Sociology* 18, no. 1 (2003): 219–38.

Schofield, Victoria. *Bhutto: Trial and Execution*. London: Cassell, 1979.

Segal, Jeffrey. 'Judicial Behavior'. In *Oxford Handbook of Law and Politics*, edited by Gregory Caldeira, R. Daniel Kellerman, and Keith Whittington. New York: Oxford University Press, 2008.

Segal, Jeffrey, and Harold Spaeth. *The Supreme Court and the Attitudinal Model Revisited*. New York: Cambridge University Press, 2002.

Shafqat, Sahar. 'Civil Society and the Lawyers' Movement of Pakistan'. *Law and Social Inquiry* 43, no. 3 (2017): 889–914.

Shah, Aqil. *The Army and Democracy*. Cambridge, MA: Harvard University Press, 2014a.

'Constraining Consolidation: Military, Politics and Democracy in Pakistan (2007–2013)'. *Democratization* 21, no. 6 (2014b): 1007–33.

'Pakistan: Voting under Military Tutelage'. *Journal of Democracy* 30, no. 1 (2019): 128–42.

Shah, Nasim Hasan. *Memoirs and Reflections*. Lahore: Alhamra, 2002.

Shambayati, Hootan. 'Courts in Semi-democratic/Authoritarian Regimes: The Judicialization of Turkish (and Iranian) Politics'. In *Rule by Law: The Politics of Courts in Authoritarian Regimes*, edited by Tom Ginsburg and Tamir Moustafa, 283–303. Cambridge: Cambridge University Press, 2008.

Shambayati, Hootan, and Esen Kirdis. 'In "Pursuit of Contemporary Civilization": Judicial Empowerment in Turkey'. *Political Research Quarterly* 62 , no. 4 (2009): 767–80.

Siddiqa, Ayesha. *Military Inc.: Inside Pakistan's Military Economy*. Ann Arbor: Pluto Press, 2007.

Siddiqi, Faisal. 'Public Interest Litigation: Predictable Continuity and Radical Departures'. In *The Politics and the Jurisprudence of the Chaudhry Court*, edited by Moeen Cheema and Ijaz Shafi Gilani, 77–130. Karachi: Oxford University Press, 2015.

Siddique, Osama. 'Judicialization of Politics: Pakistan Supreme Court's Jurisprudence after the Lawyer's Movement'. In *Unstable Constitutionalism: Law and Politics in South Asia*, edited by Mark Tushnet and Madhav, 159–91. New York: Cambridge University Press, 2015.

'The Jurisprudence of Dissolutions: Presidential Power to Dissolve Assemblies under the Pakistani Constitution and Its Discontents'. *Arizona Journal of International and Comparative Law* 23, no. 3 (2006): 622–715.

'Legal Education in Pakistan: The Domination of Practitioners and the "Critically Endangered" Academic'. *Journal of Legal Education* 63 (2014): 499.

Pakistan's Experience with Formal Law: An Alien Justice. Cambridge: Cambridge University Press, 2013.

Sidhwa, Rustam. *The Lahore High Court and Its Principal Bar: 1866–1988*. Lahore: Maktaba Jadeed, 1989.

Staton, Jeffrey. *Judicial Power and Strategic Communication in Mexico*. New York: Cambridge University Press, 2010.

Stepan, Alfred. *Rethinking Military Politics: Brazil and the Southern Cone*. New Jersey: Princeton University Press, 1988.

Stokke, Olav. *The Interplay of International Regimes: Putting Effectiveness Theory to Work*. Lysaker: The Fridtjob Nansen Institute, 2001.

Stone, Alec. *The Birth of Judicial Politics in France*. New York: Oxford University Press, 1992.

Taharia, Jose. 'Judicial Independence in an Authoritarian Regime: The Case of Contemporary Spain'. *Law and Society Review* 9, no. 3 (1975): 475–96.

Talbot, Ian. *Pakistan: A Modern History*. London: Hurst and Co., 1998.

Teitel, Ruti. 'Humanity's Law: Rule of Law for the New Global Politics'. *Cornell International Law Journal* 35, no. 2 (2001): 355–87.

Tezkur, Gunes Murat. 'Judicial Activism in Perilous Times: The Turkish Case'. *Law and Social Inquiry* 43, no. 2 (2009): 305–36.

Trochev, Alexei. *Judging Russia: Constitutional Court in Russian Politics 1990–2006*. New York: Cambridge University Press, 2008.

Trochev, Alexei, and Rachel Ellett. 'Judges and Their Allies: Rethinking Judicial Autonomy through the Prism of Off-bench Resistance'. *Journal of Law and Courts* 2, no. 1 (2014): 67–91.

Tsebelis, George. *Veto Player: How Political Institutions Work*. Princeton: Princeton University Press, 2002.

Tudor, Maya. 'Explaining Democracy's Origins: Lessons from South Asia'. *Comparative Politics* 45, no. 3 (2013): 253–72.

Tyler, Tom. 'Law and Pyschology'. In *Oxford Handbook of Law and Politics*, edited by Keith Whittington, R. Daniel Kellerman, and Gregory Caldeira. Oxford: Oxford University Press, 2009.

Urribarri, Raul Sanchez. 'Politicization of the Judiciary via Informal Connections'. In *Legitimacy, Legal Development and Change: Law and Modernization Reconsidered*, edited by David Linnan, 307–22. New York: Routledge, 2012.

Vanberg, Georg. 'Constitutional Courts in Comparative Perspective: A Theoretical Assessment'. *Annual Review of Political Science* 18 (2015): 167–85.

'Establishing Judicial Independence in Germany: The Impact of Opinion Leadership and the Separation of Powers'. *Comparative Politics* 32, no. 3 (2000): 333–53.

Politics of Constitutional Review in Germany. New York: Cambridge University Press, 2005.

Vondoepp, Peter. 'Political and Judicial Assertiveness in Emerging Democracies: High Court Behavior in Malawi and Zambia'. *Political Research Quarterly* 59 , no. 3 (2006).

Waseem, Mohammad. 'Constitutionalism and Extra-constitutionalism in Pakistan'. In *Unstable Constitutionalism: Law and Politics in South Asia*, edited by Mark Tushnet and Madhav Khosla, 124–58. New York: Cambridge University Press, 2015.

'Judging Democracy in Pakistan: Conflict between the Executive and Judiciary'. *Contemporary South Asia* 20, no. 1 (2012): 19–31.

Waseem, Zoha. '"Brothers in Arms"? A Police–Paramilitary Partnership in Pakistan'. *Policing and Society* 31, no. 2 (2021): 131–47.

Webber, Jeremy. 'Culture, Legal Culture and Legal Reasoning: A Comment on Nelken'. *Austin Journal of Legal Philosophy* 29 (2004): 27–36.

Whittington, Keith. *Political Foundations of Judicial Supremacy: The Presidency, the Supreme Court and Constitutional Leadership in US History.* Princeton: Princeton University Press, 2007.

Woods, Patricia. *Judicial Power and National Politics.* Albany: SUNY Press, 2009.

Woods, Patricia, and Lisa Hilbink. 'Comparative Sources of Judicial Empowerment: Ideas and Interests'. *Political Research Quarterly* 62, no. 4 (2009): 745–52.

Zedner, Lucia. 'In Pursuit of the Vernacular: Comparing Law and Order Discourse in Britain and Germany'. *Socio-Legal Studies* 4 (1995): 517–34.

INDEX

CAMBRIDGE STUDIES IN LAW AND SOCIETY

Culture in the Domains of Law
Edited by René Provost

China and Islam: The Prophet, the Party, and Law
Matthew S. Erie

Diversity in Practice: Race, Gender, and Class in Legal and Professional Careers
Edited by Spencer Headworth, Robert L. Nelson, Ronit Dinovitzer, and David B. Wilkins

A Sociology of Constitutions: Constitutions and State Legitimacy in Historical-Sociological Perspective
Chris Thornhill

A Sociology of Transnational Constitutions: Social Foundations of the Post-National Legal Structure
Chris Thornhill

Genocide Never Sleeps: Living Law at the International Criminal Tribunal for Rwanda
Nigel Eltringham

Shifting Legal Visions: Judicial Change and Human Rights Trials in Latin America
Ezequiel A. González-Ocantos

The Demographic Transformations of Citizenship
Heli Askola

Criminal Defense in China: The Politics of Lawyers at Work
Sida Liu and Terence C. Halliday

Contesting Economic and Social Rights in Ireland: Constitution, State and Society, 1848–2016
Thomas Murray

Buried in the Heart: Women, Complex Victimhood and the War in Northern Uganda
Erin Baines

Palaces of Hope: The Anthropology of Global Organizations
Edited by Ronald Niezen and Maria Sapignoli

The Politics of Bureaucratic Corruption in Post-Transitional Eastern Europe
Marina Zaloznaya

Revisiting the Law and Governance of Trafficking, Forced Labor and Modern Slavery
Edited by Prabha Kotiswaran

For EU product safety concerns, contact us at Calle de José Abascal, 56–1°,
28003 Madrid, Spain or eugpsr@cambridge.org.

www.ingramcontent.com/pod-product-compliance
Ingram Content Group UK Ltd.
Pitfield, Milton Keynes, MK11 3LW, UK
UKHW020358140625
459647UK00020B/2533